TREES

OF THE BRITISH ISLES
IN HISTORY & LEGEND

TREES

OF THE BRITISH ISLES
IN HISTORY & LEGEND

J. H. WILKS

FREDERICK MULLER

First published in Great Britain 1972
by Frederick Muller Ltd., Fleet Street, London, E.C.4

Copyright © 1972 J. H. Wilks

Printed in Great Britain by The Anchor Press Ltd.,
and bound by Wm. Brendon & Son Ltd.,
both of Tiptree, Essex

SBN: 584 10311 5

It's Not Too Late to Save Our Oaks

By John Ennis

They are steadily disappearing from
the countryside. Whether
they survive or not depends on us

at the board, moving the iron slowly, slowly, as cigarette ash fell on to the clothes. I finally confided to a sympathetic friend, my fingers shaking just a little as I struck another match, "I'm worried that I'm smoking too much."

"Then give it up," she said.

She was right, of course. Whenever you find yourself agonizing over something you can actually do something about, you're not worrying—you're just deceiving yourself. *Make a list*. Most of us walk round with a large, foggy cloud of worries hanging over our heads, some of them old friends, some of them near strangers. If you sit down, make a list and really examine them, you may be surprised. For a month last summer I worried steadily about my second son, who was on a camping holiday. Finally, when I wrote down all the faceless worries, I discovered that "appendicitis attack" was in the crowd. Since he'd had his appendix out

years ago, I discarded that one—along with "typhoons." As I read down the list, I kept lightening my pack and feeling better.

Another day, when weighed down with concerns, I made a two-column list: Worries, and What to Do About Them. My list of worries was a long one, ranging from "pollution" to "Jeannie's teeth." Then opposite each I entered something that was in my power to do immediately: "Write to MP *today*"; "Ring Scouts about old newspapers"; and even that terrifying phrase "Ring dentist." The major worries I carried still, even after the small gallant actions had actually been taken. But at least some part of the worry had been turned into worry power.

If we can get our worries working for us, instead of the other way round, we may eventually find ourselves having less worry to work with. But let's not worry about *that* until the time comes.

Heart-strings

The late General de Gaulle was sitting with his wife one evening watching television. Suddenly the room resounded with the notes of the *Marseillaise*. The general listened, deeply moved; then, with languid eyes he turned to his wife sitting beside him and whispered, "Listen, dear, they're playing our tune." —*Domenica del Corriere*, Milan

Groom With a View

A company director was telling friends his plans for his unmarried daughters. "I've put aside a £5,000 dowry for Lily, who is 20, a £10,000 dowry for Rose, who is 25, and £20,000 for Violet, who is 30."

"Sir," said an ambitious young man, "do you have a daughter who's 50?" —*Economic Daily News*, Taipei

CONTENTS

ILLUSTRATIONS

COLOUR PLATES

INTRODUCTION

The literature of trees ranges from the recorded myths of antiquity to the learned treatises of timber research scientists in our computer age. Intelligent races have always known the value of their forests, not merely as a material asset but also for the religious personifications that seemed vested in the great flora. Indeed, all civilizations have cherished them in poetry and religious allegory. This legacy of the tree is still apparent even in the more sober writings of the latter-day arborists and conservationists, though it may now appeal only to a minority audience. The most prosaic would agree that trees, apart from their functional and structural attributes, are natural works of art, possessing dimensions that no other living things display. As single specimens on open land, large spreading trees challenge the artist and excite the poet. The mathematically-minded find problems of purchase and strength to tease them, the apparent paradox of grace and strength often seeming at odds with the rules and formulae of the theory of structures, yet never in conflict. In their natural state, trees owe nothing to man for their growth and development, being self-generating and self-supporting, only asking space for their fulfilment. Little wonder that their appeal is so universal.

It is pertinent at this juncture to offer a brief history of the forest scene in the British Isles throughout the centuries since the Roman occupation. The individual trees, those in avenues, sites of lost trees and their surviving legends will be dealt with in respective chapters.

Before the Roman invasion of Britain the forest dominated the land. Two-thirds of the lowland and the gentler slopes of a spongy terrain were densely carpeted with oak, birch, Scots Pine, ash, hazel, beech, hornbeam and maybe sweet chestnut. Among them grew thorns and brambles, viciously impeding the paths of the ubiquitous Celts in their attempts to make clearings for their settlements and primitive agriculture. Pliny the Elder, in *Natural History*, referred to the state of barbarism existing in the British Isles at the time of the Roman invasions. He accused the Druids of tree worship, forgetting that his own pantheon owed much to the forest-oriented gods in his own mythology. Rome named the mighty oak *esculus* and consecrated it to Jupiter, the laurel to Apollo, the olive to Minerva, the myrtle to Venus and the poplar to Hercules. Pliny wrote that the mistletoe was sacred to the Druids, as was the oak on which it grew (today it is not normally a host for the mistletoe, yet it may have been in those days). All the rites were performed with oak leaves, and they believed that whatever grew on oaks was sent from Heaven, signifying that the deity had chosen that tree. The mistletoe was fetched with some ceremony on the sixth day of the moon, for at that time it had most influence. They named the plant All-Heal, and prepared sacrifices and feasts under the oaks which were decorated with the parasite plant; two white bulls were produced and, dressed in white, the priest reached up the tree and cut the mistletoe with a golden knife. Having placed the plant in a white cloth, the priest ordered the sacrifice of the animals, while the attendant worshippers begged their god to bestow upon them his gifts in return. The Druids believed that this sacrament rendered other animals fruitful, and after liberal decoctions of the plant had been dispensed to the gathering as an antidote against poisons the ceremony ceased.

Apart from the technical knowledge which the legions bequeathed to the then Romanized inhabitants, a few new species of trees appear to have been introduced, though whether by accident or intent is not known. According to the Reverend T. Whittaker, the Romans were responsible for the introduction of the lime, plane, box, elm and poplar. He assures us that the sweet chestnut was included with these newcomers, and that the white mulberry, fig and service trees were to be found planted in the gardens of Roman villas. Another writer, Daines Barrington, at the turn of the nineteenth century, refutes any claims that the above trees were introduced as early as the first centuries A.D. Caesar, in his *Commentaries*, stated that he found the woods in Britain to contain the same trees as those in Gaul, with the exception of the abies; his remarks have given rise to a good deal of controversy, some authors supposing that he meant abietem, (Scots Pine), which is a native of Britain. But the Romans had designated the Silver Fir as abies. Caesar had erred in not noting Pliny's description *Pinus sylvestris* alluding to the Scots Pine. The only reason for the misunderstanding could be that the pine was originally called Scotch Fir, and that the word abies, being considered to signify fir, was taken without further examination to apply to that tree.

The Romans did not enclose forests or create forest boundaries. They were content to extract the necessary timber for building their galleys, especially in the region of Chester, a town liable to siege from the native inhabitants who had taken refuge in Wales. An historian declares that the legions had iron furnaces in the Forest of Dean, and that through that area ran one of their great highways. Great heaps of cinders containing smelted ore were left by the Romans near their quarrying operations. Significantly, in the forest is a town named Cinderford.

The destruction of the Roman influence in Britain and the thundering entry of the Saxons completely enlivened the forest scene. Hardy hunters from infancy, the newcomers pursued the wild boar and deer throughout the length of the woods, recounting their exploits in bardic form. The Anglo-Saxon chronicler, Asser, in his *Life of Alfred*, points to the enthusiasm the Saxons had for burnishing weapons of the hunt, the test of manhood being in the skill, courage and proceeds in hunting. Kings and nobles, billmen and bowmen, "thralls and all" participated in the pleasure of the kill. Woodlands were vast in those pre-conquest days; the Saxon noble built his castle or hall in the forest from the oaks around. He lived a remarkable mixture of the hard and soft life in accordance with events, indulging in coarse behaviour and entertaining lavishly. A roaming musician or the occasional holy pilgrim would appear on the scene of entertainment, embellishing the story-telling with song or a tale of miracles. Such orgies would cease promptly at a summons from the king for assistance, or to repel attacks from the roving bands of robbers who often too confidently flaunted the licence that harassed authority had granted them.

Among the settlers in the sylvan scene were the early proselytizing monks. They selected pleasant, well watered sites, probably in forest clearances, and by the time of the Norman invasion had obtained nearly one-third of the useful land. In the eighth century A.D. the first regal claims to tracts of woodland appear. The word "forest" referred to those areas reserved for the king's pleasure, although the materials and grazing in woods were still free for all. Later the term implied tracts including woods, leas and villages, in which the king reserved the chase to himself.

The word "forest" is clearly defined legally in *Manwood's Forest Laws*. The edition published in 1598 reveals that a "forest was a certain territory of woody ground and fruitful pasture, privileged for wild beasts and fowls of the forest, chase and warren, to rest and abide in, in the safe protection of the king for his princely delight and pleasure. It was bounded and marked by irremovable meeres and boundaries, either known in record or by prescription. It was replenished with wild beasts, and well stocked with verdure for their welfare. There are certain laws, privileges and offices belonging to the same, and not to any other place." But Blackstone is terser: "Forests were waste grounds belonging to the king, replenished with all manner of chase and venery, which were under the king's protection for the sake of recreation and delight." The forest laws in our records were passed during Canute's reign in 1016. They were severe and savage, and further enforced by successive kings.

The few historians of the mid-eleventh century denounce William I for his tyranny and further legal expropriations. Their testimonies are of great value, although criticized by modern "enquirers", whose objects seem to be to devalue any genuine writings of that time. Henry of Huntingdon, writing of the Conqueror, says that anyone killing a stag or boar had his eyes removed, and none dared complain. The king cherished the beasts as if they were his own children; churches and villages were destroyed to ensure uninterrupted habitation for deer. The guise of a great political strategy has been offered as the excuse for William's obsession to impound most of the south-western part of Hampshire, then named Ychtene or Ytene, and today known as the New Forest. Towns, hamlets and ancestral halls were swept away, and the people driven out. No compensation was given. Domesday Book records one hundred and eight places, manors, villages and small settlements, forcibly abandoned and destroyed; the annexation of the terminations *ham* and *ton* to some woods in the forest today might be taken as evidence of the former existence of hamlets and towns erased by the king's fancies. Predictably, the people of the forests wished that God would ordain tragedy for William, his relatives and descendants. No doubt they thought their prayers were answered when Richard, the second son, possibly illegitimate, was gored to death by a stag while hunting. Then, after his accession, William Rufus died spectacularly by the arrow of an unknown archer, believed to be a certain Walter Tyrell.

By the dawn of the thirteenth century the clergy and nobles, who also suffered from injustices of the Royal Forest laws, were counting their grievances. This general disaffection largely culminated in the signing of *Magna Carta* in 1215. Shortly after that date the weak and vacillating Henry III was obliged to issue the *Carta de Foresta*, which, in as graceful a manner as the times would allow, solemnly "restored the stolen forests to the nation's subjects". The all important clause in the charter stated that "no man from henceforth shall lose either life or limb for killing deer; but if any man be taken herewith, and convicted for taking our venison, he shall make a grievous fine; and if he have not, he shall be imprisoned a year and a day, after that time he shall be liberated if he can find sureties, and if not, he shall abjure the realm."

An interesting clause relating to outlaws noted that "all that be outlaws of trespass within our forests since the time of King Henry our grandfather, unto the first year of our coronation shall come to our peace without let, and shall find to use sureties that from henceforth they shall not trespass in our forests". Robin Hood and his band of legendary followers may have become mere ghosts in Sherwood Forest by this time. Too late to become beneficiaries even had their political sins been forgiven them!

A free-for-all right to the produce and game of the forest did not follow from these easements. Meddling with the king's deer, either by chase or removing cover vegetation, was a serious offence; numerous petty offences, such as clearing warrens and waste woods, for which a government today might issue a grant, were dealt with at certain forest courts, held in forty-day cycles. The "Motes" were local courts, similar to the magistrates courts of today, the "Swainmote" was a type of Middle Assize which dealt with cases which could be substantially proved. The "Eyre" Court, usually held three times a year, represented a central criminal court and heard serious cases. Verderers were appointed as judges, the juries consisting of a dozen freeholders who were recommended by wardens, high-ranking officials administering the king's forests. Large and important trees, usually oaks, often overlorded the smaller alfresco courts, perhaps adding dignity to the occasions, silently computing the false statements and injustices issued, absorbing tales of freebooting, poaching and timber-fiddling.

But the Forest Charter marked the turning point in history towards the dilution of regal authority, and although the determined efforts for complete disafforestation lingered until the fourteenth century the chase remained very much the sport of the monarchy and the privilege of the aristocracy.

A heavier demand on the timber, the destruction of church property and the dwindling worship of the hunt saw the insidious first decaying of forests in Tudor times. Elaborately panelled architecture, timber for stronger enclosures for cattle and the constant demand for shipbuilding timber, weaponry and smelting material sacrificed many of the finest trees; even those oaks with distorted trunks and huge bifurcated forks were required for the decorative prows of the men o' war. Yet the Navy must not be blamed entirely for that necessary sad depletion: the population steadily increased and the general progress, especially in agricultural methods, improved considerably with the advancement of skill in the wood crafts, thus accelerating the erosion of these resources. Those forests and private properties from which extractions were made later replenished themselves with oak by natural regeneration, and the lessons learned from wars were to germinate in the first policies of woodland management. Charles I tried to resuscitate some of the old forest laws as a source of income for generous gifts to his cronies, but in 1640 a *Limitation of Forests Act* was passed, eliminating completely the royal whimsy for such levies.

John Fitzherbert wrote on the protection of stool-shots in woods, and the sowing of seeds. An Amenity Act was passed which restricted the felling of trees of small size, in order that a continuity could be assured, and the first practices of planting trees in devastated areas began. The diarist and court official John Evelyn published his *Sylva, or a Discourse of Forest Trees, and the Propagation of Timber in His Majesty's Dominions* in 1664. His work encouraged landowners to reinstate and replant neglected woodlands for the materials required in shipbuilding and home timber demands. A revolution in improved land husbandry and farming techniques released agricultural labourers for more sophisticated instruction in forestry practice. That same process is being repeated today, although it results in the exposed appearance of large hedgeless tracts of land with block forests tending to monopolise the upward slopes.

During the last two centuries, huge plantations of trees have been added by the large landowners, either for the benefit of the nation or for their own enjoyment. In Georgian times it was fashionable to establish timber for investment; the Victorians were not so committed to growing trees for commercial reasons, though they were acceptable as game cover. From this time onwards Britain received all the world's flora into her gardens, estates and arboreta; explorers, botanists and adventurous nurserymen wandered into the contrasting new territories which were opened up to them by better methods of inland travel and the advantages of the faster propeller-driven steamships which did not expose the tender plants and seeds to a long journey by sail.

In 1838, J. C. Loudon completed the fullest and most intricate work ever attempted on the subject, *Trees and Shrubs of Great Britain*, or, if you prefer the alternative musically sounding title, *Arboretum et Fruticetum Britannicum*. The work is full of precise information on propagation, culture and management of most woody plant life known up to his day; it is written in the best taste, full of amusing anecdotes of forestry practice, and has many quaint illustrations. It was, though, a somewhat deterring exercise to readers, the four text volumes taking some time to absorb.

In 1906, Elwes and Henry privately published their fulsome *Trees of Great Britain and Ireland*, an expensive work which had a limited distribution to subscribers dedicated to arboriculture and forestry. Although these writers describe meticulously all the species collected by that date, their work is superior to that of the erudite Loudon chiefly because of the addition of about four hundred large photographic plates of important specimen trees from all parts of the world, and their wider opportunities for world travel. In the preface of this tree encyclopaedia we are warned of the popularity of the conifer and the neglect in ensuring a substantial continuity of broadleaved trees—a progressive argument still.

The nostalgia for the deciduous native trees of Britain creeps into much of the descriptive literature written since the First World War and the growing concern for a more balanced tree cover has been echoed by Richard St. Barbe Baker in his *Sahara Challenge* and *Green Glory*. He does not hesitate to caution the farming community in Britain of the short-term gains to be had from a prairie-like policy, resulting in the wholesale extraction of hedgerows and the major trees in the landscape.

That patient and once under-financed body, the Forestry Commission, has experienced half a century of dour work which may yet be appreciated. The block coniferous forests criticized by the national aesthetes from time to time are gradually becoming accepted by the public, although some years will pass before the immigrant pine cone is revered as emblematically as the acorn. Apart from the substantial advice given to private woodland owners, the Commission produces topographical and technical literature on the forests. Research stations and libraries are available for general facility by appointment. Records are kept of the largest trees known by that indefatigable and enthusiastic research officer Alan Mitchell, to whom much of the present resurgence of interest in trees is due. Voluntary bodies add their quota of articles on the importance of increasing the green cover of the land, especially in areas where new towns are springing up, and in the derelict parts where spoil heaps have been left as a legacy of the Industrial Revolution. The Arboricultural Association, the Royal Forestry Society, Men of the Trees Society and the Civic Trust all produce *Journals* which will doubtless form the material for some future John Evelyn of our age.

But we have reached the day of the computer, even in forestry and planning. The knowledge of the forester has been digested by the machine, resulting not only in economic selection and permutation of trees but also in the planting and removal. Any literature or guidance from this source may be enlightening to the commercial grower, but certainly unexciting to the sylvan admirer.

Having used seven-league boots to skip over the ever-changing scene in this brief history of our trees it may seem something of a miracle that any single tree of sentimental or historic interest should have survived such bulldozing tactics, in fact or in legend. Yet the efforts of those who have troubled to record the *obiter dicta* of our island story, not unworthily through the lore of our trees and woodlands, have found powerful responses in the hearts of many. This has sustained me in the task of collating the many items from my researches and presenting them here for the benefit and, it is hoped, pleasure of both confirmed tree lovers and those who wish to enjoy perhaps the grandest of Nature's gifts.

Among those kind people who sent me information on folklore and details of odd trees tucked away out of popular places were lords, ladies, politicians, artisans and children. The University College of London were extremely helpful in allowing me to examine their research into the folk-lore of trees and the B.B.C., which accepted correspondence for me from interested listeners, has also been of great assistance. I owe most to my good friends Arnold Croot who patiently helped me to organize the book and corrected some very "woodsy" grammar, and Maurice Gould, who assisted in research and taking photographs. Alan Mitchell, who knows the location and sizes of more trees than any man in these islands, but is extremely wary of legend and hearsay, balanced the book with his facts and figures of the grandest trees existing and a list of places where we can all look at great collections of international trees.

J. H. W.

Chapter One

Landmark, Boundary and Marker Trees

Although forests and woodlands still covered most of these islands in the Dark Ages and after the Conqueror's time, great clearings had been made for homesteads, agriculture and monastic estates. Oak and thorn fell to the axes of the husbandmen and the fertile forest floor was slowly transformed by the plough into the pattern recognizable today. The population, perhaps little more than three million in the thirteenth century, was concentrated in the south and Midlands. The scattered northern communities, because of the generally harsher terrain, settled in the alluvial valleys, shrewdly carving out homesteads among the natural shelter belts of the surrounding forest. These latter were exploited by the hunter, the woodman and the charcoal burner; the Crown, of course, often arbitrarily reserved large tracts of forest for the chase.

Mediaeval society was a static one, although there was a steady traffic in trade between neighbouring towns and villages. Except where Roman roadways still survived in part, travel was primitive and hazardous, often meandering muddily or dustily along the river valleys, or trailing over exposed moorlands. The usages of the chase and of trade had established halting-places at strategic points along the routes, often identifiable by a prominent tree or a conspicuous grove on a hilltop, where a clearing could conveniently be made and defended. At such places the seeds of a local economy would soon germinate. The farrier, the tinker, the wheelwright, the carpenter, the baker, and soon the first inn-keeper, would set up in business. And thus a social community would be born. It followed that this entity would be known by its customers in distinctive terms of its prominent tree or grove—or sometimes by the name of one of its personalities, famed for a craft or ill-famed for banditry.

B

Edward I, to mitigate anti-social activities, encouraged the clearing of cover undergrowth from the thoroughfares but, to his credit, decreed the preservation of the larger forest trees.

"Mile" trees were common features, even though distance mensuration was sketchy, and were often marked or numbered accordingly, in their local context.

Thus, not only were "place-names" conceived in this fashion, but social events—political, religious, judicial, and even the half-remembered, grass-rooted pagan festivals—often centred around revered trees. Sometimes the place name was a complex one, a combination of tree site and river crossing, the name of a popular landowner, or perhaps the dark dregs of a witch's brew of legend and unrequited hate. Often the lore of a tree would be so compulsive that it was replaced in perpetuity when death or accident removed it. In some cases a commemorative stone sufficed for its recollection, such as the Rufus Stone near Cadnam in the New Forest. And, indeed, cases are extant where the remains of an historic tree were dug up and resited in another part of the village, with a protective fencing placed around.

The landscape thus became peppered with names derived from such idiosyncratic sources. Also, there were centre-of-forest trees, centre-of-county trees, and eventually a supposed centre-of-England tree. The permutations were endless, for we had county boundary trees, as well as those which straddled the meeting points of three counties.

Approximately a third of the place-names in the British Isles originated in these ways. Thorngumbald in Yorkshire is said to have described the location of a Mr. Gumbald's house, a toothless gentleman who lived near a thorn tree, or among thorn bushes. But Barking, once in Essex and now part of the Greater London Council, has nothing to do with dogs: in 735 A.D. it was Berecingum, denoting "birch tree dwellers". Birkenhead in Cheshire was a headland covered with birches.

Many are obvious derivations, such as Oakhampton, Oakley and Sevenoaks. Old English, Old German, Norse and Celtic words for our best known tree, the oak, are hidden away in the guises of *ac, ake, aig, aik, eik,* and in the French *chêne.* Some examples are Acton in London, Savernake in Wiltshire, Malaig in Inverness county, Chenies in Buckinghamshire. Also in Scotland the Gaelic *darach* gives the same clue, and in Ireland *derry.* The Celtic counterpart *derw* is common in Wales, springing from Druid, the ancient priest of the oak ritual. Derwentwater, in Cumberland, describes "oaks by the stream".

Place-names with "ash" as prefix or suffix are legion, although the meaning of some are not so obvious, such as Aspatria, Cumberland, construed as "Patrick's Ash". With "Asp" and "Aps", the aspen tree is often indicated, not ash as sometimes claimed. For instance, Aspley in Bedfordshire, and Apsley in Hertfordshire depict "aspen trees by the field". Yorkshire is dotted with towns and villages originally sited in orchards. Appletreewick, the "orchard beside the farm", is typical. Boxmoor is self-explanatory. The two villages of Ewhurst, one in Surrey, another in Sussex, were built in yew-groves, and Hazelton in Gloucestershire was the "farm in the hazelwood".

"Lind" signifies the lime tree. Lindfield in Sussex means "lime tree land", and Lindsell in Essex tells us that huts were once built among lime trees, probably the native species of small-leaved lime. Mappleton in Yorkshire is so named because a pioneer farmer set up among a grove of field maples; Mappowder, Dorset, for the distinction of a settlement among maples near a slope. Plumpton in Lancashire and Sussex and Plumtree in Nottinghamshire are three more illustrations where farms became known for their orchard-tree environments, or perhaps for their subsequent investment in fruit trees following the Roman introduction of continental varieties.

Willows were known as "salls" to ancient homesteaders, thus settlements near willows have the "Sal" prefix. When Sarum was moved to its new site, its ancient name was dropped in favour of the more descriptive one of Salisbury because of its associations of the place of willows on the banks of the Avon. And we know Sallins, in County Kildare; Salperton in Gloucestershire was the "farm by the stream of willows", and Sallahig in County Kerry as the "place of the willows". Willows are still "sallies" to the Irish today.

The elder tree was known as "scawen", and Boscawen, Cornwall, implied the "house by the elders".

The thorn merits a catalogue to itself. With the exception of the oak, both in its pagan and its Christian connotations, no other tree has been so revered.

The ubiquitous hawthorn, insignificant in size by forest standard, is unmentioned in folklore until the advent of Christianity, when legend has it that Joseph of Arimathea, c. 60 A.D., planted his hawthorn staff in the chosen ground at Glastonbury, Somerset, whence began the miracle of the flowering thorn at Christmastide.

Where place-names incorporate the thorn tree, the origins appear to be in farms or homes where thorn trees grew, not necessarily implying sacred themes. One town taking its name from a single tree is

Thorne in Yorkshire. Many place-names are even more obviously synonymous. For instance there are twelve towns and villages named Thornton, mostly in the North of England, all originating from associations with the thorn. An interesting example is Thornton-le-beans, meaning the "farm where the thorn trees grew by the beans".

Often areas and towns would take names from locally known woods or from the clearings made in them by early agriculturists. "Weald" and "wold" meant forest lands; Cotswold portrayed "forest in the hills". The great eighty-mile stretch of woods from central Kent into Sussex and Hampshire was known as Andreds-weald after the Saxon title, anglicizing an earlier Roman description Sylva Anderida. "Worth" and "Worthy" defined an enclosure, and exceptionally signified a homestead or manor, where a place had been cleared to make way for buildings. Hamworthy in Dorset reveals the "village in the clearing". But "Worth" could also apply to a place where trees did not flourish on a site selected for a house. Thus Harmworth in Nottinghamshire, a "homestead on stony ground". "Hurst" and "Frith", seen in Billingshurst, Sussex, and Duffield Frith, Yorkshire, both implied forest or wood. The Cornish "gweath", found in Trengweath, pictured a village among trees. The old forest areas of Ireland can often be traced by the suffix or prefix "derry", the Erse-Celtic vernacular for oak trees. Londonderry and Derrygrogan are but two of a host of examples.

H. G. Stokes, in his admirable little book *English Place-names*, mentions three interesting examples of landmark trees which became centres for folk gatherings. A place in Lancashire, he says, once sported a tall poplar tree which received admiration from so many that it became a meeting place. It swayed so gracefully in the wind and served as such a noticeable landmark that the town of Waver-tree, now part of Liverpool, grew up around it. Aintree, not far from here, remains mysterious in origin, but tradition supposes that an oak, a complete "loner" and a survivor from a mediaeval forest, acquired such local lore that the community around claimed it as their "ain tree". Poplar, now part of London, was once a village divorced from the city and became settled upon marshy land which played host to aspen trees. The town was christened after the dominant tree at a time when, perhaps a thousand years ago, the land was drained to make way for the growing port. Some have said that the nearby Limehouse area derived its name from the linden or lime tree, but that association seems a little tenuous. The existence of limekilns there probably deserves the credit.

Salcombe Regis Thorn. Saxon Boundary Marker Tree.

A close study of tree-names could give us a computed picture of our former woodlands and forests. No great detective powers are called for to infer that tree-names imply the existence of such trees in their respective localities in historic times. Difficulties arise when a starting-point is needed, and several alternative language queries crop up.

More proof of tree species existing in these islands before Neolithic times has been arrived at by scientists using Carbon 14 testing in recent years than has been revealed by all the arboricultural studies over two thousand years. The study of pollen grains and what has become known as the "pollen count" reveals that many of the exotic trees introduced into these islands in past centuries were common-place in earlier warmer periods. Sir Arthur Tansley's *British Islands and their Vegetation* graphically describes the cycle of the appearance and disappearance of oriental and occidental species according to climatic changes.

The Roman god Terminus was represented as the custodian of fields and landmarks and the promoter of goodwill among men. From this stems an annual celebration of marking the boundaries, when respected elders of certain Scottish and English parishes walk around the established areas, halting at certain places and performing ceremonies to impress the evidence of old-established boundaries upon the memories of both old and young. The custom was inaugurated about 800 A.D. by Avitus, Bishop of Vienna, and has continued as a celebration by the Christian church during Rogation Week to this day in certain parishes. The parish priest, accompanied by his flock and churchwardens, "beat the bounds" of the parish, stopping at appointed trees.

Mostly oak, for there are exceptions, these became known as Gospel Oaks, under which passages from the gospels were recited, imploring the blessing of the Almighty on the fruits of the earth and for the preservation and rights of the parish. There were known Gospel Oaks at Stoneleigh, Warwickshire; Avington, Hants; Huntingfield Park and Lavenham, Suffolk; and at Lapworth in Worcestershire. The best known one today is that at Polstead, Suffolk, where only a sapling oak grown from an acorn from its parent remains. The remains of the old tree are still to be seen decaying and have not been interfered with since it collapsed in 1956. The ceremony had been conducted under the old Polstead Gospel Oak for a thousand years, and the annual service which commemorates the tree is still held. The oak, which measured thirty-two feet in circumference, stood in Polstead Hall Park, just outside the churchyard. Polstead has a profane memory in the shape of Maria Marten's gravestone, resting place of the lady who mysteriously disappeared well over a century ago and was found murdered in the Red Barn near the oak.

A walk along the old Windsor Forest road from Ascot for about three miles to Binfield will end at an old oak which marked the centre of Great Windsor Park hundreds of years ago. Fifty years ago the road to the tree was merely a stony track with ditches on both sides. The inn nearby is the Stag and Hounds, a name which may have signified a halting place during deer chases in the days of the first Elizabeth. In the same county, Berkshire, is the Boundary Oak at Swallowfield, standing near Bound Oak Cottage. At one time, before the county boundaries were changed, this oak spread over meeting points of no less than four counties: Wiltshire, Hampshire, Berkshire and Surrey.

The boundary line between Somerset and the parishes of Lynton and Brendon in Devon is marked by a tree known as Hoar Oak. Records state that an original oak marked the division from the time of Domesday until the tree fell in 1662. A sapling grown from one of its acorns was planted in its place, but the matured tree fell in 1916. A successor was again planted, and the Hoar Oak of today is fifty-five years old and thriving.

Gilbert White, in his *History of Selborne*, describes the Pleastor Oak, which used to mark the boundary of the Pleystow, or playground for the children of the village. White said that the tree had a short, squat body, with huge horizontal limbs extending to the extremity of the play-area; it was surrounded by stone steps with seats above them. Much resorted to on summer evenings, it is said that this pleasant place attracted both the old, who sat in grave debate, and the young who frolicked and danced before them.

An Ordnance Survey Map of 1831 marked the Three Shire Elm at Pebworth in Gloucestershire. The tree was described as a specimen which "overhung three counties and three parishes, Cleeve Prior, Worcestershire, Salford Priors, Warwickshire, and Pebworth itself". In 1958 the O.S. pinpointed the spot as Three Shire Elms, indicating that the original elm had gone, although the boundary area contains a number of trees, no doubt self-generated from the root system of the fallen tree. Three Shires Oak Road at Smethwick recalls a famous tree, the branches of which were said to stretch into three counties, Staffordshire, Shropshire and Worcestershire. The tree was felled by Smethwick Corporation in 1908. A local builder named Rollason photographed it before it was cut up and used the picture as an emblem for his business trade mark.

The parishes of Devonshire have consistently used the tall-growing Wellingtonia Gigantea to mark their boundaries. Few are more than a hundred years old today since their introduction from the Sierra Nevada was not until 1851, when the seed was sown in the Exeter nursery by Veitch, taking two years to become a visible plant. As a boundary tree, the Wellingtonia has every attribute—height, evergreen branchlets and a tapering stature, with firm roothold.

The sycamore which stands close to the parish church in the Somerset valley town of Dulverton is probably the largest in the West Country. Although the tree is locally reputed to be about eight hundred years old, it must be an overestimate, as it has always been assumed that the sycamore is not a native tree and was not found to be widely distributed until the middle of the sixteenth century. The present girth of the trunk at four feet from the ground is 16 ft. and its height is approximately 70 ft., but it is a magnificent wide-spreading tree which dominates the west end of the churchyard.

In 1845 the churchwarden was instrumental in preserving the old tree, then known as the Belfrey Tree, after a hurricane and lightning decapitated and split some of the branches. He engaged a local mechanic to brace the split branches together with iron chains and girders. The work was effective and new shoots have since grown into large branches which have filled up the lost centre. They now overtop the battlemented tower. The original practical but rather heavy ironwork is not visible today, and only discerning scrutineers will observe the marks where the metal bands encircled the limbs. New modern wire bracing has replaced old-fashioned methods; it is less harmful to use a threaded bolt fixed into a drilled hole through a branch and use flexible wire for supporting limbs than to clamp throttling metal halters around them, which cuts off the sap-flow and weakens the wood. The tree, which I consider to be between three and four hundred years old, has recently received the above modern treatment. It is only because of the sympathetic treatment and endowment received from certain West Country private individuals that it is in such good condition today.

Near the famous windmill at Chailey, Sussex, is a yew tree which is claimed to stand in the centre of the county, but its site in relation to the irregular outline of Sussex does not qualify it. The boundary has changed over the centuries especially at the Hampshire border. Today we should search for a more eligible centre tree between Haywards Heath and Twineham. In the same county, at Burpham, is a fine cluster of pines known as the Seven Sisters, close to a fifteenth-century tower. The practice of naming groups of pines Seven Sisters is of unknown origin; there are village greens, commons and many open spaces which have similar plantings over England, but invariably there are only six trees as one has died. Any attempt to grow a seventh always appears to have failed. The number seven is well known in Christian mythology as representing the Seven Gifts of the Holy Spirit. This was usually symbolized by seven doves and possibly it is with this that the Seven Sisters is synonymous.

A few miles north-west of Herstmonceaux is the small village of Cowbeech. The hamlet took its name from a large beech tree believed to be close on three hundred years old. Standing on land which formed part of the old Cow Farm, this tree was recently threatened with "treatment" by the Central Electricity Generating Board to allow a free passage for their high-powered overhead grid lines, but after much local protest the Board agreed to re-route the lines to avoid interfering with the shape of the old landmark.

"Lightning Oak," Haileybury College, Herts. Tree exists.

Hertfordshire still contains a few famous marker trees. In the grounds of Haileybury College is Quitchell's Oak, standing on what was known as Quitch Hill in the Middle Ages, the name stemming from the dialect word "queach", meaning a thicket. A post near the tree carries a plaque: "This tree was recorded in 1634 as the boundary corner of St. Margaret's Parish (formerly Thele)." Another tree in the grounds is the Dumb-Bell Oak, a boundary oak so called because of its strangely shaped trunk, which has a waist between thicker portions above and below, giving it something of the appearance of a dumb-bell. Another oak, on the boundary between St. Margaret's and Great Amwell Parishes, has a ring sunk deeply in its trunk. Local tradition has it that Dick Turpin tethered his horse to the ring while awaiting the arrival of coaches on the Hertford–London Road. Another tree in the college grounds with interesting connections is the Lightning Oak, which stands in full vigour today. Struck by lightning in 1898 it appeared dead and the following year was considered for felling. In 1900 it recovered, seemingly more healthy than before its ordeal. In 1904 a plaque was placed on the bole with the inscription *"Saepe Jovis Telo Quercus Adusta Viret.* Ovid" (Often the oak burnt by Jove's bolt flourishes). In 62 years the cambium and bark tissues of the tree have grown over the plaque, which is now completely concealed. A new plaque placed on the tree in May 1966 describes the history and reveals the location of the old plaque.

Perhaps the most famous oak in Hertfordshire was Goff's Oak at Theobalds, a tree referred to by J. C. Loudon as being thirty-two feet in circumference in 1844. It gave its name to an inn nearby and to the village which may soon be absorbed by the proposed new town of Flamsted End. In the inn was a figure of the oak accompanied by the following printed account: "This tree was planted in A.D. 1066 by Sir Theodore Godfrey (or Goff'by) who came over with William the Conqueror". The skeleton remains of the tree were still preserved *in situ* until two or three years ago. They stand about a mile north-west of Cheshunt Church on the south side of the common. Close by, in Beaumont Manor, there is an ancient oak reputed to be a twin planting. A story goes that one of the early owners of the present manor house (the previous one having been burned down in Elizabethan days), put his last shirt on a horse, which, failing to win, was shot by Major Grant and buried at the side of the oak. The groom promptly committed suicide with the same weapon, since when both he and the horse are said to haunt the manor. The original Goff's Oak collapsed in 1950, leaving but a short piece of trunk, and is perpetuated by a young oak sapling nearby. A plaque nearby describes the foregoing events.

William Gilpin, in his *Forest Scenery* (1791), gives the following notice on the Magdalen or Great Oak of Oxford: "Close by the gate of the water walk of Magdalen College, Oxford, grew an oak which perhaps stood there as a sapling when Alfred the Great founded the University. This period only includes a space of 900 years, which is not great for an oak. It is a difficult matter to ascertain the age of a tree. The age of a castle or abbey is the object of history; even a common house is recorded by the family who built it. All these objects arrive at maturity in their youth, if I may so speak.

"But time gradually completing the oak's growth is not worth recording in the early part of its existence. In youth it is only a common tree, afterwards when it becomes remarkable for its age, all memory of years is lost. This tree, however, can almost produce historical evidence for the age it boasts. About 500 years after the time of Alfred, William of Waynfleet expressly ordered his college (Magdalen) to be founded near the Great Oak, and an oak could not, I think be less than 500 years of age to merit that title, together with the honour of fixing the site of the college. It was afterwards badly damaged in the time of Charles II, when the walks were laid out and its roots disturbed. The spread of the tree was 50 ft. in every direction from the trunk, and under that magnificent pavilion 3,000 persons could have sheltered. In 1788 the oak, then a ruin, fell after the main taproot decayed. A chair was fashioned from part of the healthy timber remaining and given to the president of the college." At least part of the Magdalen Oak remains today.

In Yorkshire are two famous landmark trees which, although squat and distorted, could be of considerable age. They are both ash trees which have found sustenance in the inhospitable cracks of limestone rocks. The first is worthy of special interest to those who travel the road between Chapel-le-dale and Ingleborough, for it seems to be growing directly out of stone. The second is high on Brimham Rocks overlooking the Vale of York and Nidderdale, where its hilltop position gives it no protection from the fierce winds which sweep over the moors. The ash is a strange tree, intolerable of any interference by man, and always short lived if its roots are disturbed. Yet it will survive bleak blasts and thrive as a hermit, providing it has sufficient light with water and the right minerals freely, though not excessively, available. The survival of random seed in inaccessible places can also be seen in the Avon Gorge at Bristol where Corsican Pines have formed natural plantations in the cracks of limestone rocks. The parent trees were planted about forty years ago on the gentler slopes above, on an area known as the Downs, and it appears that this natural propagation succeeds far better than any efforts of man. Stories are told of landowners firing shotguns loaded with seed of various species into the most precarious places in attempts to mimic Nature, with negative results.

Sixty years ago the Selly Oak stood at the junction of the main street of the town of that name with Oak Tree Lane. The original tree took up a considerable part of the pavement with its large and gnarled root system. A well-loved landmark admired by residents, it was doomed to go to make way for road improvements in 1908, but the plan met such opposition that there was a postponement, followed by the canvassing of the views of nine hundred local inhabitants. More than seven hundred voted for the tree to be saved; the remainder expressed no opinion. J. G. Ledsham, Lord of the Manor and claiming the tree as his property, supported the reprieve. But unfortunately a new development plan for house building hastened an inevitable decision to "modernise the existing amenities" by deciding on the widening of the footpath and road. Thus the old oak was finally cut down and the butt placed in Selly Oak Park.

At Knockholt, in Kent, 770 ft. above sea level, stand beech trees which can be seen as far away as Harrow School and from Leith Hill in Surrey. They are also visible from Crystal Palace ground. "Knock", or "Noke", claimed to be an elided version of "an oak", while "holt" means wood. Doubtless beech would have predominated on the higher ground, while oak, largely absent nowadays from the village area, did at one time have prior claim to the title. Another great group of Kent beeches crowns Idle Hill overlooking the Darent valley. Eight hundred feet above sea level, they are the highest objects in the county. In Wiltshire the highest point is Liddington Hill, crowned by a clump of half a dozen ancient beeches. Here Richard Jeffries, the poet from Swindon, would recline and compose his observations of nature; he found the company of trees inspiring and called them his "thinking places".

Not until about 1720 did milestones appear on the trackways of Britain. Not one paved highway had been constructed since the Roman occupation, and any levelling or rut filling, clearance of overgrown vegetation and "dust-laying" on the thoroughfares apparently fell to the voluntary labour of the landowners, transporters using heavy horse-wagons and the early passenger coach operators. Improvements were then begun, water pumps for sprinkling dusty surfaces were installed on the main network roads, ditches for draining off surplus water at the sides of the highways were more frequently maintained, and the first turnpike roads appeared. Toll gates arrived about 1750, when the laying of dust, some cambering of road surfaces, drainage and other justifications for toll charges had been effected. The original "toll-house" was often arboreal in the shape of a road-landmark tree, and although no such sentry-boxes exist today there were several oaks associated with a rather haphazard manner of collecting dues, and there's little doubt that before the Turnpike Act became law in 1773 a fair number of self-styled "wardens" at "tree-stations" claimed that their sections of passable road were due solely to their own labours meriting private reward.

Large hollow oaks served well, for convenient peep-holes could be cut out to face both ways. The collector, observing his oncoming customers well before their arrival at the entrance to his "patch" of road, would wave the wayfarers down, lest they pretended ignorance of the toll and speeded up to avoid payment.

One of these trees is a mere vestige today, the Turnpike Oak at Northaw, Herts. Another, at Boddington, in Gloucestershire, stood near the turnpike road between Tewkesbury and Cheltenham and may have been used for tolling. At the base the tree was 54 ft. in circumference, and in 1783 its hollow trunk was formed into a room and wainscoted. It had noticeably small leaves, like a hawthorn, and was burned to the ground in 1790, either by accident or design.

It became common practice in the nineteenth century to plant an ash and a sycamore together at strategic points, especially at hazards on roads. The combination became known as John and Mary, and was recognized as an old form of warning of crossroads or of a main road ahead. There may be nothing of deep significance here (although the protective associations of the "Beloved Disciple" with the Virgin Mary have been invoked, but with little conviction), and there is little in folklore to support a reason why these two species should represent danger. Ash and sycamore, being fast-growing trees with prominent features, easily established on most soils, or even between rock crevices, no doubt were convenient as cheap markers and cost little to install.

Mile trees were common two centuries ago and are shown on many old maps. Andrew's and Day's map of Wilts, dated 1773, marked mile trees planted by the Earl of Pembroke, and on the ridge south of the modern A30 Salisbury to Shaftesbury road six lime trees belonging to this group still exist in good condition and are reckoned to be 250 years old.

In the Avon valley north of Salisbury there are three elms reputed to be mile trees. The first is near Great Durnford Church, but is now dead. The second is a mile on towards Salisbury, at Netton, and stands in the grounds of Elm Tree Cottage; the third is at Salterton Farm, exactly a mile from the last elm, and is in a good state.

Lillington, a suburb of Leamington Spa, recently lost its traditional "Centre of England" tree, an oak. It was a neglected monument, seldom treated with respect and irreverently used as a bill-board. A large branch fell across the highway, exposing sufficient hidden rot to merit condemnation, and the tree was felled. There have been other claimants to the supposed "centre". Meriden, in Warwickshire, has set up a memorial stone to the effect. Copston Magna, another contender for the honour; also Minworth, where schoolboys of King Edward's Grammar School, Birmingham, claim to have proved that that is the "centre" by mathematical demonstration. The centre is continually in dispute. On a murky night during the Second World

War, two air-raid wardens, bored with inactivity, embarked on an experiment to find the exact centre of England: they cut out two cardboard map replicas, one for England and the other for England and Wales, and with the aid of handy instruments in their H.Q. (a drawing office) found the centres of gravity. The results were:

Centre of England   1½ m. S.W. of Higham
Centre of England and Wales   3 m. West of Sutton Coldfield

Surely it is now fitting that the Ordnance Survey Office should salute the singular by-product of the Civil Defence of the British Isles by ceremoniously planting two trees? Gog and Magog would not seem inappropriate names. "Gog", in Gaelic, does at least signify a "nodding of the head", and could be read either as official approval or as a monument to the historic mood which prompted the exercise.

The Crouch Oak, a venerable tree even in decay, stands adjacent to the small estate which takes its name from that tree in Addlestone, Surrey. It formerly marked the boundary of Windsor Forest in a S.E. direction. Tradition states that the first Queen Elizabeth dined beneath its shade. The girth at 2 ft. from the ground is 24 ft., and at a height of 9 ft. the principal branch, itself as large as a tree, shoots out almost horizontally from the trunk to a distance of 48 ft., and was known to have been even longer.

Before the enclosure of the Manor of Chertsey in 1808 this oak stood on open common, but it is now surrounded by railings in the Princess Mary's Village Homes estate. This protection was given to preserve it from a practice which accelerated its decay, namely that of having the bark peeled off by lovesick women in the belief that drinking the liquor boiled out of it would operate as a love charm. The "Crouch" probably refers to the low stooping form of the chief branches. A local story recalls that Elizabeth I narrowly escaped death from a stag at bay near the tree, being saved by the devotion of her huntsman who himself perished on the animal's horns. The Crouch Oak lies about eight miles from the boundary of Windsor Park.

Cranborne Chase lies partly in Dorset and partly in Wiltshire and on the boundary between the two counties grew the Larmer Tree, an old wych elm, a native tree of Britain, which marked a favourite stopping-place for King John when he visited his hunting box at Tollard Royal. The meaning of "larmer" is not known, but it may have meant a "chase" or "rush". Only the stump of the original tree remains, but an oak has been planted nearby with a suitable plaque.

Near Blandford, Dorset, there once grew an ancient tree by the name of Damory's Oak. It measured 68 ft. in circumference at the base, and at 17 ft. from the ground the trunk still measured 16 ft. in girth. As it decayed and became hollow, good use was made of it by an old man who set up an ale-shop within; indeed, he lived within this cave among his stocks. In 1703 a violent storm shattered the huge crown above the hollow bole, and yet, forty years later, it still displayed limbs 75 ft. long from its main fork. In 1755 it was felled and sold for £14 for firewood—a strange inversion of values. Today it would have only a nuisance value and the labour cost involved in converting the tree would probably be chargeable to the owner of such a patriarch.

Between 1620 and 1630, two Silver Firs were planted by the Duke of Argyll at Roseneath in company with many other trees being introduced at that time. In 1906 Henry Elwes visited them and disclosed that they each girthed over 22 ft. at base and rose to a height of 110 ft. Adam and Eve, as they were known, stood out as landmarks important enough to attract thousands of visitors from all parts of the world. To quote from *Roseneath Past and Present*, by W. C. Maugham, in 1893:

"The trees in front of Campsail House are the special glory of Roseneath. Their fame has endured for generations. These are two grand specimens of their tribe, their huge trunks, gnarled and massive, and having all the solidity and seeming indestructibility of granite rock, their great roots fixed deeply in the mossy soil. Probably not in Europe are there to be seen two such magnificent and venerable firs as these celebrated big trees of Roseneath. Giants which lift their verdant crests above their companions of the grove. What a tale they could tell of the many visitors of all ranks of life who have stood in their majestic presence, and gazed upon the spreading boughs which so long have wrestled with the wintry tempest!"

Since that time the two trees have slowly died back, yet withstanding the terrific gales in their nakedness, witnessing the collapse of their neighbours one by one. In the great hurricane of 1968 Eve fell, leaving Adam alone amidst the thousands of petty conifers planted around its petrified roots. The last measurements of Adam alive were a girth of 29 ft. at base and a height of 130 ft. Eve had been a little less at 22 ft. by 124 ft. The outline of Adam's branch structure in its starkness can be compared with a photograph Elwes produced in 1906.

Part of the Downs area above Bristol is known as Whitetree. It

"Adam and Eve" a few years ago before "Eve" fell. Adam still stands dead. Roseneath, Scotland.

takes its name from the practice of painting the bole of a certain wych elm which stood by the side of the roundabout on the main road between Bristol and Westbury-on-Trym. A hundred years ago there was no street lighting on this space of over 200 acres covered with trees, many of them wych elms very much alike. Coachmen and travellers often had difficulty in knowing exactly where to turn off to cross the tracks on the Downs when they returned late at night. One such man, Hurley, coachman to a certain large household just off the main road, hit upon the idea to whiten the tree near his destination, making it easier for him to pick it out in his coach-lamps.

In 1956 a roundabout and road improvements were planned and the tree, its trunk painted annually as custom even after lighting had improved the situation considerably, was felled to allow more road-

Dulverton Sycamore.

space. However, the area still had to justify its name, and consequently another elm close by was painted in the same way to maintain tradition. This tree, now daubed regularly by the local authorities, has reacted in strange ways to the treatment, for it will hold its leaves until the end of December some years, and come into leaf later than its fellows in the following late springs. There is no proof that the layer of paint affects the growth of the elm in this way; possibly the new effects of more and closer traffic have influenced its antics; salt spray, exhaust fumes, more people walking around the base of the tree; all these new experiences can affect the welfare of a tree in different ways. Nevertheless, the new White Tree perpetuates the name of the district, and is adapting itself to a new environment.

If we take note of modern road names and avenues, house names, and even public houses, we find a grand list of tree titles, though in most cases we discover that the qualifying trees no longer exist. Modern developers, however, persist in naming their estates with evocative woodland and tree names, perhaps as a sop to their consciences for the pitiably few trees their bulldozers have spared. Or is there perhaps hope for a growing appreciation of trees in those nostalgic references to "Firs Estate", "Yew Paddock", "Sylvan Way", etc?

Whereas our ancestors chose to live with their dark, mysterious woods, or honoured the survivors of their clearings, we of the twentieth century hug their empty, apocryphal names to our guilt-ridden bosoms. There may yet come a time when trees are allowed to resume their roles as markers, mile trees and gathering places as our leisure culture becomes more atavistic. Already the trend can be discerned in our "nature trails" and the like, and in the growing membership of societies, such as the Men of the Trees and the Arboricultural Association.

Subconsciously, many motorists do use trees as markers on their journeys. Perhaps they may not appreciate them as trees of a species on a first sighting, but familiarity with the passing landscape may well breed an awareness of what is left of their heritage. Movement and subtle colour changes are, possibly in certain cases, trendily psychedelic reminders of their own natures still in rapport with primæval things. Is the thought more valid than mere fantasy that would dwell on the revealed opening of these doors of a new perception? But, at the least, it would surely be better to barter the token values of a saner civilization in the green shade of our mother forests than to wrangle over the small coins of our lives under the neon lights of the present.

Dulverton Sycamore.

Chapter Two

The Tree in Literature

Until 1796, in the Little Park, Windsor, once part of that great forest, stood Herne's Oak, an unimpressive structure more dead than alive and long retained because of its weird and uncanny links with a strange legend of haunting by a certain Herne, who hanged himself from the tree. Vague tradition claimed that Herne was a keeper in the forest in Elizabeth's reign, and that he dabbled in witchcraft. He had taken his own life in remorse, and was to haunt the glades forever. Shakespeare used the background of this tree as the scene of the tricking of Falstaff in the *Merry Wives of Windsor*; the folk-lore of the forest was not lost on so perceptive a playwright. In his lifetime, such scenes found a ready response in Tudor audiences:

> *"There is an old tale that Herne the Hunter,*
> *Sometime a keeper here in Windsor Forest,*
> *Doth all the winter time at still midnight*
> *Walk round about an oak with ragged horns.*
> *And then he blasts the tree and takes the cattle,*
> *And makes milch kine yield blood, and shakes the chain*
> *In a most hideous and dreadful manner."*

Herne the Hunter also has a ballad. A certain R. B. Brough composed fifty verses for him in 1853. Some say that Herne's ghost, wearing stag antlers, haunted the oak at midnight. His spirit became the leader of a wild hunt and he is described as being dressed in a deerskin, mounted on a coal-black stallion preceded by an owl in full flight. This owl may be associated with Tutursel, which flew before Woden, the leader of the hunt in north European versions. During this century the spectre of Herne has been reported twice, once before the Great War of 1914, followed by another appearance heralding the economic crisis in 1931. Thus any appearance is

Herne's Oak. Old print.

traditionally accepted as a warning that the nation is in danger, or that the royal family is threatened.

The trivial aspect of Shakespeare's life is often commented upon, and though the record is lean enough, local lore insists that he was a member of a "drinking team" at Stratford-on-Avon. Villages close by held ale-swilling competitions, a parallel to the gregarious activities of our modern darts teams. The drunkenness of the work-people of the Stratford and Bidford areas was doubtless due to the high standard of wages earned in the local quarries. Returning from one such bout against a team at "Drunken Bidford", as the village was known, and deserted by his three stupefied team-mates, Master William found the company of a crab-apple tree on the banks of the Avon and fell asleep beneath it.

Shakespeare retold the story of that night's repose some years later at the Falcon Tavern in Bidford, revealing that he had dreamed his plot for *A Midsummer Night's Dream* and concocted a rhyme about the people and places with whom and where he spent such inebriating and adventurous evenings:

Piping Pibworth, dancing Marston,
Haunted Hilborough, hungry Grafton,
Dredging Exall, Papist Wrixford,
Beggarly Brown, and Drunken Bidford.

The Sidney Oak.

The Crab Tree became famous after this incident, and although it no longer exists boxes of its wood are still preserved as precious relics. The tree was marked on an early Ordnance Survey Map, and even as late as 1943 the site was pinpointed as being on the right of the main road from Bidford to Stratford-on-Avon on local maps.

There are several trees of note at Penshurst Place, Kent, the birthplace of Sir Philip Sidney. Some misunderstanding prevails over the origins of the title of the Sidney Oak, which Lord de L'Isle believes to be nine hundred years old. It may have been Sidney's favourite tree, but if so we dispute the opinion that it could possibly have been the tree planted to commemorate the poet's birth, an argument reinforced by Ben Jonson's lines:

That taller tree, which of a nut was set,
At his birth where all the Muses met.

Those words allude rather to a beech than an oak. Southey was of the opinion that the Sidney Tree had been destroyed:

Upon his natal day the acorn here
Was planted; it grew up a stately oak,
And in the beauty of its strength it stood
And flourish'd, when its perishable part
Had moulder'd dust to dust. That stately oak
Itself hath moulder'd now.

Yet a Sidney Oak is still firmly implanted there today, and it is accepted as that tree. Like the oak, Sidney was described as a being whose spirit was too high for the court, and whose integrity was too stubborn for the cabinet. Both Landseer and Nasmyth have portrayed the tree, and three lesser known artists have used it as a subject. A writer in *Country Life* in 1897 gave its girth as 33 ft. at one foot from the ground and 27 ft. at six feet.

The overtures of the poets in this vicinity were not entirely made to Sidney's Oak, for local information rumours that Edmund Waller tried to impress his love to "Saccharissa" upon another oak at Bidborough nearby:

"Go, boy, and carve this passion on the bark
Of younder tree, which stands the sacred mark
Of noble Sidney's birth."

Saccharissa was, of course, Dorothy Sidney, Countess of Sunderland. She had been residing at Bounds, an estate in this part of Kent.

Waller and Dorothy Sidney met many times under the oak, later known as Bounds Oak. Waller has his own tree, in the garden of a house at Coleshill, Amersham, Buckinghamshire. It is still known as Waller's Oak.

After the poet Cowper died, papers were found among his property mentioning the girth of oaks in Yardley Chase and at the Lodge, Castle Ashby, Northamptonshire. A favourite oak was the Yardley Oak, over 22 ft. in girth, and another at the Lodge of 28 ft. Hayley, in his *Life and Writings of Cowper*, rejoiced in the discovery of a jotting which referred to a poem of 161 lines written about the trees in the Chase at Yardley. Alas! That contribution has never been discovered.

Another oak in the drive around the Chase was traditionally known as Judith, as it had been planted by William the Conqueror's niece, and although a dead wreck it was meticulously described by Cowper. No doubt the poet had ventured to other parts of the Salcey Forest, in which the Chase fell, to meditate on those two gargantuans Gog and Magog, great specimen oaks at that time of 32 ft. and 31 ft. in girth. In 1959, both these patriarchs of Salcey were dead and dry, yet still majestic in their petrified state. Although balding, Salcey Forest was sufficiently inland to escape a main deforestation for the construction of ships, the difficult and long journeys to shipyards acting as deterrents to comfortable profits for the various negotiators in the wood trade. A pattern of retained oakwoods, some stagheaded, with a smattering of naturally regenerated trees has been a legacy left to Midland counties, although certain entrepreneurs will probably find a use for what remains, unless our sense of values genuinely changes. Perhaps Cowper allows us some encouragement in the last line of an unfinished poem addressed to the Yardley Oak:

> *Yet life still lingers in thee, and puts forth*
> *Proof not contemptible of what she can*
> *Even where death predominates. The Spring*
> *Finds thee not less alive to her sweet force*
> *Than yonder upstarts of the neighbouring wood*
> *So much thy juniors, who their birth received*
> *Half a millennium since the date of thine.*

The Meynell Langley Oak, Derbyshire, reflects the passing of history in the Meynell family. A poem by Godfrey Meynell, written in 1820, records the ancestral losses at home and abroad from the Conqueror's time, through Crécy and up to the Parliamentary Wars. The oak's career is compared to the fortunes of the family residing at

Langley Hall today. Most of the oaks on the estate were mutilated by Cromwell's men, but the structure of this one oak, its girth and other proportions, defied destruction completely.

The Meynell Langley Oak stands alone, the main feature of the place, and has become symbolic of an old family clinging to the land. Acorns still appear on the tree, but they are difficult to propagate, although several trees have been successfully rooted locally. At the adjacent house, Kedleston, there remain many old oaks. A few lines from Meynell's poem are typical and harmonize the history:

> But days and years a change will bring, my head shows the stag horn,
> Though my arms are broad and my leaf is green in summer's early morn.
> Newcastle's Duke next claimed the soil, a daughter ends her race,
> And once again I viewed a change in this my long-loved place.
> King Charles the Good should have ruled the land, but rebels held the sway
> And my noble Duke gave his helping hand, to ward the blow away.

At Clifton Grove, in Nottinghamshire, is a fine avenue of mixed oaks, elms, and beeches, planted two centuries ago and stretching for more than a mile. Its grandeur is immortalized by the county poet Henry Kirk White in his poem *Clifton Grove*, and in prose by his depressing legend of the *Fair Maid of Clifton*.

The opening of Edward Thwaites' epic poem *King of the Woods* is a simple introduction to a tree which saw the assembly of bowmen from the farms around Pott Yeats in Littledale, Lancashire, on a morning in 1513:

> In Pott Yeats Wood at Littledale
> There stands an ancient oak,
> As King of the Woods it is known
> To all the local folk.
> Regal it is, its massive trunk
> Is sixteen feet in girth,
> Great boughs extending all around,
> Tower above the earth.

The long march of the bowmen ended at Flodden Field, where they overcame the Scots and saw the death of James IV of Scotland. The land close to the oak was given to Robert Baines, a standard bearer to Mounteagle of Hornby Castle, in recognition of his bravery at that battle. To this day one of the fields at Pott Yeats is known as "Flodden".

London has few literary trees, but one little-known specimen still

Wood Street Tree.

flourishing is at the Cheapside end of Wood Street, a plane tree referred to by Wordsworth in his verses on Poor Susan. While standing in Wood Street listening to the singing of a thrush in the tree she has visions of the country:

> *T'is a note of enchantment: what ails her? she sees*
> *A mountain ascending, a vision of trees:*
> *Bright volumes of vapour through Lothbury glide,*
> *And a river flows on through the vale of Cheapside.*

The mention of a tree in any printed or painted work prompts the student to seek it out. But when the Fyfield Elm occurs in Matthew Arnold's *Scholar Gipsy* he will be disappointed to know that the tree, which stood between Abingdon and Fyfield in Berkshire, has been lost. Before its decay, it was 36 ft. in circumference, though the trunk was hollow. Known once as the Tubney Elm, Arnold illustrated the delightful scene around the tree in a couplet:

Maidens, who from the distant hamlets come
To dance around the Fyfield elm in May.

We may wonder if Old Crome's Oak, or the Poringland Oak, as the painting is titled, still exists. John Crome's work will certainly survive his tree, although an old oak in Carr's Lane in the Norfolk village is still declared to be his original subject.

Dickens was more concerned to describe the shrill and windy elements in grotesque backgrounds to grim scenes than to give particulars of trees. But in *Oliver Twist* he allows Bill Sykes and Oliver to rest under a yew tree at Sunbury, Middlesex, en route to their proposed robbery at Shepperton. "As they passed Sunbury Church the clock struck seven. There was a light in the ferry-house opposite, which streamed across the road and threw into more sombre shadows a dark yew tree, with graves beneath it. There was a dull sound of water not far off, and the leaves of the old tree stirred gently in the night wind. It seemed like quiet music for the repose of the dead." The Sunbury Yew, immortal and impartial, guarding sanctity, yet allowing Dickens a licence to lend a shelter for profanity.

Walt Disney always believed in location work and his live-acting films were often shot on original sites, even if the stories were fictional. Old Romney, in Kent, with its ancient yew tree, supplied a spectral and impressive backcloth for his harrowing scenes in the film *Dr. Syn*; perhaps that tree *has* encountered similar affairs of double-dealing and smuggling, and the script centred upon it no doubt echoed previous performances held long ago before the camera saw its first image.

Eynsford, a pretty little village in Kent, celebrated the first Arbor Day in England at the commemoration of Queen Victoria's Diamond Jubilee. Some of the trees planted on the annual Arbor Day still remain; they were planted in such a way that the initial letter of the name of each tree would together form words and sentences. There were five sets of these, and from the station into the village on the left-hand side the following quotation from Browning's *Rabbi Ben Ezra* may be spelled out:

The best is yet to be
The last of life, for which the first was made.

In the meadow on the left-hand side of the village going towards the mill from Little Mote Gate, the trees planted in the year of the Queen's death were arranged to form the line from Tennyson:

She wrought her people lasting good

Each letter of every word commences the name of the species of tree and the formation is as follows:

S ycamore
H ickory
E lm

W alnut
R obinia
O ak
U lmus
G ingko
H ornbeam
T horn

H orse Chestnut
E lm
R obinia

P oplar
E lm
O ak
P oplar
L aburnam
E lm

L iquidambar
A sh
S ervice Tree
T horn
I lex
N orway Maple
G uelder Rose

G um
O ak
O ak
D amson

Most of these trees are in the Towercroft Meadow. Their names are set out in full as this is the only example still preserved complete. Elsewhere, one set of eleven trees has now only five survivors, and of four trees planted where the War Memorial stands only the lime remains. The Arbor Day trees were generously tended by the late Elliot Downs Till, a villager who spent a good deal of his life preserving and restoring the beauty around him.

That most famous of Shropshire trees, the Royal Oak, which sheltered the refugee Charles II, and which will be discussed later, has been featured so much in literature, from Evelyn's *Sylva* to the

The Caerwys Tree, Flintshire. Bards composed their odes here underneath the sycamore tree, and hurried with them to the old town hall across the way where the Eisteddfod was held. Replacement planting.

modern historical novel *Royal Escape* by Georgette Heyer, that a simple passing reference to Cowley's lyric will be sufficient:

The Royal Youth, born to out-brave his Fate,
Within a neighbouring oak maintained his state,
The faithful boughs in kind allegiance spread
Their shelt'ring branches round his awful head,
Twin'd their rough arms, and thicken'd all the shade.

Many trees were favourite haunts of writers. Alfresco thoughts were no doubt illuminating, and suited well to the moods of the naturalist scribe. Aubrey de Vere usually wrote his poetry while ruminating under an oak in Little Heaven, a place in the Adare Forest, Limerick. W. H. Davies was known to spend many of his working days under an oak tree, about which he wrote in an ode, *The Old Oak Tree*. This specimen is quite healthy today, and stands in the village of Sevenoaks Weald, Kent. Davies spent hours leaning on a gate here, staring at the tree and watching children climbing it. While living there he completed his *Autobiography of a Super-Tramp*.

The charm of Gilbert White's nature reportage will long outlive the electronic tape recordings of wild-life of our time. In his *History of Selborne*, there is a touching description of an oak and its tenants in Losel's Wood. White says the oaks in the Hampshire wood were of singular value because of their peculiar growth, tall and tapered like firs, but standing close together. They had very small crowns, no large limbs, were about 60 ft. in height and only a foot in diameter at the smallest ends. In the centre of this grove grew the Raven Oak which, by contrast, bulged out into large excrescences about the middle of the stem. A pair of ravens had fixed their residence on it for a number of years. Local youths had attempted to get at this eyrie, and the difficulties in reaching the birds' abode only whetted their ambitions. When they reached the overhang they found it comparable to a severe climb and had to admit defeat. The ravens built their nests year after year in smug security, until the day came for the tree to be felled. It was February, when the raven usually sits, and the dam was upon the nest; the saw was applied to the butt, wedges inserted in the opening, and the woods echoed to the heavy blows of the beetle and the mallet. The tree began to nod, yet still the raven sat. At last, when the tree gave way, the bird was flung from her nest, and though her maternal affection deserved a better fate she was whipped by the boughs which brought her dead to the ground.

White describes many of the trees around Selborne, especially that

Thomas Moore's Tree, Vale of Avoca, Eire

stalwart known as the Selborne Yew, which still guards the church. He stated that it was 23 ft. in circumference, and it shed great clouds of dust—a male tree. It stands today as an epitaph to Gilbert White.

At Dalilea House, Moidart, in Scotland, the Jacobite bard Alasdair Macdonald planted an oak in 1745, no doubt imitating the practice of the Welsh poets and minstrels of Elizabethan times. The Bard's Tree still stands.

The attraction of a tree in a strategic setting, such as the sycamore at Caerwys, Flintshire, was not overlooked when Elizabeth I ordered the first official Eisteddfod to be held in that village in 1568. Before that time a scrabbly affair had taken place as an annual event and dated from the twelfth century. The practice of issuing trade certificates to minstrels and various craftsmen on these occasions highly enhanced the proceedings. Contestants sat around the tree, the centrepiece of the arena, and having composed their songs to suitable harmony, memorized or written their odes, the eager students would flit across the highway to the old town hall where the Eisteddfod examinations were held. Only qualified persons were henceforth permitted to meander across the country, benefitting communities with their songs or playing the harp. The original practices of this gathering were discontinued for a long period after Tudor times but were resumed in 1819. The old tree, known as the Caerwys Tree, eventually had to be removed in the interests of road safety, but a new planting has been made on the original site in reverence to those small beginnings.

On State Forest property at Coole Park, Gort, in Co. Galway, is a very large copper beech which has suffered the indignity of some distinguished memorials. Prominent guests have carved their initials on the smooth receptive grey bole. Time will probably heal the scars made by George Bernard Shaw, W. B. Yeats, A. E. (George) Russell, Sean O'Casey, E. M. Forester, Katherine Tynan Hickson, J. M. Synge, James Stephens, J. B. Morton, Violet Martin and Eva Gore-Booth, all at the invitation of Lady Gregory. No great damage has really been caused by these subscribers as the carvings have been carried out over a period of time, and no doubt such illustrious graffiti will ensure the conservation of the tree. The beech is known locally as the Autograph Tree.

At Rathdrum, Wicklow, is the skeleton of a tree beside which Thomas Moore, Ireland's greatest poet, wrote the *Meeting of the Waters*. The specie is not known, though the structure of the stark crown resembles hawthorn, a tree of high esteem in Eire, especially

Nannau Oak or Spirit's Blasted Tree. Old print.

if isolated. Well railed to protect it from souvenir hunters, this frail monument marks the site where the bard composed much of his work and is well known as Thomas Moore's Tree. The village of Rathdrum is at the point where the Avonmore and Avonberg rivers meet—a setting with an audible emotional swell suited to Moore's metre.

The Nannau Oak, which was wind-thrown in 1813, is still whispered about in the neighbourhood of Dolgelly. Sir Walter Scott referred to the tree in *Marmion*:

> *All nations have their omens drear,*
> *Their legends wild of woe and fear;*
> *To Cambria look—the peasant see,*
> *Bethink him of Glendowery,*
> *And shun the Spirit's blasted tree.*

Among the Welsh, this oak was celebrated for centuries as the Hobgoblin's Hollow Tree, the Haunted Oak and the Spirit's Blasted

Tree; it stood on the estate of Sir Robert Williams Vaughan, of Nannau Park. In the troubled times of Henry IV the Welsh chieftain, Owen Glendower, turned to the advantage of his race the rivalry in the English factions of Red and White Roses and in 1400 restored the independence of a large part of Wales. This attractive figure, who revived the great attributes of Llewelyn the Great, became the victim of conscience from the day of the following incident: Glendower and Howel Sele, a cousin and secretly a follower of the House of Lancaster, accompanied by a friend named Maddoc, set out on a hunting trip on the Nannau estate. Howel, seizing his opportunity for treachery, feinted at taking aim at a passing doe, only to release his arrow directly at Glendower's breast. But his intended victim wore armour hidden below his clothing and the arrow slipped embarrassingly to the ground. Owen then grappled with Sele till life seemed to have left him. A pact of silence between the two friends was struck and Howel Sele's body, whether stunned or dead is not known, was hustled into the hollow of the oak with some difficulty, and there it remained. Some say that Glendower, on his death-bed, implored Maddoc to reveal the grave; others, that forty years passed before the skeleton of Sele was uncovered, still gripping a rusty sword in his hand.

After the fall of the tree, the owner of Nannau Park had a variety of utensils made from its wood, which was of a beautiful dark colour, approaching ebony. There was scarcely a house that did not have an engraving of the tree framed in its wood.

Selbourne Yew.

Chapter Three

Trees of War

The Brythonic invaders probably introduced iron smelting to these islands shortly before Pytheas, the Greek traveller from Marseilles, recorded his visit here in about 325 B.C.

Thus the native weapons and implements, first of wood, then progressing through the era of bone, stone, flint, to the comparative sophistication of bronze alloy from tin and copper, soon gave way to the stronger and more readily available iron. In smelting the abundant ore, large quantities of fuel were required. The forests seemed limitless, yet the demands of the new and efficient technology became insatiable, and so began the first ruthless exploitation of our natural timber resources. The great forests of the Sussex Weald, the Midlands and the Severn Valley became more and more depleted.

The process went on in a mad geometric progression until the middle of the eighteenth century, although coal had been surface-mined as far back as the fifteenth century, and had even been used by Londoners for domestic heating. John Evelyn, at the close of the seventeenth century, was one of the few with the vision and voice to articulate eloquent warnings about the depredations, and to urge conservation before the point of no return was reached.

The combustibility of certain woods and their charcoal values is outlined in the following table of comparisons suggested by J. C. Loudon. (Similar values had been arrived at empirically by the primitive smelters over the preceding centuries):

	Combustibility	*Charcoal Value*
Beech	1,540	1,600
Scots Pine	1,536	1,724
Hornbeam	1,655	No figure given
Oak	1,497	1,459

Stonewall Park Oak.

	Combustibility	*Charcoal Value*
Alder	985	885
Aspen	970	988
Willow	808	No figure given

Note: Loudon does not give a maximum figure for either of these relative tables, but it is surmised as 2,000.

It can be demonstrated that there is a direct relationship between these factors and the present-day distribution of tree species. The higher the factor, the scarcer the trace of the original indigenous specie in certain areas. For example, the high charcoal value for Scot's Pine may account for its relative scarcity in Southern England (where the first smelting began). Again, the pattern of Roman campaigns and settlements is reflected in the scarcity outline of pine forests. This situation is similarly traceable in latter centuries in Scotland, during the era of Norse and Danish settlers. Interesting to note, too, that the sheer bulk of required fuel meant that it was more economical to transport the ore to the forests, rather than the reverse. This is borne out by evidence recently discovered in Scotland, where neat piles of overgrown cinders have been noticed on the sites of original pine forests.

In Plantagenet and Tudor times the iron foundries began to proliferate, but it wasn't until Elizabeth I became disturbed on account of the depleted forests, ostensibly because of the harm to shipbuilding but no doubt also by her love of the chase, that the first steps were taken to control the wastage and conserve what remained.

In 1581 she gave assent to an act preventing smelting and conversion of timber in the surrounds of London, the industry having crept insidiously from Sussex and Kent into Surrey and the Thames area. The Weald of Kent was exempted, for a time, as it seemed inconceivable that those large woodlands, over 100 miles long by 25 miles wide, could ever be substantially eroded. But by 1585 there were growing doubts about this, and finally the Queen's advisers recommended an Act for the Preservation of Timber in the Wilds of Sussex, Surrey and Kent, to place restrictions on the felling of large trees for charcoal making and iron smelting, because "it is thought that the great Plenty of Timber which hath grown in those parts hath been utterly decayed and spoilt and will in short be utterly consumed and wasted unless some convenient remedy therein be not timely provided". Thus the great woods of the Weald had a stay of execution so that in 1660, when Charles II made his entry into London, over 200,000 acres of trees still remained in Sussex.

However, the demands of the smelters persisted. In 1635, 50,000 men were still employed in over forty blast furnaces, and although there was a reduction in the number of kilns in the early years of the Merry Monarch's reign, the claims of the industry were yet consistent. The blight of deforestation continued over Scotland and England, for as long as there were woods left the smelters and iron-forgers regarded them as their rightful fuel supply.

But the growing use of coal, and the opening up of iron mines in the north of England, caused the southern iron industry to wane. The last surviving smelting furnace in Sussex was at Ashburnham, which closed in 1809. So at last the forests which had supplied the nation with the fuel to forge progressive tools and the weapons of war and defence now became mere place-names and cyphers of their former grandeur, and had their first reprieve.

One could argue that if trees didn't exist weapons would not have evolved from their simplest form. By the same reasoning, man could not have survived without trees, their shelter and climatic influences. Wood, undoubtedly, has shaped his history. The shields and coracles of the ancient Britons were made of osier—a wood associated today solely with wicker work and basketry. The lightweight aspen, a wood with little virtue now, was used for shields and bucklers, because, when struck, it acted as a cushion, and neither cracked nor pierced easily. Where the birch grew profusely, universal use was made of it; domestic furniture and utensils, dwellings, carts, fences and ropes being fashioned from its bark. The wood was formerly used in the Highlands for arrows, and the bark, on the sea coast, peeled off for the making of boats.

Apart from the oak, the indigenous yew tree must claim a high place on our list of *armorum arbor*. There is little doubt that the archer's bow is of very ancient origin, and was originally used without any form of string. Arrows of a very simple form were merely pressed on to a length of pliable wood, one end of which was often fixed in the ground, when the arrow was thus released at the target. The structure and whiplike nature of small trees bending in the wind must have inspired the idea, and man saw the advantages of the missile projected from safe vantage points. Historians differ in their theories regarding the use of the bow. Some state that the men of the Early Iron Age used it, others that it was unknown until early Saxon times. The Eastern civilizations had various forms of bows for many centuries earlier, and their weapons were fashioned from many different woods—laburnum, birch, and sometimes ash on the west of the Holy Land, and from various exotic trees peculiar to the lands of Egypt, Persia and Assyria farther east.

Early bows of the Saxon period were doubtless made from the yews growing in Britain. Again, writers contradict each other about the part of the tree from which the bow was cut; some arguing that the branches of the trees were the raw material, while others claim that the boles, having strength and durability and an enduring pliability, were used. The best bows did not come from British yew trees, but were imported in ships bringing wines from Spain and Venice. Royal Statutes were passed forbidding the export of yew-wood, and obliging all incoming vessels to import ten bow-staves of yew with every butt of wine.

Two kinds of bow were in use by the dawn of the thirteenth century, the long-bow and the cross-bow. Known as an arbalest, the cross-bow was not only much shorter than the former, but mounted upon a stock, and released by a trigger. The great fame our countrymen acquired in archery arose from their skill with the long-bow. This lethal weapon varied in length from 5 ft. 8 in. to 6 ft., with a bend, when strung, of 9 or 10 in. Its power was proportionate to the archer's strength, its range regulated by his height, and the weapon was generally tailored to suit the physical capability of the owner. The string of the bow was of silk or hemp, again imports, although sometimes the stems of climbing plants or hair were used. To receive the notch of the arrow the string was thickened at the midway point. The shaft itself was made either of hard or soft woods, ash, oak and birch being chosen by the fletcher, according to the purposes for which the arrow was intended. Goose-wings supplied the feathers, and in length the arrows varied between 30–36 in. At short range the shaft was drawn back level with the ear; for long flight the notch and string were pulled back to the chest, the archer keeping both eyes fixed on the target until his arrow had struck home.

In the thirteenth century, everyone earning less than 100 pence a year from his land was obliged to possess a bow and arrow, together with other arms. Archery was considered so important that when John Lyon founded Harrow School one of five articles which he added to the statutes was: "You shall allow your child, at all times, bowshafts, bow-strings, and a bracer, to exercise shooting". August 4th was set aside for trials of skill, the victor receiving a silver arrow. Edward II ordered the use of the long-bow, and in the reign of Richard II an Act was passed to compel all servants to practise shooting on Sundays and holidays. The reason for these urgent commands for archery practice was that, because standing armies were unknown, the crown depended upon levies of the barons' retainers being trained and disciplined for battle. An Act of Henry IV laid down that arrows were to be steel-tipped, and those not so equipped would be forfeited and the makers imprisoned.

The feathers of arrows were to consist of two white and one brown or grey, thus at once showing the archer how to place the arrow. Another Act, this time of Edward IV, ordained that every Englishman must own a bow equal to his own height, and that butts were to be erected in every township for the use of the inhabitants on feast-days. Absentees were to be fined a halfpenny.

In the sixth year of Henry VIII's reign, employers had to provide a bow and four arrows for each male servant, stopping the purchase money from his wages piecemeal. Thus was the civil defence of Britain of those times built up. It was the skill of the English archers that enabled Henry II to gain a footing in Ireland, and the name of Strongbow, borne by the leader of the expedition, attests the high repute in which the weapon was held. Crécy, Poitiers and Agincourt were won with the yew long-bow, the most popular weapon throughout the long civil strife between the rival houses of York and Lancaster in the Wars of the Roses. It was highly esteemed long after gunpowder had prepared the way for a complete change in the science of war. Several kings of England were noted for their skill with the bow. Henry VIII shot as well as any of his guards, and Charles I practised archery with considerable success. Charles proclaimed in the eighth year of his reign that the fields near London should not be enclosed to prevent archery practice. Public exhibitions of shooting continued throughout the reigns of Charles II and James II, and an archers' division, until just over a century ago, formed a branch of the Artillery Company. From the time of the first Elizabeth the yew did not figure so prominently in sea power, for the use of gunpowder, very reliant on the supply of charcoal, caused another page to be written in the story of trees.

Whereas the ancient Britons were the first to use oak for ship-building, cypress, alder, pine and silver fir were invariably preferred by the Romans. Britain always had a navy of sorts from the beginnings of her history. The ancient name of Britain, according to the Welsh Bards, was Clas Merddin, "the sea-defended green spot", and we read that before its invasion by Julius Caesar in 52 B.C. a naval engagement took place between the Romans and the Veneti, the latter being aided by the Britons, or Cymry, in which the allied vessels, solidly built of oak, stoutly resisted the beaks of the Roman galleys. Sails were made of skin, and their anchors were attached to iron chains or cables.

The Saxons were noted for their prowess in piracy, and seem to have kept up a formidable marine strength. Their vessels were single-masted, carried one square sail and had curved bottoms, their prows and poops being decorated with wooden images depicting the heads or tails of mythical monsters. King Alfred, by 874, had many ships, some of which carried sixty oars; all were known to have been of oak. William the Conqueror's invading fleet of 900 boats was apparently inferior in quality to those of the Anglo-Saxons, so he set great value on their Navy, and after his conquest gave privileges to the Cinque Ports. King John, in 1214, was the first to claim dominion of the seas. He issued a mandate to his admiral ordering him to arrest and make prizes of ships found in English waters.

In 1380 the first cannon was used aboard. In Henry VII's reign the first three-masted vessel was launched, and in Henry VIII's time many ships were built and dockyards were established at Woolwich, Deptford and Portsmouth.

At this time the laws for the preservation of oak timber began to be enforced, but it is difficult to say exactly when oak plantations were first laid down. In William III's reign another statute was passed empowering commissioners to enclose 2,000 acres in the New Forest for the growth of naval timber, and 200 more (for the space of twenty years). From that period, government plantations of about 6,000 acres of young trees have nominally been kept up.

Although good, clean lengths of oaks were constantly required from large standard oak trees, there was always a steady demand for the crooked parts of the trees, for particular purposes in shipbuilding. Great care was taken by tree-fellers that the twisting crowns of oaks were not damaged when dropped on the forest floor. This meant that the top branches were carefully lowered beforehand by ropes and blocks. The brushwood having been removed piecemeal, the largest arms were sawn off at certain distances from the bole; scaffolds erected, and pit-saws braced together. The body was then cut half-way through at the bottom, or basal area of the tree, and then the whole trunk sawn down the middle vertically, between the arms remaining. The first section was then allowed to fall on to a suitable cushion of brushwood, so that it would not split or be damaged. After that the remaining section of tree was felled in the same

manner. The same method of conversion is today thought of as an
"innovation" of the modern timber industry, where standing timber
is "planked" by mechanical and mobile woodsaws.

The market for "knee" timber meant that stunted oaks of neglected woodlands also had a market. Various methods of growing bent
and twisted trees were devised, which included tying them together
or grubbing trees on one side so that the trunks were laid prone, and
the living side branches facing the sky would continue as upright
"trees".

The larch was used for shipbuilding timbers, especially on the
Tay from 1810 onwards, and its timber was considered shot-proof.
Larch "knees" had much strength and durability, and, had that tree
been introduced to our islands much earlier than the early eighteenth
century, it could have ousted the oak for naval purposes. The knees
of vessels had a number of strong bolts passed through them, generally of iron, to secure the beam ends to the sides of ships. Larch was
more suited to withstand the auguring and seating of the metal, as
it did not split when the bolts were driven home. Also the resinous
gum of the wood prevented the oxidization of the iron.

The elm, so beloved by the undertakers, is extremely durable
underwater, and many men o' war had keels made from it. Boxwood,
an extremely hard and heavy wood which sinks in water, was employed for the intricate parts of shipbuilding, such as pulley-blocks
and pins, wheels and shivers.

The charcoal and heat values of various woods have already been
mentioned. From the thirteenth century onward there arose a further
demand for pre-treated wood for making gunpowder. Subtle mix-
tures of saltpetre, sulphur and charcoal were stockpiled for different
grades of explosives, to suit a range of weapons from cannon to
muskets. The stocks of muskets were invariably made from walnut.

John Evelyn mentions that the demand for walnut was so great
that imports had to supplement the dwindling native variety. The
price of walnut trees rose so high that large specimens could fetch
about £600 each. In France, in 1806, the manufacture of muskets
required about 12,000 trees annually, and in consequence a great
many plantations were made by landowners, and prizes were offered
for the most successful achievements by the Society for the Encouragement of Arts. Monsieur A. M. Michaux, in a letter dated
December 1834, stated that he had planted a nursery of between five
and six acres for the government in the Bois de Boulogne consisting
of 30,000 walnut trees for transplantation, which at the time he

wrote were from 20–30 ft. high. In Britain, the enthusiasm for planting the walnut has never been impressive. Local superstition has tended to adhere to the belief that the man who plants a walnut never lives long enough to see it bear fruit!

So timber has been one of man's greatest aides in his warring throughout the centuries. What of the other side of the picture—the depletion of the forests and man's neglect to replenish them? To some extent the countryside can heal itself, and although the process of natural selection is itself another kind of warfare, harmonious recovery usually follows if Nature is left to its own devices. Not so the thoughtless and selfish selections of man. The few enlightened rulers I have mentioned, who encouraged the private landowners and the state to popularize certain timbers in plantations, are worthy of our gratitude, for their foresight was probably of paramount importance to us. Mercifully, trees will never determine our destiny in war again, except perhaps in the freakish human survival after a nuclear holocaust. Should a few tree species also survive and escape harmful mutation there might be some prospect of continued human tenure of this earth; without the life-nurturing forests, there could be no tolerable future for us.

Many trees have been recorded as having connections with sites of battles, skirmishes and revolts, and some have even been planted to commemorate such events, though not always at the particular location. The following examples I quote are not all still flourishing or preserved.

Straddling the playing fields of Wellington College, near Finchampstead, Berkshire, is a grand avenue of Sequoia Wellingtonia Gigantea trees which John Walter, the founder of *The Times* newspaper, planted in 1869. Growing in double file, there are fifty-five of these American stalwarts in dignified formation on each of two sides of Wellingtonia Avenue, which runs from the college to Finchampstead Ridges. The Iron Duke died in 1852, the year of the discovery of the great redwood trees in Sierra Nevada. His fame was influential enough to cause the substitution of the more apt botanical name "Washingtonia" to that of "Wellingtonia". In the grounds of the college is a cedar under which is interred a hoof of his famous charger Copenhagen, which he rode at the Battle of Waterloo.

Although I am not allowed to divulge the actual site of a lime tree in a rectory near Royston, Hertfordshire, I can say that it has a ring sunk in it to which the Iron Duke would tie his horse when visiting his youngest brother, in the years from 1812 to 1822. The Hon. Gerald Wellesley was incumbent for this parish during those years. The wood around the ring has to be cut away regularly to prevent it from becoming completely grown over and burying the metal.

On Bucklebury Common, in Berkshire, an avenue of oaks over a mile long was established by Lord Bolingbroke to commemorate the Marlborough victories. He planted them at a time when Queen Anne visited his manor house, since demolished. On this land Cromwell encamped in 1643 with 20,000 men, in preparation for the crucial confrontation with Charles I at the Battle of Newbury.

In the same county is a mulberry tree at Long Wittenham, under which Oliver Cromwell used to be entertained by certain friends and upholders of the Parliamentary cause. John Hampden's parents lived in the neighbouring village of what is today Clifton Hampden, and that in itself might seem to lend some authenticity to the story. Hampden, an English patriot, opposed Charles I, especially on the issue of "Ship Money" tax. The mulberry tree itself fell over, but its roots continued to thrive.

The Verney family of Claydon, in Buckinghamshire, had for centuries a tradition of public service and allegiance to the crown. Claydon House, with its great cedars and oaks, the latter of unknown age, was visited by Charles I at a time when "the wooden walls of England" required more timber than ever. It was probably the young Edmund Verney who offered the oaks on the estate to the king, but whoever the donor it is certain that the monarch himself considered the trees 300 years too old at that time. Some of those ancients still stand today; one specimen, though not tall, being 36 ft. in girth at its base.

Another tree with Civil War associations was the Boconnoc Oak. It stood on the downs near the park of Boconnoc, Cornwall. Some years ago it was reported that only a stump remained marking the place where Charles Stuart won a battle and where he planted his standard. Legend persists that he was fired at when performing the ceremony, the ball passing through the tree and that, after the incident, the leaves changed almost to white. Another popular tradition is that the leaves turned a very pale green after the king's death. In Polwherel's *History of Cornwall, 1826*, there is a note: "Near to the gate of Rookwood Grove, leading to Boconnoc Parsonage, there remains the stump of an aged oak, in which the King's Standard was fixed. The upper part of the tree was broken off in the wind in March

1783, about 9 ft. above the ground. Within the memory of the oldest inhabitants of this county, it had produced scarcely any other than variegated leaves which had originally changed colour after an attempt to assassinate the king while receiving the sacrament under its branches. The shot was said to have passed through the tree, and a hole made by the woodpeckers was shown in confirmation of the tale, probably from the king having been actually shot at when in the hall-walk and a fisherman killed who was gazing at him."

At Lanhydrock, about five miles from Boconnoc, is an avenue of beeches, two rows on each side of the drive to Lord Robartes's gate-house. During the Civil War the Royalist owner was imprisoned by Cromwell in his own battlements, and afterwards in London. During his captivity in the city he issued orders for the avenue planting to be carried out. A story goes that on one of Cromwell's destructive forays near Dalton-le-Dale in Durham he rode within a mile of that tiny village, and tradition says that the large chestnut tree that concealed any sign of the church saved the inhabitants from interference, for he promptly turned back, thinking that a place without a church was too insignificant for his attentions.

At Fontmell Magna, Dorset, is a large, old, pollarded elm in the centre of the village. At one time the preaching cross stood at the side of the tree, and a seat encircled the base. The two additions had given the tree the double titles of Cross Tree and Gossips' tree. Originally this elm, which I consider to be at least 400 years old, may have been one of the gospel trees referred to earlier, and there are records to substantiate that Cromwell destroyed the cross. The seat would have accounted for the second title. But even that has now gone, probably through damage caused by the elm's continual expansion in ring growth. The house standing in the shadow of the tree is named Cross House.

Another of Cromwell's victims was Sir Benjamin Tichborne, who resided at West Tisted, Hampshire, in one of the Dower houses. A once famous oak tree in a field near the house sheltered him from Cromwell's troopers, but a short time later, while hidden in the priest's-hole beneath his roof, he was shot accidentally by one of his own troopers who was cleaning his gun. Sir Benjamin's Oak, as it was known for centuries, is only one of a number of trees which offered respite, whether temporary or otherwise, from Cromwell's hue and cry. The Tockholes Oak, in the village of that name in Lancashire, was a mere shell in 1958. Standing in a farmyard near the ancient parish church, it was only 12 ft. high and girthed about

10 ft. A tale of a Royalist using the hollow as a hiding place has never been substantiated, but a skirmish did take place nearby in this strangely isolated hamlet wedged between the heights of Darwen and Rivington. Relics excavated in a nearby field known as Kill or Kiln were identified as horse skulls, human bones, cannon balls and fragments of weapons used in 1642.

In Henley, Oxfordshire, are two trees noted by the Henley Historical Society. The first, Rupert's Elm, is in the town at Northfield End, at the junction of the Marlow and Oxford Roads, facing a row of houses which formerly formed the Bell Inn, a coaching inn with stabling for a hundred horses. From this tree Prince Rupert hanged a Roundhead spy during the Civil Wars. The second, named Big Oak, is in reasonably good shape for its age and is the tree in which Charles I hid when he escaped from Oxford disguised as a servant. Another oak, renowned as a refuge from the Roundheads, was at Blythburgh in Suffolk, close to the home of Sir John Rous, where he hid for several days, his wife feeding him clandestinely. In the years after, Sir Robert Rous and some of his friends would gather together at night around the tree to pledge the king across the water. Two other trees, however, lay claims to have hidden Cromwell himself— an oak at Bannerhill, near Leek Wootton, Warwickshire, which was apparently capable of concealing eight men, and another, somewhat shattered, tree at Shustoke, Coleshill, in the same county. At Edge-hill are many fine beeches planted by Saunderson Miller of the Neo-Gothic Movement. They are known as King's Crown. The land on which they stand is a spur known as Knowle-end-Charles, where the king is supposed to have "examined the plain below with his prospect-glass" before the battle. Miller first planted a ring of trees, but eventually extended the undertaking along the whole ridge.

There are three important oaks in Shropshire traditionally associated with wars: the Watch Oak, at Wroxeter, by the side of the Shrewsbury–Iron Bridge Road and about seven miles south-east of Shrewsbury, has a plaque stating that it was used as a look-out post during the Civil War. The Shelton Oak, $1\frac{3}{4}$ miles WNW of Shrewsbury, by the Holyhead Road, is marked in Gothic characters on the 1 inch Ordnance Map, and it is believed to be the tree from which Owen Glendower watched the progress of the Battle of Shrewsbury in 1403. Historians disagree with this claim by local residents, pointing out that Glendower was detained in South Wales at the time of the battle.

After the decisive Battle of Worcester, on September 3rd, 1651, the fugitive Pretender, later to become Charles II, succeeded in finding refuge at Boscobel House, Tong, in Shropshire, a property rented from the Giffard family by William Penderel, a Royalist. Charles first reached Whiteladies, a house built on the site of an old convent, near to Boscobel. The hunt for the royal fugitive was so keen that the king spent an entire day, September 4th, in Spring Coppice, a wood on the Boscobel estate, wrapped in a blanket but wet and cold and cheered only by the fidelity of Richard Penderel, a brother of the tenant. The constant drizzle during that day may have discouraged the Roundhead pursuers. At night, he was removed to Hobbal Grange, Richard Penderel's house, where he changed his clothes and continued on his hazardous flight. About five o'clock on the morning of the 6th he and his guide arrived at Boscobel House. It was here, in company with Colonel Carlis, that the well-known oak tree adventure took place. After some refreshment they concealed themselves in the branches of the oak, a tree that had apparently been pollarded and had thrown up a number of thick leading shoots, well covered in leaves. It was not hollow, and had been cut back only three years previously. Here they remained during the whole of the day, the king dozing off, his head on a cushion the Penderels had provided. That night Charles and his protector descended and made their way back to Boscobel House, secreting themselves in the cheese-room, their way of escape ensured, by way of a chimney, back to the oak should Cromwell's men send another search party to the house.

The events that followed are legion, terminating in the escape to France. From the alfresco concealment in the Royal Oak have sprung numerous legends, traditions and ceremonies. Oak-apple Day is the best known ceremony commemorating the restoration of the monarchy in the person of Charles II on May 29th, 1660. Unfortunately for our tourist industry, the original tree does not exist today, but is supplanted by another tree, supposedly grown from an acorn from the oak, which stands near the site of the vanished royal tree. John Evelyn, in *Sylva*, wrote that the original tree was killed in his time, 1704, by people who persisted in hacking off boughs until the tree was destroyed.

Loudon, who stated that the tree at Boscobel was in Staffordshire (Boscobel is on the border between Shropshire and that county), confirms that "the Royal Oak was prematurely destroyed by an ill-judged passion for relics and a huge bulk of timber consisting of many loads was taken away by the handful". About 1750, Dr. Stukeley, a celebrated antiquary, mentioned that the Royal Oak was standing in his time. "A bow-shot from Boscobel House, just by a horse-track passing through the wood, stands the Royal Oak, into which the King and his companion climbed by means of a hen roost-ladder, when they judged it no longer safe to stay in the house, the family reaching them with victuals with the nut-hook. The tree is now en-closed with a brick wall, the inside whereof is covered with laurel, of which we may say, as Ovid did of that before the Augustan palace, *mediamque tuberee quercum*."

The earliest records of the tree were given by the Reverend George Plaxton, Rector of Donington, which was in the Parish of Boscobel in the late seventeenth century. He recorded: "The Royal Oak was a fair spreading tree, the boughs of it all lined and covered with ivy. Here in the thick of these boughs, the King sat in the daytime with Colonel Carlis, and in the night lodged in Boscobel House. So that they are strangely mistaken who judged it as an old hollow oak,

Frenchmans' Oak, Winchfield, Hants.

whereas it was a gay and flourishing tree surrounded by a great many more and, as I remember in Mr. Evelyn's History of Medals, you have one of King James I or Charles I, where there is a fine spread oak with this epigraph, *Seris nepotibus umbra*, which I leave to your thoughts. . . ." The poor remains of the Royal Oak are now fenced in by a handsome brick wall, at the charge of Basil Fitzherbert, Esq., with an inscription over the gate, upon a blue stone in letters of gold. The enclosure was put up about twenty or thirty years ago, but the place deserved a better memorial. The English translation from the Latin reads:

> "This most highly favoured tree, planted by the God through whom kings reign, to afford shelter to His Majesty King Charles the Second, was enclosed with a wall by Bazil and Jane Fitzherbert, as well to preserve to posterity a memorial of the auspicious event as to be a token of their own steadfast loyalty."

In a little book on Boscobel by the Reverend G. H. Cope, published in 1951, the oak standing now is questioned as being a seedling from the original:

The Royal Oak

"It is a matter of dispute whether the tree surrounded by iron railings in the adjoining field is the original tree in which Charles hid, or its successor. The third Earl of Bradford (1814–1894) made a statement dated May 6th, 1878: 'When the wood was cut down, the tree into which the King had climbed was left standing, and was regarded with pride and affection. It has been known from father to son from that time until this. As to its being a substitute of any sort, least of all an acorn from the original tree, I discard the idea as ludicrous and absurd. I have known the tree myself for half a century, and it looks very much now as it did then. My father used to say that he had heard his father and grandfather speak in the same sense and the recollection of the tree by his grandfather would easily carry him back as far as 1740, which would be less than ninety years after the King sat in the tree.' When the Evans family came into possession of the property the remains of the old wall surrounding the tree were pulled down and iron pallisades put up. An inscription was added in 1817 saying that the existing tree had sprung from the original Royal Oak. About thirty years afterwards, Miss Evans, being persuaded that it was the identical oak that had sheltered the King, altered the inscription to: 'This Tree, under the blessing of Almighty God, the

King of Kings, had the honour of sheltering from his foe His Majesty Charles II.'

"It therefore seems unlikely that the present tree was grown from an acorn of the original tree, as it appears to be more than 300 years old, seeing that it has made no growth recently, but has slowly declined for the last sixty years."

One doubtful snippet of opinion about the escapade has recently been put forward, viz.: that Charles took a pigeon into the tree and allowed it to fly off at the time when Cromwell's troops were searching below. The act was timed to deceive the soldiers into thinking that no one could possibly be in the tree, since a pigeon flew out at their approach.

From all the circumstances it appears that the tree now standing at Boscobel is a direct descendant of the Royal Oak, and that it is a transplant of a sapling grown from an acorn of that tree in 1660, about the time of the Restoration, as nearly on the same site as the remains of the original would allow. There are many plantings from the acorns from this tree in parts of the British Isles, although few seem to have had plaques placed upon them recording the fact.

One such planting is in the Dropmore Arboretum in Buckinghamshire, at the west end, close to the great avenue of cedars of Lebanon where a flourishing oak may be seen on a sloping bank. Originally, a plaque, now disappeared, was placed here with the inscription:

THIS TREE
RAISED FROM AN ACORN
OF THE OAK WHICH SHELTERED
CHARLES THE 2ND AT BOSCOBEL
IS PLANTED AND CHERISHED HERE
AS A MEMORIAL,
NOT OF HIS PRESERVATION
BUT OF THE RE-ESTABLISHMENT
OF ENGLAND
THE TRUE SOURCE
OF HER PROSPERITY AND GLORY

Another is in the old cemetery in the village of Netherseale, near Burton-on-Trent. Recent correspondence from Mrs. Nancy Groves informs me that she has at her new home seven oaks growing from acorns collected years ago from the existing tree at Boscobel. More interesting still, that she is a recipient of the Elizabeth-Yates-

Penderel Trust Pension, which was settled by Charles II in perpetuity on his saviours and their descendants. Thus, royal descendants of the Boscobel Oak are now in her garden at Whitchurch in Hampshire.

A magnificent oak at Irton Hall, Holmbrook, Cumberland, recalls the conflict between Lancastrian and Yorkist in the Wars of the Roses of the fifteenth century. The Hall, now a school, still proudly displays Henry VI's Oak on the front lawn. It is about 45 ft. in height and 14 ft. in girth at 3 ft. up the bole, a portion of the tree being hollow. It was in this cavity that Henry VI took refuge after the Battle of Muncaster. A servant at the Hall gave food to the king while he was hiding in the tree. Later the man's loyalty to Henry was discovered, and he was executed.

In Sheriff Hutton Park, ten miles from York, there still stands part of an oak, fenced off, known as the Warwick Oak. An old book on Sheriff Hutton sets out: "In the Park are many fine oaks of venerable appearance. One of these, partly blown down many years ago, is said to have been standing in the reign of Richard III, and was titled 'Warwick Oak', from having been the limit to which the unfortunate Earl of Warwick was permitted to extend his walk whilst a prisoner in the Castle. There is a local tradition of the elders of the village that there was a subterranean passage between the Castle and the Park, but for what its purpose was is entirely unknown."

Although the best yew bows came from the Continent in mediaeval and Tudor times, the supply was inadequate to equip the whole force of the standing army and the militia, so large numbers of yews were planted in the homeland. Even so the species must have become seriously depleted by Plantagenet times. The natural indigenous groves of these slow-growing conifers had therefore to be felled very circumspectly. The demand resulted in primitive forms of woodland management—at least in differentiating between the sexes of the trees, and in learning correct felling procedures to ensure natural regeneration. Husbandmen soon observed that seed falling on to the ground did not always germinate, but that regurgitation of the seed by birds was more effective; the juicy aril being digested, the hard seed rejected, a percentage of these "droppings" germinating after two or three years.

All over the British Isles today we can find strange glades of yews of varying ages, legacies from our warlike economy. These were often venerated for superstitious reasons that have baffled later inquiry. The most interesting groves are still evident in the South of England.

Badbury Rings, Dorset.

At Hod Hill, near Shroton, Dorset, areas of the yews still grow where their prototypes were planted after the Battle of Agincourt to ensure vital supplies of bows.

Four miles North of Chichester is a coomb known as Kingley Vale, where yews of different ages grow thickly. A tradition notes that yews were planted here about the beginning of the ninth century, to commemorate a defeat of the Vikings by men of Chichester. The grotesque and sombre antique trees permit nothing to grow beneath their dim canopy. Rain rarely reaches the earth through the evergreen crowns, and the sunlight seldom penetrates to the soft, composted floor. The coomb covers more than 200 acres, and the oldest trees grow at the bottom of the valley. At one time the belief that the grove had been an ancient pagan preaching site was so strong that few would venture near their eerie cloisters after daylight hours. The coomb slopes over 600 ft. upwards to a plateau, the top of Bow Hill, from which there is a view of Chichester Harbour.

In the village of Rufforth, near York, yews were planted in a field adjoining the churchyard in 1644 to commemorate the local men who died at the Battle of Marston Moor. Thirteen yews still remain, near-immortal reminders of nameless men—more fitting than a

E

scratched memorial on a stone. At Portchester Church, Portsmouth, near the castle, is a yew of no great age, though extremely well grown for its 150 years. During the Napoleonic Wars, French prisoners of war, were held in the garrison near the church. Part of their duties included nearby maintenance work. During their break-times they were allowed to cook their meals on the side. Alas, a wood-stove was lit too close to the old yew which guarded the church and the tree was destroyed by fire. After the indignation and the apologies came practical suggestions for requital. The remains of the tree were grubbed out by the P.O.W.s. A smaller yew tree was purchased for one shilling and threepence locally by the Frenchmen and carefully planted in the hole. Further reminders of the naval history of Nelson's time are at Catherington, Horndean, Portsmouth, where there are many trees planted by Captain Hood.

A well-known landmark still stands a mile out from Winchfield, near Odiham in Hampshire, known as Frenchman's Oak. During the Peninsular Wars, French prisoners, who were billeted close by in cottages near their work of quarrying, had this oak as their ''parole'' limit for recreation. Attempts have been made to preserve the slowly decaying tree, and it has been lopped and propped to prevent further breakages. A similar oak occurs at Whitchurch, near Tavistock, again a ''limit'' tree, known as the Honour Oak.

Between Blandford Forum and Wimborne in Dorset is the famous avenue of beeches bordering the road alongside the Iron Age hill fort of Badbury Rings. At one time there were 364 trees on one side and 365 on the other side of the road. Here again we see a reminder of the planting labours of French P.O.W.s of the same period. In summer, the interlinked branches across the roadway form one of the longest natural tunnels known, allowing the occasional shaft of sunlight across the busy highway. The avenue is still in fairly good condition, although the occasional tree has either died back through competition from its fellows or lost branches in the high winds that strike the ridge from the south-west.

Leading from nearby Shapwick to Badbury Rings was a Roman road, and many strange scenes must have been witnessed here before the strongly held fort finally fell to the all-conquering Romans. The massive earthwork on the hilltop, covering eighteen acres at an altitude of over 300 ft., is surrounded by three great ramparts, 30–40 ft. in height, with ditches between. A silent and mysterious place, whose flat summit, now thickly wooded, might once have known ruthless siege and savage defence, and perhaps the rites of the Druids.

The Seven Men of Moidart.

An awesome place that has its ghosts. Some years ago archaeological students, camping out on the summit, were disturbed by the clash of metal, the sound of marching men and shouted military orders in a strange tongue. The camp is reported to have been abandoned in panic and one of the students suffered a mental breakdown.

Many French prisoners were quartered in Scotland, and 190 officers, billeted in Selkirk, in whom Sir Walter Scott took a great interest, would know well a small hawthorn tree, Penny Row, or the Prisoner's Bush, between the Bridgelands road and Lindean Kirkyard. Known also as the Uile Bush, it stands on the spot where a mile post was erected to mark their recreation limit in the years between 1812 and 1814. The local authority recently took steps to protect it by fencing.

Farther North in Glen Moidart are six large beech trees planted to commemorate the landing of the Young Pretender, Prince Charles, in 1745. They stand in a line parallel to Loch Moidart near the place where the Prince landed during the second Jacobite Rising. There were originally seven trees, one having succumbed to gales, but a smaller tree, a more recent planting, now rises, to make up seven. Known as the Seven Men of Moidart, they celebrate the seven men who accompanied the prince, but the exact date of planting, or by whom they were set out, is uncertain.

Somerset and Dorset were the backcloth for the staging of two remarkable and romantic adventures during the seventeenth century. Firstly, that of the future Charles II's flight after the Battle of Worcester, as we have seen earlier, and then of his illegitimate son, James, Duke of Monmouth. Monmouth's act was over in the short space of four weeks, in the June and July of 1685, and during that period he brought fame to two trees. Apart from several trees upon which his followers were hanged after the Bloody Assizes, these two, like the luckless Duke, are but a memory, the victims of unkind fates, crumbled into obscurity. After the Duke's landing at Lyme Regis on June 11th, 1685, with eighty supporters, the company made its way to Taunton, stopping en route at Whitelackington Park at the invitation of the Speke family. Under a large sweet chestnut tree, the motley company was hospitably entertained by Speke. The Duke of Monmouth Tree was marked on the OS map of Whitelackington Parish in 1887. An extract from *The Speke Family*, by one Matilda Pine Coffin, reads:

"The Chestnut tree in Whitelackington Park was blown down on the 3rd March (Ash Wednesday) 1897.

Its size was: Diameter at foot   12 ft. 3 in.
               Girth mid-trunk   25 ft.
               Girth top   25 ft.
               Height from bole   17 ft.
               Total height   49 ft.
The age of the tree has been computed as bordering 800 years."

After the disastrous Battle of Sedgemoor, Monmouth fled towards Cranborne Chase. He managed to reach Woodyates with Lord Grey. and a German officer. There they left their overworked horses, disguised themselves and planned an attempt to reach the coast. At Horton nearby, and in open country, the Duke found himself alone, the German Buyse having been captured. In the garb of a shepherd, the bedraggled fugitive was eventually captured in a ditch below an ash tree, which stood until the latter part of the nineteenth century and was propped from all sides to ensure that its near-lifeless bole would not topple. In the end the tree rotted away, and the props collapsed.

Print of original Monmouth Ash at Horton, Dorset.

The site of the capture is marked today by a plaque at the side of another ash, grown in memory of the event. All that remains of the original tree are some souvenirs made in the form of ashtrays, and small panelling in the public house, named the Monmouth Ash, in nearby Verwood.

One of the last stopping-places for the crusading armies in the twelfth century before leaving from the Cinque Ports was near St. Leonards-on-Sea, Sussex. A descendant beech of great age still exists in a wood in school grounds, a quarter of a mile from the town, under which the armies rested on their marches from the western and southern parts of England. Possibly this tree merely marks the camp site, and is not the original, or maybe it is the successor of such a noted beech. But it is difficult to believe that a beech could survive eight hundred years, except in very special sheltered circumstances. An oak in the same circumstances might be accepted, as specimens over a thousand years of age are not unknown.

At Stonewall Park in Chiddingstone, Kent, close to the Sussex border, is a massive old gnarled oak, still flourishing in the company of other ancient oaks, which may very well have been imposing when William the Conqueror halted there on his way to London after the Battle of Hastings. The owner of the tree informs me that she delights in an anecdote that her husband used to quote to visitors: "If you look closely into one of the hollows you may see the Conqueror's sandwich papers!" This ancient specimen is a survivor from the old Forest of Andredsweald, spared by the ironworkers of an earlier age. At Great Yeldham, Essex, is another patriarchal relic of an oak, which was shown on maps in 1777 as The Great Oak and marked the ford in the river at a road junction.

The Yeldham Oaks, which once formed part of the Forest of Essex, were nearly all felled for shipbuilding purposes in the tenth century. Records show that the Great Oak was alive in 1865, having attained a girth of 30 ft. and a height of 80 ft. The trunk, which is all that remains, was encased and preserved by public subscription in 1949. The young oak planted nearby commemorates the marriage between King Edward VII and Queen Alexandra in 1863.

A magnificent ruin of a sweet chestnut tree, of great age and a popular subject for many antiquarians, is in the grounds of Wymondley Bury in the parish of Little Wymondley, Hertfordshire. It is mentioned in Gilpin's *Forest Scenery* and Clutterbuck's *History of Hertfordshire*. In 1789, the girth at 5 ft. from the ground was 42 ft. An engraving in 1798 shows that the main trunk was broken off about

20 ft. from the ground, yet it still grows strongly today. The local supposition is that the tree is over a thousand years old. This may well be so, as the present moated Tudor house is on the site of a former Norman manor house, where there was earlier a Saxon stronghold.

In Ireland, at Scarva, Co. Down, are the remains of an immense sweet chestnut, which William of Orange stood under to review 30,000 Protestant troops in 1690, immediately before the Battle of the Boyne. At Enniscorthy, Co. Wexford, is a black poplar tree standing at the corner of Slaney Bridge. A plaque attached to the tree reads: "The Cotton Tree is 250 years old. Tradition holds that

Bole of Prince of Orange's Oak at Teigngrace, Devon.

some of the British cavalry tied their horses to it after the Battle of Vinegar Hill in 1798. In Irish the title is Crann Critheac, which means 'Quivering Tree'."

Not the least singular tale of oak trees is the following about one which was taken to war. In the garden behind the Old Rectory at Westwell, Burford, in Oxon, the home of the late Lord Redesdale, formerly Captain the Hon. Bertram Mitford, R.N., is an oak tree grown from an acorn by his old family seat at Moreton-in-Marsh. The acorn was potted and taken to sea by him at the beginning of the 1914 War. A plate adjacent to the tree (finally transplanted to its present site in about 1927) gives its life history and wartime adventures. It was aboard his ship during the chase of the German cruiser *Emden*. It even shed its leaves with the changes of climate during its voyaging. After one action and a gale, it was repotted in stokehold sweepings. But it survived both the hazards and the exigencies of war, and made landfall in 1918. In 1928 it had only reached five or six feet in height, but in more recent years it has attained 20 ft.

So the curious stories could continue. Many are not so well documented as the foregoing; we don't, for example, know the reasons for the planting of certain commemorative trees, or for the conservation of trees associated with escapes, hidings, defence and ambush, and they must be regretfully omitted from the catalogue. There are tales of complex clumps of trees, sometimes on a large scale, planted to illustrate battle formations, both naval and military. For instance an aerial view of Blenheim Palace grounds *might* show plantings depicting the formations of officers and men at Marlborough's battles, while at Amesbury, in Wiltshire, the great beech clumps could represent Nelson's main van at Trafalgar. In many cases the landscape of our islands reflects the history of our wars, and has been affected by them, but this is another story and outside our terms of reference.

Chapter Four

Crime and Punishment

There must be profound significance in the fact that throughout man's history crime in all its facets has been faithfully and meticulously recorded. Indeed, in numerous cases the sites of crimes have been commemorated, even venerated, in no less degree than the holy places. The significance is more remarkable in that crime and revered places are more often than not synonymous in story and location: political murders; lost causes; Robin Hoods in varying guises; evangelism; martyrdoms; crucifixions. The same is true of myth as of history.

Could it be that at least part of the significance of man's compulsion to remember the events of his "crimes and punishments" is a harking back in his racial memories to that Last Day in Eden when God's edict took effect, and that he still clings to the hope that expatiation may yet be possible if his sins be confessed and atoned for? Or is it but the eternal gesture of defiance out of the strange duality of his nature?

All we know is that the events are archetypal; the unceasing conflict between good and evil, and its commemoration, "lest we forget". Sin, and its retribution; true love, and its consummation. Or, should the twain meet, tragedy or comedy, according to the whim of the puppet-master. At times, when the contest was unequal, or the gods grew weary, it was ended summarily and satisfactorily by a whiff of magic.

In context, the study of the nature of punishment and its instruments graphically reveals the development of man's sophistication in the lethal uses of his artefacts, if not of his humanity to his kind; the graph curve of his precocity anchored to the base earth of his nature.

The salt of his nature is the savour of his spirit, and it is with the latter attribute that man has discovered grace in the pursuit of his soul, as will be seen in several of the following stories of historic trees.

Hankford's Oak near Bideford.

It is perhaps singularly fitting that trees should symbolize our archetypes, inasmuch as they evoke our origins yet have a promise of growth and an intimation of immortality, so long as the roots are nourished.

Poetic justice would best describe the odd happenings below two oak trees, still alive. In the parish of Monkleigh, near Bideford, Devon, Hankford's Oak stands on land which was once within the great park of Annery House. There lived Sir William Hankford, Lord Chief Justice of England from 1414–22. The story is told that Sir William instructed his gamekeeper to shoot any intruder in the deer park who did not answer correctly to his challenge. One night, shortly after, the judge, wandering forgetfully under the oak, was himself shot, not having replied to his retainer's challenge.

Two hundred years later at the Keeper's Oak, Bramshill, Hampshire, there was an ironic repetition of such an accident; the irony being that the rôles of master and servant were reversed. The master, Dr. Geo. Abbot, Archbishop of Canterbury, shot his gamekeeper after issuing decisive orders to him to shoot on sight "any trespasser or poacher".

A strange story is told of the Corstorphine Sycamore, which is still in fine shape after several centuries' growth in a tiny garden in a very busy Edinburgh street. Known also as the White Lady, it leafs a pale gold in spring, as distinct from the customary brilliant green of the common sycamore. Two legends exist about this fine tree, dating as far back as 1679; the evidence that it existed then having been substantiated by several writers. Elwes wrote of the tree in 1906: "The tree has a romantic history, as being the only survivor of an avenue which formerly led to an old manor house belonging since 1376 to the Forrester family. James Baillie, second Lord Forrester, who took an active part against the Commonwealth, and became involved in difficulties on account of a heavy fine laid on him by Cromwell, is said to have quarrelled with his sister-in-law on August 26th, 1679, and to have been murdered by her at the foot of the tree." An alternative tradition adhered to by other chroniclers a century earlier runs: "The tree grows near the corner of Dovecot Road and Sycamore Place, and is in the grounds of what used to be the estate of the Forresters. It is a very old, large and beautiful tree; at some time during Cromwell's purges upon the estate of the second Lord Forrester, the latter's daughter would meet her lover beneath this tree. Her father, discovering that the suitor was an unsuitable match, slew him one night at the meeting place. After the event, the leaves of the sycamore turned white, and in the years following the daughter's death there were tales of her haunting the scene of the murder."

Measured in 1905 as being 11 ft. in girth, it has grown little since, being now about 70 ft. in height and 12 ft. 4 in. around the bole. The Reverend William Gilpin mentions the dovecot attached to the tree at the turn of the nineteenth century, still surviving to this day. Grafts from the tree can be got from nurseries under the name of the Corstorphine, or Golden Sycamore.

A very wide-spreading yew grows at Whittinghame, East Lothian. Although it has but a girth of 11 ft. 2 in. (an expansion of only 1 ft. since Elwes measured it in 1906), the spread of the outer lower branches is over 120 yards. Beneath this sombre shade Sir Archibald Douglas and others are said to have plotted the murder of Darnley, Mary Queen of Scots's second husband. Its branches droop to the ground like an immense umbrella. On one occasion three hundred school-children stood comfortably between the short trunk, only 12 ft. in height, and the inside of the canopy.

Certain remarkable sycamore trees in Scotland are called Dool Trees. They were used by the powerful barons for hanging their enemies and recalcitrant vassals upon, hence the name dool, or grief trees. One of these is at Blairquhan, in Ayrshire, on an estate once belonging to the powerful Kennedy family. Originally there were two of these sycamores, but only one has survived, now 45 ft. high and 17 ft. in girth. In 1850, J. C. Loudon received the following particulars of the two trees from Sir David Hunter Blair: "They are in great health and vigour, and are probably nearly three centuries old. The date on the old coat of arms of the Kennedys in the adjoining court of the castle is 1573."

Other hanging trees once stood at the old castle of Cassilis, a seat of the Marquess of Ailsa, on the banks of the River Doon. There is one survivor, last used as a gibbet for the execution of Johnny Faa, a gypsy, and seven of his men, hanged for abducting the Countess of Cassilis. The Cassilis dool tree was more remarkable for its spreading branches and luxuriant foliage than for its girth.

Another dool tree, a mere relic, is at Invergarry Castle, on which Mac' Ic Alasdair, Chief of Glengarry, hanged malefactors. At Mains Farm, Kincardine, Perth, near the ruined Kincardine Castle, is an ancient yew named "Jeddart Justice". The origin of the name is obscure but it appears that there was a lynch-law tale of "hanging first and trial afterwards".

About twenty-two miles from Selkirk, near Ettrick Water and not far from the Tushilaw Inn, is the remains of King James V's Castle, once a stronghold of the Douglas family. It was captured by the king from Adam Scott, a border thief who strung up his victims on an ancient ash tree. In 1527, James and his forces made a dawn attack by a difficult narrow track over the wild hills and took Adam unawares, finally hanging him on his own Gallows Tree. The original tree perished in a fire, but its remains could be seen for years among the rubble of Tushilaw Tower. As late as 1955 a tree was reported growing on this very spot, said to be an offshoot from the old roots.

The Abbot's Oak, at Woburn, was an English "dool" tree. Unremarkable as a tree, its associations are, however, interesting. From its branches the Abbot and Prior of Woburn, the Vicar of Puddington, and other "contumacious persons" were hanged by order of Henry VIII. Dodds, in his *Church History of England*, states that Roger Hobbs, the Abbot of Woburn at the time, "nobly disdaining to compromise his conscience for a pension, as most of his brethren did, and as many others who do not wear a cowl at the

The Abbot's Oak, Woburn Park, Bedfordshire. Tree exists.

present day, resolutely denied the king's supremacy, and refused to surrender his sacerdotal rights. For his conduct he and the others were hanged on an oak tree in front of the monastery." He was drawn to the place of execution on a sledge, as was customary with State prisoners. A jury at Woburn, Bedfordshire, had found the victims guilty of high treason for having spoken in public against the marriage of Henry VIII to Anne Boleyn. On a board nailed to the tree were painted the following lines:

"Oh, 'twas a ruthless deed, enough to pale
Freedom's bright fires, that doom'd to shameful death
Those who maintained their faith with latest breath,
And scorned before the despot's frown to quail.
Yet 'twas a glorious hour when from the goal
Of papal tyranny the mind of man
Dared to break loose, and triumph'd in the band
Of thinders roaring in the distant gale!
Yes, old memorial of the mitred monk,
Thou liv'st to flourish in a brighter day
And seem'st to smile, that pure and potent vows
Are breathed where superstition reigned: thy trunk
Its glad green garland wears, though in decay
And years hang heavy on thy time-stained boughs."

A favourite of John Bunyan was an old oak at Samshill, a hamlet near Harlington, Bedfordshire. The farmhouse where he preached no longer exists, but until recently an old, stag-headed oak marked the spot where the famous tinker-preacher dared to hold services. Bunyan held his last service under the oak before his arrest by his old enemy Francis Wingate and subsequent removal to Bedford Gaol.

Bedfordshire has another tree symbol of the hope of peace and goodwill, instigated by Adolf Hitler! An Old Boy and famous sculler of Bedford School received an oak sapling from the Führer at the Olympic Games of 1936. Hitler, in presenting it to the champion, said he hoped it would be planted "as a witness of common friend-ship". The tree was established in the grounds of the old school, where it still flourishes.

Pedom's Oak is in a remote part of Mugglewick Common, in Co. Durham, near the Northumberland border, on a farm named after it. A story goes that Pedom was a local sheep stealer who, until the hue and cry which followed his sporadic marauding raids died down, used to keep the stolen animals in this huge hollow oak near his farmhouse.

At Poole, Dorset, and adjoining the Westbourne suburb of Bournemouth, is a locality still called Lilliput that boasts an old pine tree, reputed to have been the meeting place of the notorious smuggler Gulliver and his gang, where their schemes were hatched and the proceeds distributed. Dean Swift immortalized the smuggler of Lilliput in *Gulliver's Travels*.

In 1834, six agricultural labourers from the village of Tolpuddle, Dorset, were sentenced to transportation for seven years to the then

Bunyan's Oak, Lower Samshill, Westoning, Bedfordshire (c. 1 mile east of Harlington, Bedfordshire). Taken 1962.

Martyrs' Tree, Tolpuddle, Dorset.

penal colony of Australia, for administering an oath, illegal under the Mutiny Act of 1797. It may be that the whole history of the trade unions' rise to power stemmed from the meetings of the "Six Men of Dorset" which used to be held beneath the sycamore, which still stands by the side of the village green. The lot of the agricultural labourer in the 1830s was an unenviable one. In Dorset the labourer's wage was nine shillings a week, later to be reduced to eight, then seven. Finally, in 1834, a further reduction to six shillings was threatened. George Loveless, a man of outstanding character, called a meeting against this exploitation. They haggled with the employers and were supported by the Vicar of Tolpuddle. Promises were made, but none kept. The men then turned for support to the Grand National Consolidated Trades Union, led by Robert Owen. Two dele-

Portchester Yew.

gates from this fast-growing organization arrived at Tolpuddle, and as a result the Friendly Society of Agricultural Labourers was formed.

The employers and magistrates became apprehensive, fearing a repetition of the riots and rick-burning of the 1830s. The result was the arrest of Loveless and his six closest associates. They were imprisoned at Dorchester in February 1834 and sentenced at the Assizes. The "crime" for which the men were punished was that of organizing themselves into a "sworn union", although trade unions were no longer illegal as such since the Act of 1824. But the oath procedure had laid them open to the charge under the Mutiny Act. The sycamore, which has been badly lopped in the past, is probably nearly two hundred years old. It is completely hollow, though still topped with a healthy growth on its mutilated leading branches. Known as the Martyr's Tree, its girth is 17 ft. 10 in.

In February 1969, the tree was in poor condition, the bole being split through its hollow from the main fork to the base of the trunk, and a fungus thrived in the dark interior of the ivy-covered trunk. Later in 1969 the T.U.C. was belatedly advised that the tree appeared dangerous and might have to be felled. A survey was made by the National Trust and a parish meeting resolved to ask the Secretary of the T.U.C. for help in preserving the tree. Some preservationists stated they would have the tree conserved, even if it meant pickling it *in situ*. Eventually, tree surgeons began operations on it and banded the trunk to prevent a complete splitting of the main body. The hollow trunk was cleaned and filled with vermiculite, removing the rotten contents in the hollow. The brave new growth in the crown of the old pollard was thinned and cleaned, the ivy removed, and the historic tree given another lease of life.

There are several remaining examples of tree gibbets from the time of the Bloody Assizes in the seventeenth century. The aftermath of the Monmouth Rebellion gave rise to impromptu "splinter" trials. These were held throughout Somerset and Dorset, usually being presided over by the infamous Judge Jeffries. Men condemned as followers of Charles II's bastard son were executed on makeshift gallows. Trees at cross-roads or track-junctions were preferred. In the parish of Silton, Dorset, is "Wyndham's Oak", about 200 yards east of the church, from which two of the Duke's unfortunate followers were hanged. The oak takes its name from Judge Wyndham, who lived in the nearby manor house and died in 1682. The Judge used to have a seat in this hollow tree, but it is now gone.

F

Yew Grove at Kingley Vale.

Another tree, an elm, is railed around at Wrington, Somerset. Two men, Branch and Cross, were executed from this tree in 1685. It stands at a cross-roads on the outskirts of the village towards the gradient of Redhill, and is known locally as Branch's Cross. Roper's Lane runs alongside.

Vestiges of an old elm can be seen in a retaining wall at a road junction at Corston, near Bath, and the strongly growing stool-shoots from the old stump are still preserved on a nearby triangular plot. This tree is also traditionally associated with the Monmouth Rebellion. It may have been used as a hanging tree after a local Assize, or it could be linked with the account of a clash between the Duke's men and the soldiers of James II. The Heddon Oak, between Crowcombe and Stogumber, Somerset, is the best known of the hanging trees. There is no doubt that some of Monmouth's men were strung up from this ominous-looking oak, which again stands at minor cross-roads in the picturesque part of the Quantocks. Three men from Stogumber and three from Crowcombe were supposed to have been executed here after the Taunton Assize. A legend says that few will pass the tree after darkness, as the creaking of swinging bodies can be heard on the boughs that grow horizontally over the road.

In the large Somerset parish of Withycombe and Old Cleeve there is the remnant of another requisitioned scaffold, Felon's Oak. Here there is no tradition of the Rebellion. It is said that the tree was used for hanging "thieves, highwaymen and murderers". The title Felon's Oak is often incorporated in the postal address of nearby houses, and the tree is illustrated on picture postcards. Only a century and a half ago criminals were still hanged from trees in public places. Four Elms Road in Cardiff, adjacent to the Newport Road, is named after such a place, though the old gibbet trees have gone. But there is no doubt that they were used for that purpose, and for crimes which to-day might qualify for a fine of a few pounds.

Four trees in Eire have similar morbid associations: in Co. Cork, Coolcower, is the Hanging Tree, two miles East of Macroom, adjoining the Cork–Macroom Road. The legend of this field maple tells of a former landlord in Coolcower who attempted to hang a Papist during the days of persecution, but failed because the tree was not high enough. He therefore shot his victim. Since that event the tree has ceased to grow but is still alive. In Killarney Forest, Kerry, grows an oak known as the Crooked Tree, from which in the late eighteenth century a local girl is reputed to have hanged herself. Since then, it is said, no one will fell it or even cut its branches.

The Heddon Oak, Crowcombe, Somerset. Hanging tree during Monmouth Rebellion. Three men from Crowcombe and three from Stogumber supposed to have been hanged from it by Judge Jeffries' men. At night it has been said that you can hear the creaking of the limbs from swinging bodies.

Turpin's Oak at Finchley.

Half a mile from Newcastle West, on the main Limerick Road, is an ash also known as the Crooked Tree. Many hangings were carried out on it in 1798.

Located in Ardcarnorisk Townland, three miles west of Wexford, near the River Slaney, is an oak tree which has no such evocative name. Under it a duel was fought between two men named Alcock and Colclough. The latter was killed. Alcock's sister was betrothed to Colclough and following the duel became insane.

Although he was "Bloody Mary's" lieutenant in the persecution of Protestants, Sir Anthony Browne founded a fine school at Brentwood, Essex, in 1557. A grim reminder of those times stands today at the roadside immediately in front of the new school buildings. It is the Martyr's Oak, where Protestants were burned at the stake during Mary's turbulent reign. Today it is carefully preserved and protected by railings.

In the same county, at Paglesham, Nr. Rochford, there were three old elms known as the Old Maids, which were used by smugglers in the eighteenth and nineteenth century for storing their contraband, brought up the River Roche by rowing boats. Only one of these trees now remains.

Dick Turpin is said to have been born in the north of the county of Essex, at Hempstead. The highwayman, along with the smuggler and the outlaw, had perhaps the lowest status in contemporary annals of crime and the glamour attaching to a man like Turpin is a product of Hollywood and Wardour Street. Plain thief and murderer, in his beginnings a butcher in Whitechapel, he teamed up with the notorious Gregory Gang, soon qualifying as leader by his daring and cunning. This unlovable, pock-marked thug is now memorable chiefly by the number of trees associated with his luckier exploits. The famous ride from London to York is probably fictitious, although an oak in Thirsk was known as Turpin's Oak. He doubtless changed his manor of operations to the north very promptly when it got too hot in Herts and Essex for him. At his reputed birthplace there was a ring of trees which have since become known at Turpin's Ring, although the only record of events there appears to have been that of a cock-fighting arena.

For some years Turpin confined his maraudings to the Bath and York roads into London. At Bedfont Green another Turpin's Oak appeared. This was on Hounslow Heath in Middlesex, where the mounted robber would pounce on coaches using the nearby Staines road. At Haileybury College, Herts, is another oak, with a counter-sunk ring in the bole, where it is recorded that Turpin tethered his horse on occasion while awaiting victims. It is said that Turpin would often join his accomplices at this point, or at Amwell, and after the robberies would make for the shelter of Hertford Heath nearby.

Until mid-Victorian days there stood an old oak on a green space opposite the Green Man public house at Finchley, on the road to Barnet. This also was known as "Turpin's Oak". It was centuries old and in the first stages of decay during the highwayman's day. His custom was to hide behind this tree in ambush. Being close to the road, a tree as large as this was ideal since it could conceal both him and his horse as well as protect him from pistol shots. The oak was used by other thieves for the same purpose—lesser fry who perhaps hoped to have the blame shifted on to their more notorious contemporary should they be apprehended and charged elsewhere. For years after Turpin's execution in 1739, a variety of pistol-shot was extracted from the bark of the oak.

A dead highwayman was seldom given sacraments or a grave in a churchyard. Often he was roughly buried near the place he was killed, or close to the gibbet. At Boxmoor, near Hemel Hempstead, Herts, there is a group of chestnut trees beside the Bourne End Road under which two weatherbeaten stones mark the graves of two such unnamed footpads.

A hold-up in a more romantic vein occurred at Grizzy's Clump, a walled group of fir trees in a field beside the Great North Road at Kyloe, Northumberland, in 1685. Sir John Cochrane's sister, Grizel, dressed as a man, held up the London mail and seized the death warrant of her brother, who had been sentenced for a part in the Earl of Argyll's rebellion. The respite allowed Sir John sufficient time to obtain pardon from James II.

At Moyles Court, Ellingham, in the New Forest, Hampshire, grew a gigantic oak, 20 ft. in girth, near the watersplash and footbridge. Dame Alice Lisle lived at the Court at the time of the Monmouth Rebellion; she was the wife of one of Charles Stuart's judges. After her arrest near the oak, for complicity in the Rebellion, she was charged at Winchester with harbouring two Monmouth sympathizers after the Battle of Sedgemoor in 1685. Thirty years before, and nine years before he himself was murdered, her husband, Judge Lisle, had sentenced to death as a rebel one John Penruddock. This man's son, Colonel Penruddock, now took revenge and brought Alice Lisle to her death. The unpleasant Judge Jeffries, who bullied the witnesses at her trial into the foregone verdict, ordered that she be dragged on a hurdle to her death by burning. The indignant clergy of the cathedral protested, and the sentence was delayed for some days. In this space of time James II modified the sentence to one of beheading, which was carried out on September 5th, 1685.

The Naked Man is a stark and withering oak trunk near Wilverley Post, Lyndhurst, in the New Forest, standing alone amid sparse bracken and typical open forest tract. It is fenced, resembles a man with two arms, and from one aspect is popularly supposed to depict a man engaged in an act of nature. Some say the relic earned its name from the gruesome fate of a highwayman who was allowed to hang from the tree until the rooks had picked him to the bone. More cryptically, it is also known as the Tree of Good and Evil Knowledge. The first reference to it was 180 years ago, when it was said that a certain Mark Way, highwayman, who held up coaches at a nearby hill, was the true historic genie of the tree after his hanging, and from whom these strange mutations have stemmed. During the Second World War a tank knocked the stump down, whereupon it

"Naked" Man, Wilverly Post, New Forest.

Fairmead Oak, Epping. Tree gone.

was promptly re-erected and concreted in. Would-be pilgrims are referred to the Ordnance Survey 1-inch map for its exact location.

Returning from the Holy Wars of the twelfth century, Crusaders would bring souvenirs, among them seeds and plants. Many individual trees of new and probably unidentified species found their way to churchyards, village open spaces and to private estates. The mulberry, oriental plane, walnut and chestnuts were probably here long before the dates so sacrosanctly claimed by the arboricultural historians. Sweet chestnuts, although here much earlier than mediaeval times, were popular food, and a seed which would travel well. Some might be planted especially, or be accidentally dropped, eventually germinating as seedlings. On Chipperfield Common, near Kings Langley, Herts, is a large sweet chestnut standing near the "Twelve Apostles" pond on the left of a fragment of the common beyond the second "mound". Here the belief has been handed down that Richard III rested, and tethered his horse to a low branch of this Crusader's tree. Further, that he cursed the women of the village for laughing at his malformed body and mocking his awkward walk so that no woman of Chipperfield should inherit anything from her husband, nor would more females ever be born. But the story goes that the curse proved effective only on the successive inmates of the nearby manor house, where no children were born for many generations.

The mystery of the churchyard yew deepens when we consider the strange phenomenon displayed by one such tree, the third on the right of an avenue leading from the gate of St. Brynach Church, Nevern, Pembs. Approximately seven feet from the ground there is a natural "gash" in the yew which from time to time exudes a substance resembling blood. This lends support to a local legend that a man (perhaps a monk) was hanged from the tree, while protesting strongly of his innocence of an alleged crime: "If you hang me guiltless as I am, these trees will bleed for me." Another legend is that a condemned man's hand was cut off for some local crime against the forest law. Resinous substance from yews is certainly rare, though various slimes are known in elm, cherry, and of course, the resinous pines. In this case the possibility of rainwater running down the branches of the tree and becoming trapped in the reddish heart of the gashed yew and emerging coloured makes some sort of sense. But a reddish plasma resembling blood is unusual, and worthy of closer study.

For the details of the next two accounts dealing with trees in

Shropshire I am indebted to University College, London, for allowing me to make use of information collected during their Survey of
English Folklore. The individual research was carried out for the
College by Miss Judith Molinoli, of Madeley, Shropshire. The first
of these is Wiggin's Tree, Bridgnorth, Salop.

"On Wednesday, 26th November, 1912, between six and seven
o'clock in the evening, Mr. Wiggin, a miller from Ardington, about
two miles from Bridgnorth, was murdered between that place and
his own house. He was returning from Wolverhampton Market and
was met by a footpad about a mile from his home. It is supposed that
on his making a stout resistance, the villain drew a pistol and shot
him; the ball passing through in a direct line just below his heart.
It seems that the assassin was alarmed by Wiggin's cries for he made
off without taking any property, which consisted of between £50 and
£60 in notes. It is conjectured that, after being shot, the unfortunate
man pursued his murderer for about a hundred yards, but fell
exhausted. Someone from a local turnpike house heard his cries and
helped him to the house, but Wiggins expired within a short time."
(Extract from the *Salopian Journal*, Vol. 19, No. 984.)

Wiggin's Tree was an ash which was cut down for road-widening
purposes in 1957. Between the period of the murder and that time,
there had been rumours that the site was haunted by Wiggin's ghost.
Once a year the youths living nearby would make a pilgrimage to the
tree to see Wiggin's blood on it—a patch around a hole in the bark
coloured red, and in the shape of a cross. Wiggin's murderer was
never discovered, although the reward of £200 offered stood for a
long time.

The second is Brewer's Oak, two miles North of Shifnal. The tree,
which may still be standing, is at Brewer's Oak Farm, so named as
far back as 1780, when Brewer himself farmed land on the opposite
side of the road to the Duke of Sutherland. It appears that the oak,
which stood on the Duke's property, was marked for felling with the
axe. Brewer objected to these arrangements, being fond of the tree,
and negotiated with the Duke's agent to buy the oak and the piece
of land about it, and indeed they are both part of Brewer's farm
today. Local enquiries however have revealed that there was something uncanny about the tree. Old suppositions that Brewer committed suicide, and that the tree held some ghastly secret, couldn't
be dismissed. Brewer's gravestone could not be found in the local
churchyard, and the mystery remains.

In 1955, an important oak in Epping Forest was burned to the ground. Known as the Fairmead Oak, it was the tree under which Henry VIII stood and waited to hear the guns from the Tower of London informing him that Anne Boleyn had been executed. But perhaps the grimmest blood curdler of all trees was at Tyburn, used as a gibbet for 600 years until 1783, when hordes of offenders from petty thieves to murderers died in batches, half-a-dozen or more at a time, gawped at and jeered at by huge crowds. The place has the history of a morgue: Claude Duval, Jonathan Wild, the fourth Earl Ferrers, the unearthed bodies of Cromwell, Bradshaw and Ireton; Tom Clinch, and two of Charles Stuart's judges. All kept the hangman busy, and the grisly occasions spawned a fashionable and often profitable entertainment that stained the conscience of England for centuries. The tragic associations of Tyburn became too much for local folk in this part of Middlesex. The small village took a new name from the dedication of the parish church. So Ty-burn became Mary-bourne. But, soon, Marybourne was felt to lack grace, and so the definite article was borrowed from the fashionable French, and Marylebourne was conceived—to grow up ingloriously as Marylebone. No clear record has come down to us identifying an actual tree. All that is certain is that for several hundred years a series of man-made gibbets were in use, no doubt in the interests of efficiency.

Lastly, in the context of this chapter should be mentioned trees where court leets were held to administer the forest laws, or to decide parish business and property disputes. The earliest record is of the Wapentake, a Saxon word meaning "a taking of weapons". At such meetings a vote was usually taken by a brandishing of weapons to support some proposition, or as a sign of fealty to the local overlord. An oak tree was the site of a Wapentake at Headingley, Leeds. This survived until a few years ago; but a sapling oak has replaced it. Known as the Skyrack, or Shire Oak, a public house in the district is probably on the site of an oak tree used as a meeting place in Saxon times. An extract from John Waddington-Feather's *Leeds* records: "A list of men capable of being mustered for the army was drawn up for the Leeds area in 1529. This 'Musters in the Skyrack Wapentake' (note that the old Norse administrative term was still in use) lists the men available and liable for service, together with the pieces of armour, which would belong not to individuals but to the township as a whole."

On the south side of the fifteenth-century church at Headcorn, Kent, stands a hollow oak, centrally propped and having a girth of 33 ft. Some estimate its age as over 1,000 years, and it is probably one

Oak at Headcorn, Kent.

of the few survivors of the great forest of Andredsweald that defied the axes of our forefathers. Apart from the probability that it was a "court" tree, legends exist that King John held bull-baiting contests around the oak. The proximity of the oak's large, venturing crown to a small chamber on the south side of the church used to imprison the occasional wrongdoer, once enabled a prisoner to escape by way of one of its accommodating branches.

In 1960, the Vicar and members of the parish became aware that the tree was deteriorating, and, considering it a valuable relic of the past and a tourist attraction for the village and church, they obtained the advice of the Kent County Council. Treatment was carried out. The shell of the old tree, amazingly still supporting very heavy yet healthy growth, was cleared of all rotten and worm-infested wood, the upper part of the tree thinned, the props replaced and the wires from the central strut tensioned correctly. The tardy yet expert treatment of this tree should prolong an historical link between two societies ten centuries apart.

Another Kent tree is the Bonnington Oak, in the village of that name. Known as the Lawgiver, it is now a dying shell. Another oak is to be planted *inside* when the time is considered suitable, to perpetuate its claim as an "ancient Court Leete tree", according to Samuel Bagshaw's *Directory of Kent*, 1848, which also states that here was the "meeting to choose new boarsholders or constables for Bonnington & Hamme".

A survivor from the dense Forest of Middlesex, which for hundreds of years covered the hills overlooking North London, is the Minchenden or Chandos Oak, now preserved in a small public garden next to Christchurch, in Southgate. The tree was illustrated on a map of 1582 and described as the meeting place of the Edmonton Hundred Court. Dr. James Beattie, a friend of Dr. Johnson, recorded that in 1772 he visited the Chandos Oak. It was a notable sight in those days. Its branches then spread over an area 100 ft. in diameter, the trunk being 20 ft. in girth. By 1900 a surge of growth had increased the girth to 27 ft., the spread to 136 ft. and the height to 80 ft. Estimates of age vary, some giving it a generous 800 years. Prints of it appear in Loudon's *Arboretum Britannicum*, 1853, and in Strutt's *Sylva Britannicum*, 1822. The Minchenden Oak is represented in the Borough's coat-of-arms, and the motto *"Ex Glande Quiercus"* (from acorn to oak) bears reference to the growth of Southgate from a very small community to its present proportions.

---⚬⚬∞∞∞∞∞⚬⚬---

Chapter Five

Trees as Symbols
of Religions

I n his beginnings Man, in zoological terms an improbable survivor
in the enveloping jungle, somehow contrived a precarious compromise with a hostile environment. He feared, yet defied, his far more
competitive neighbours to the significant point of exploiting their
more advantageous endowments of hides and furs to further his own
desperate needs. That he survived at all is the never-ending wonder
of his descendants—in particular, the anthropologists and zoologists
of our day. Those long odds, we are told, were fortuitously shortened
by the advent of that curious mutation from the ape, the "hominid".
This hypothetical creature, by inference, assured his future and ours
by the chance of being born with an instinct that prompted him to
reach for a stone or a stick in an emergency or a necessity and so
found he had invented a weapon or a tool.

There are, of course, those who still maintain—though more and
more diffidently—that man's story is one of devolution rather than of
evolution; that he bears the scars rather of a fall from grace than of
a scramble up the fossiliferous rocks out of the primordial swamps.
But our present purpose is not to contend but to hold up the looking-
glass of mythology and through it to examine the age-old beliefs concerning his origins, especially those associated with trees. And, not
surprisingly, there are many.

Consider, for instance, the legendary belief that two trees were the
progenitors of the human race. This belief, variously dressed, has persisted in widely separated cultures ever since man became articulate
about the nagging question of his beginnings. A variant is the tree-of-
life theme, implying that all things derived from a tree, being not
only sustained but sheltered by it. From this image of protection and
continuity can perhaps be inferred the later more sophisticated cult of
ancestor worship. There would seem to be echoes of the latter in the
theologies of ancient Egypt, Greece and Rome. The shapes of dead

trees might graphically have evoked the memory of a hero, or saviour of the tribe, to minds inclined by their nature to anthropomorphic imagery. From such ideas the first commemorative statues might have been fashioned, conceptions already stylized by the fortuitous likeness of the tree shape.

With his improved tools his evolving iconography would take on the permanence of stone, and so first a tradition, then a form of worship, would become established, grafted on to the symbolic everlastingness of the tree. In a similar way it is possible to identify the Doric column in the first order of Greek architecture with the tapered tree-trunk posts and massive beams of earlier structures. Even the Doric flutings, taken uncompromisingly straight down to the foundations, would seem to echo the buttressing effect of the roots emerging from the ground. The same faithfulness to the structural qualities of trees is evident in the columnar temples and funerary buildings of Egypt, the Minoan architecture of Crete and the Mayan and Incan cultures.

And, at the risk of overstraining the simile, the branching growth of the tree could symbolize the ramifications of pagan theologies, or the hierarchies of the gods. Many of the legends became, as it were, transliterated into those of the Christian era, as, for instance, the Tree of Jesse. Fertility cults and Festivals of the Solstices became metamorphosed into the epic or traumatic events of the Christian calendar: the red-berried thorn with the mortification of Christ; the swastika, or ancient sun symbol, thought by some authorities to link the concept of Apollo with the Cross of Christ.

There are many legends which invest trees with oracular properties. No doubt this arose not only from the self-evident life of the tree but from its deep-rooted characteristics, suggesting wisdom, also its conformity with the cycle of nature, with its mysteries of death and re-birth, with flower and fruit in season—all unvarying sermons of constancy and integrity, in contrast with the wayward ways of man. His acknowledgment of these observed qualities was expressed in symbols—the fruit-tree branches as used in their religious rites both by the Celtic Druids and their Teutonic successors; the veneration for the mistletoe from the belief that the life of its host became invested in the parasite at the onset of winter. It also followed that the mistletoe became an emblem of fertility. Branches of it were kept indoors during the winter months to ensure the life and fortunes of the family.

Yet another interesting custom concerns the veneration of the Norway Spruce at Christmastime. The story goes that a poor forester sat huddled near his log-fire with his family one bitter winter's night when a shrill voice was heard calling plaintively outside in the blizzard. He opened the door and there stood a child, shivering and obviously starving. The forester carried him into the warmth of the hut and he was given food and warm clothing. Later, his young son gave up his bed for the distressed child whom they thought to be a foundling. Next morning heavenly choirs were heard singing around the cottage. The child arose from his bed and smiled at them, his face shining with an unearthly light. He was, of course, the Christ-Child. He blessed his benefactors, but, before departing, plucked a twig from a spruce tree, planted it firmly in the ground, and said as he did so that it would always bless the forester and his family with winter fuel.

The winter solstice—Christmastime—the still moment of expectancy for both pagan and Christian, had many tree symbols. The best known is undoubtedly that of the holly. Like so many other tree symbols it is pre-Christian in origin. During the Feast of Saturnalia the Romans used to send boughs of it, together with presents, to their friends and relatives. The meaning of the custom is obscure but so widespread and entrenched was the ritual that it persisted into Christian times; even churches were bedecked with it. The symbolism underwent a sea-change, becoming an allegory of the Crown of Thorns, with the red, drop-like berries signifying the Blood of Christ. Northern converts knew it as the Christ's Thorn, and later, of course, as the Holy-tree. (This spelling appears in an early ballad preserved in the British Museum.) It is possible that the use of the evergreen holly for religious rites may have reflected an earlier link with the Jewish Feast of Tabernacles, commemorating the moment when "the Word was made flesh and dwelt (or *tabernacled*) amongst us".

Once Christianity had become the official religion of Rome, following Constantine's edict, there was almost an inevitability about its integration with the ancient pagan customs. So facile did it seem, not only at the outset in metropolitan Rome but also in later centuries when, for instance, Pope Gregory's emissary to Britain, Augustine, found surprisingly little opposition to his evangelism, that it would seem to demonstrate the grass-roots similarities in religious symbolism; a sort of symbiosis of the images of earthy life with those of theology. Are there not echoes of this in the numerous foliate heads carved on roof bosses in mediaeval churches, and in the sculptured stone faces framed in leafy tendrils? There was also the curious ceremony from Anglo-Saxon times of Loaf-Mass, or Lammas, where the first loaf of bread following harvest was reverently buried. Or, alternatively, the first loaf was hung from the branch of an oak tree. This Bread of the Mass, later to be confused with or merged into, Harvest Thanksgiving in a more enervated theology, shows marked pagan undertones to the central sacrament of the church. Lammas Day, the first day of August, is the time of greatest bacterial activity in the soil, and, incidentally, when there begins a sudden resurgence of new leaf on the oak, a sort of second birth. Of no less significance this is also the time most suitable for the striking of cuttings of plants and trees.

After the virile oak the next in order of importance in symbolism were the yew and the hawthorn. The age-old veneration of the yew seems to have been universal, at least throughout Western Europe. The reasons for it are still obscure. Pliny thought little of the yew. He found it sapless, gloomy, and altogether graceless. In addition, its berries were poisonous, vessels made from it polluted wine, and those foolhardy enough either to sleep or even to eat under it risked grave misfortune or even premature death. Yet our forefathers planted it purposefully. Even today large numbers of yews exist, occasionally in isolated groves but more commonly as single specimens, in churchyards, cemeteries and on the great feudal estates.

One can only surmise why pagan communities planted this "tree of death". That the early Christians revered the custom and perpetuated it might be inferred from the number of churchyards possessing yews considerably older than the earliest church building on the site. Probably it represented a form of exorcism against the forces of evil in that its spreading canopy sheltered the resting-places of souls awaiting Resurrection, protecting them from the encroachment of passing seasons. On the other hand, it may be that it was St. Augustine's way of obeying Pope Gregory's instructions not openly to violate the old pagan sites (often identified by a mound or a yew tree) but to erect altars and to build churches alongside the older sacred site.

There does not seem to be any significance in the use of yew branches on Palm Sunday, despite a coincidental resemblance to the fronds of the palm. In parts of Ireland sprigs of yew were worn in hats from Palm Sunday until Easterday, while in England yew branches were carried in funeral processions, finally being placed under the coffins at interment. An even more obscure practice, in Wales, was the ceremonial planting of yews, each yew being valued at a pound after consecration. This valuation was clearly not for

Heddon Oak.

intrinsic worth since non-consecrated yews were contemporarily valued at one shilling and threepence.

The yew is notoriously difficult to date by a ring count. After about 150 years of growth the heartwood begins to decay, thus destroying the annular rings of growth. Curiously, this characteristic has little effect on the continued vitality of the tree; the sapwood and cambium layer still flourish and become self-supporting. The tree thus goes on increasing in girth and the crown branches remain healthy and unaffected. In the event of branches breaking off, the wounds are effectively healed and new shoots feather out around the bole. Indeed, one authority states that should the crown of the tree die the girth expansion would be accelerated!

Thus old yew trees are mostly hollow and their ages remain largely a matter of guesswork. This assessment is not made easier by another phenomenon—that of its ability to self-graft its own branches that may press on the bole, thus deceptively adding to the girth. Not only that but it can even ensure its immortality by propagating its own seed in the composted decay of its heartwood, thus growing its scion within its own body, to maturity. Added to all these difficulties of age assessment are the vagaries of climate, soil, water supply and other variants of environment.

On the popular concept of immortality associated with the yew it is of interest to note that the Druids, as recorded by Caesar, preached a doctrine of the immortality of the soul, the yew being their *cultus arborum*. Since the yew is a commoner kind of tree than, say, the oak in the Iberian Peninsula, whence the pre-Celtic peoples came, it is probable that they brought the cult of the yew—or at least the custom of using yew groves for their religious rites—to these Isles. In this respect it is perhaps an added significance that there is a higher proportion of yews in Welsh churchyards than in England generally.

The hawthorn, although improbably the same thorn associated with the Crucifixion, has always had strong Christian connotations. But like so many Christian symbols its ritualistic uses can be traced far back into antiquity. To the ancient Greeks it was the emblem of hope and so dedicated to the goddess Persephone; later, by the Romans, to the goddess Flora. (Modern Greeks, to this day, hang garlands of hawthorn blossom from their doorways on Mayday.) Girls carried its flowering branches in wedding processions and laid them on the altars which were lit by hawthorn-wood torches. In prehistoric times the Troglodytes tied bunches of hawthorn twigs to the dead at burial; the reason for this is obscure, although conceivably it

G

Above, *Wyndham's Oak, Stilton.* Below, *Fortingall Yew.*
Previous page, *Kett's Oak at Wymondham.*

could have been in the same context as the myth of Persephone and her seasonal return to the Underworld.

The maypole, another link between the tree-deity and fertility rites, was usually adorned with hawthorn blossom (that is, in the more southerly parts of Europe where the tree was in bloom on May-day). In parts of France the hawthorn is known as *l'epine noble*, because of associations with the Crown of Thorns legend. The super-stitious even assert that the tree groans and sighs on Good Friday. Many peasants used to wear sprigs of it in their hats during thunder-storms, to guard against lightning.

In Britain our Celtic forefathers revered the hawthorn equally with the oak and the yew. This may explain its prevalence in south-west England and Wales, as well as in Ireland.

The many legends of the hawthorn perhaps culminate for us in that of the Glastonbury Thorn, dubbed by the laborious botanist *crataegus oxyacantha biflora praecox*—the last two adjectives being the really operative ones and meaning a precocious double flowering. The legend tells us that in Somerset there was once a land called Avalon, an island on the eastern end of an archipelago, and one of a chain leading to the Mendips. It is said that Joseph of Arimathea, an old tin-trader of the Phoenician tradition, in whose tomb the body of Jesus was laid, fled his native land in the days of the persecu-tion and sought asylum in his old haunt of Avalon, bringing with him twelve followers. Led by Joseph, they climbed a hill, now im-mortalized as Wearyall Hill near Glastonbury, to survey the scene. Joseph is said to have planted his hawthorn staff in the ground as a sign that their journey was ended. As proof of the wisdom and finality of his choice the staff took root, grew apace and flowered in a miraculously short time—this despite the unpropitious time of year, the 6th day of January by the old calendar, the original Christ-mas Day. The miracle was celebrated by the building of the first Church of Christendom in an alien land and its dedication to the Virgin Mary.

Scions of the supposedly original Arimathean Thorn can be found in many parts of England. It flowers usually twice a year, during mild Novembers and Decembers and again in May; some of the trees are evergreen. A fine specimen can be seen in the foreground of St. John's Church, Glastonbury. A sprig from this tree is traditionally sent to the reigning monarch each Christmas.

In Elizabeth I's reign the offspring from the roots of the supposed original tree had two main trunks. One of these was lopped off by

Crowhurst Yew, Surrey. Bench inside with room for twelve men. Entrance made in 1820.

a vandal—possibly an iconoclast of the Reformation. It is said that as a result the vandal lost an eye and injured a leg. In Charles I's reign the remaining trunk was felled, but the stump of the tree survived until 1750. In 1800, John Clark, a Quaker from Street, near Glastonbury, marked the site of the tree with a stone engraved: J. A. ANNO D. XXXI, i.e. Joseph of Arimathea, A.D. 31.

In Ireland the hawthorn is revered somewhat differently than in England. In some places it is known as a "Mass-Tree", in others it has connotations of the saints. It often marked a resting-place for coffin-bearers. But by far the greater number of thorns, either singly or in groups, are to be found either surrounding or in close proximity to a tumulus, or tump, said to mark a meeting-place of the "little people". There would seem to be here an analogy with the Bronze Age burial tumuli or barrows (with their presumed associations of tree and ancestor worship).

There are, of course, many other tree species with religious associations, but it is the yew, the thorn and the oak which, taken together, make up an esoteric trinity of trees whose mythical roots go down deep into the genesis of man's subconscious thought processes, stirring a slow sap of speculation on the awesome nature of the dualities of the existence he has to come to terms with: darkness and light; evil and good; death and birth; how to placate the one and evoke the other. In the legendary stories that follow we shall see through his homely looking-glass something of his ethos as well as his pathos—or, if you prefer it another way, the *hominid* ghost of *homo sapiens* being yet loath to exchange his ragged, old, dyed-in-the-wool coat of many colours for a brave new cloak of man-made fibres.

Perhaps the most interesting of our famous yews are not the single specimens which dominate churchyards and burial places. Winding across the downs in Surrey and Kent are sombre lines of them tracing the Pilgrim's Way to Canterbury, a track leading by way of villages with Norman churches, many having their own venerable yews. This meandering path passes many old earthworks of vanished races. Sporadic outcrops of the indigenous yew occur all over the British Isles, although in Ireland self-sown trees are rare in the eastern part of the country. The churchyard yew, however, is commoner in the West of Ireland, due to certain historical and religious factors. Yet at the time of King John, who was also Governor of Ireland in 1185, it was recorded that the yew abounded, especially in cemeteries and sacred places, and that they were then of some antiquity. The historian Gerald de Barri, who accompanied John to Ireland, recorded that many of the large trees were trampled down and broken.

In Scotland natural growth of the yew is sparse, but here and there it can be found growing wild in the highlands. Mr. Vaughan Cornish in his *Churchyard Yew and Immortality*, has prepared some interesting maps illustrating the significance of churchyard yews in Scotland, with a special note of the journeyings of the apostle St. Ninian. This missionary advanced northwards through Ayr, Renfrew, Dumbarton, Stirling, Fife and Perth, his route following the paths of Roman campaigns and the line of the Antonine Wall. He also took a secondary route along the western coast to Fort William and Inverness, and eventually reached as far as the Shetland Isles. The establishment of churchyard yews coincides with both routes, although the contrast between the distribution and size of the trees on the east and the more prolific distribution of church yews on the west should not be attributed to St. Ninian's lesser influence on the former: it is merely that the climatic conditions on the east of the country are less favourable to yews.

When, in 1771, Thomas Pennant visited Fortingall in Glen Lyon, Perthshire, and measured the yew tree near the church as being of 56 ft. girth, it was supposed that this was the largest of them all. The legends grew. Pontius Pilate had been suckled beneath the tree when his father was a legionary during an early Roman expedition; it was an early pagan preaching site, etc. The tree is now merely a shell supporting several upright growths with healthy foliage from what appears to be the old rooting system of two older stumps, the overall height being little more than 25 ft. The tree is enclosed by walls on one of which is a framed noticeboard with the following legend:

FORTINGALL YEW TREE

This ancient world famous tree has stood in this village for many centuries. How many no-one can say accurately, but from observations made by eminent botanists it seems certain that this specimen of the primeval forest must be over 3,000 years old.

In 1796, Pennant, when on a visit to Colonel Campbell of Glenlyon measured this historic tree he found it measured 56½ ft. in circumference. Some years afterwards, De Candolle, the eminent French botanist, Baron Humboldt and several savants of our own country, visited and examined the tree. They were all much impressed by its size and age. In 1825, the limbs had fallen away from each other, no doubt due to the fact that for 200 years it had been subjected to vandalistic treatment by the village boys who lit their Beltane fires between the separated parts.

About the middle of the 19th century the local authorities were compelled to build this wall for its protection. In 1870 the late Sir Robert Christison, after a careful examination, pronounced its age to be about 3,000 years.

This celebrated yew tree is incontestably the most ancient specimen of vegetation in Europe.

Unfortunately, in attempting to assess its age we are again faced with the problem of compound trunks (and indeed others may have disappeared completely) merging and grafting themselves into each other, so measurements are of no avail. Those two (or more) trunks may have been previous offshoots from a still earlier main bole, and so the mystery remains.

Ranking high among the numerous large yews in England is the churchyard tree at Crowhurst in Surrey; it is reputed to be at least 1,600 years old. First mention of this well-known tree was made by the historian Aubrey, who stated that it measured 30 ft. around the bole at 5 ft. from the ground. Recent girth-taping of the tree by the Forestry Commission representatives give it a waist of 30 ft. 4 in., which shows how slowly old yews grow. In 1820, some villagers excavated the earth around the base of the hollow trunk and found a cannon ball, believed to be a relic from a skirmish (during the Parliamentary Wars) in 1643. Shortly after this a table and seating for twelve persons were introduced into the cavity, and the whole was capped by a door erected between the live tissues of the shell. The latter is still there, though it seems that nature is providing a "callus" rim to roll discriminately over this opening, subtly sealing off the meeting place of past committees whose deliberations *may* only have been the organizing of Palm Sunday wakes. The tree has recently been propped and chained in an effort to prolong its life.

Another village of Crowhurst, in Sussex, has an ancient yew which is railed off to prevent souvenir hunters and initial-carvers from damaging it. The Reverend Lonsdale Ragg called the Crowhurst Yew the "Caged Lion"; indeed the brown fissured bark and the metal protection do give such a zoological effect. Tree surgery has been carried out on this old monarch lately. It stands between the Manor and the church, and the general opinion is that the tree is older than manor or church, both of which began their recorded history about 1250. King Harold owned the Manor of Crowhurst at the time of the Conqueror's landing, and a legend records that the Reeve was hanged on the yew tree for failing to disclose the king's hidden treasure when requested. The tale is part of the obscure legend of the Golden Warrior. The measurements of the yew are 38 ft. in height and 27 ft. 10 in. in girth; it is a female tree.

In the churchyard of St. Helen's, Darley Dale, Derbyshire, is a renowned yew of the Peak District, having a girth of 32 ft. 10 in. at 5 ft. from the ground. Part of the legend on the attached plaque tells us that the yew is 2,000 years old and was known to the ancient Britons, "who met and sheltered under its boughs . . .".

Close to the tree near the chancel door is the lid of a Roman burial urn. A large, round, inscribed stone indicates that the tree marked a sacred site in pre-Christian times. The branches are supported from the main trunk by chains. This tree has been claimed as the finest yew in Britain. In 1817 the girth was only a little less than its present measurement. In 1888 a Mr. Paget Bowman cut from it, with a trephine, nine cylinders of wood on one horizontal line which showed 33 to 66 rings per inch radius, demonstrating an average growth of one inch in forty-six years. Like the Crowhurst, Sussex, yew it is a female tree.

The first avenue of yews to be formally planted in Britain was in 1644, by the Earl of Arundel, at St. John the Baptist Church, Westbourne, Sussex, leading from the gate to the church door. At Midhurst, some ten miles NE of Westbourne, is a curious grove in the Close Walks; these surely must be the tallest yews in Europe. Their age and history is not known. The Close Walks are situated near the town, on both sides of the River Rother. They are arranged in four

Yews at Painswick Church, Gloucestershire.

avenues forming a square of about 150 yards. There is also another grove near the avenues in which the trees are about 80 ft. in height. Many have boles clear of branches for some 20 ft. from the ground; some have a girth of 9 ft. Very little grows under the shadow of these yews, save some small seedlings of yew straining towards the light on the perimeter of the grove.

An annual "clipping ceremony" used to take place at the church of St. Mary the Virgin, at Painswick, Gloucestershire. The ninety-nine yews in the churchyard, still in remarkably neat condition, used to be clipped on September 8th, the feast of the Nativity of Our Lady and known in the church calendar as "Clipping Sunday". The following Sabbath the parishioners would march in procession around the churchyard, then join hands to form a ring about the church. They then congregated at the steps leading to the tower door to hear a sermon preached. Attempts have been made to plant the hundredth yew, but with no success. The circumstance is like that of the Seven Sisters (pines) previously referred to, when attempting to replace a dead tree.

At Packwood, Warwickshire, are yews planted to represent the occasion of the Sermon on the Mount. Grouped between six tall yews—representing the Apostles—are six taller ones representing Evangelists, and at the head of all these is the finest of the group, a single specimen representing Christ. A host of smaller yews at a lower level represents the multitude.

In A.D. 1132, certain monks dissociated themselves from the Benedictine Abbey of St. Mary's, York, in order to adopt the more severe discipline of St. Bernard, the founder of the Cistercian Order at Clairvaux, in Champagne. Ceding to their wishes, Thurston, then Archbishop of York, established Fountains Abbey, near Kirkstall, in the valley of the River Skell. For two years, the pioneer monks lived within the shelter of large yew trees, some of which survive to this day, the best known being the one close to the mill-house in the grounds south of the Cellarium. Hugh, a monk of Kirkstall, has left a manuscript story of the founding of the Abbey, which is preserved in the library of the Royal Society:

"At Christmas, the archbishop, being at Ripon, assigned to the monks some land in the patrimony of St. Peter, about three miles west of that place, for the erection of a monastery. This spot of ground had never been inhabited unless by wild beasts, being overgrown with woods and brambles, lying between two steep hills and rocks, more proper for a retreat for wild beasts than the human species. This was called Skeldale, from a rivulet of that name running through it from the west to the east. The Prior of St. Mary's, at York, was chosen Abbot by the monks, being the first of this monastery of Fountains, with whom they withdrew into this uncouth desert, without any house to shelter them in that winter season, or provisions to subsist on, but entirely depending on Divine Providence. There stood a large elm tree in the midst of the vale, on the lower branches upon which they put some thatch and straw; under that they lay, ate and prayed. The bishop, for a time, supplied them with bread, and the rivulet with drink. Part of the day some spent in making wattles to erect a little oratory, while others cleared some ground to make a garden. But it is supposed that they soon changed the shelter of the elm for that of seven trees, growing on the declivity of the hill on the south side of the abbey. They were of extraordinary size; the trunk of one of them is 26 ft. in circumference at 3 ft. from the ground, and they stand so near each other as to form a cover almost equal to a thatched roof. Under these trees, the monks resided till they had built the monastery."

At Hafodunos Hall, Llangernieuw, near Abergele, North Wales, are some old yew trees on the lawn which are famed for giving sanctuary to St. Winifred, Patron Saint of Virgins. Beneath these yews the maid Winifred found shelter for a night—the name Hafodunos meaning exactly that—"shelter for the night". She was later captured and beheaded by Caradoc for scorning him.

Overton churchyard is in a remote part of Flintshire known as Maelor. The group of yew trees there is known as one of the "Seven Wonders of Wales". Beneath the yew to the north of the western gate is the much weathered shaft of a fourteenth-century stone cross. At Gresford Church, Wrexham, is a yew estimated to be 1,500 years old. It is 15 ft. in girth and 60 ft. in height. J. E. B. Bowman, writer and Fellow of the Linnean Society, describing the tree in 1836, said it had seven main branches, most of them being divided in their upper reaches into several smaller ones. "It is a male tree, in good condition, and is reputed to be the finest of its specie in Wales."

A remarkably upright yew of great interest is the Muckross Abbey tree near Killarney. It grows within the cloistered court and has a bole clear of any branches to about 20 ft. above the ground, with a spreading crown. J. C. Loudon stated that the tree was traditionally coeval with the abbey, though there is a good deal of doubt about this opinion. He also writes that the sanctuary was in existence about 1180, which would mean that the tree is at least seven hundred years old. With its present bole diameter of less than 3 ft., attempts at calculating its age based on this factor are questionable, for, in this case, the tree is sound throughout the bole. Even allowing that the circumference of the butt could have expanded one-third of an inch per year, that would only give us an approximate age of three hundred years. Arthur Young, the travel author, writing his *Tour in Ireland* in 1780, stated that the tree was the most prodigious he had ever seen, being at that date 2 ft. in diameter at a height of 14 ft. and with a spreading crown forming a perfect canopy. By this no doubt he meant merely that the lower branches as then existing filled the cloister-walk on all sides. In 1836 another writer, Percival Hunter, described the tree as having been stripped of all its lower branches. Possibly such an interference with the general equilibrium of the tree accounts for the slender proportions and restricted growth—an interesting botanical query, which will not be resolved until the tree is felled and the rings counted at the lowest part of the basal area. Such an experiment is unlikely to occur, as the ruins of the Abbey are being preserved by the Irish Works and Buildings Department, with the tree as the central feature of the restoration. This yew is another example with unanswered questions about its history. Did it mark an original preaching site, or was a yew considered the most appropriate tree to be planted within the shrine? Or had it been propagated by chance, later overshadowing the ruins?

Recent correspondents have informed me that the Abbey was established in 1448 by Franciscan Monks led by Donald McCarthy Mor. This is, of course, 268 years later than the date given by Loudon.

In the context of trees and religious establishments are some remarkable exceptions to the ubiquitous yew that should perhaps be mentioned at this juncture. For instance, an immense pear tree at Inch Abbey, near Downpatrick in Northern Ireland. If it is correct to assume that it was planted by the monks this would mean that it must have been there before the Dissolution in 1538. There are, of course, many other pear trees, some still extant, in the grounds of religious houses. Loudon mentions some standing at Jedburgh Abbey, in Scotland, dating them at around 500 years old in 1853. The monks, apart from using the fruit for a thriving trade in perry, valued pear juice as an antidote against the effects of poisonous fungi.

The most remarkable hawthorn tree associated either with the mysterious "thorn cult" of the Belgae and Manapii or with the legend of Joseph of Arimathea was at Hethel, near Norwich. It is still standing, being adequately propped. In 1755 it measured, at 4 ft. from the ground, 9 ft. 1 in. in girth. One arm extended over 21 ft. It was at that time a compound tree growing in all directions, making a canopy circumference of 31 yards. There is no evidence, apart from its close proximity to the church, that it has any more historic interest other than its use as a boundary tree, although about 1841, in the Register of Remarkable Trees in the County of Norfolk, reference was made to the possession of a deed by Sir Thomas Beavor, bearing a date in the thirteenth century, in which the thorn is mentioned as being a boundary tree marking a meeting place in an insurrection of peasants in the reign of King John. The tree stands on a low ridge, and local tradition avers that it is older than the fourteenth-century church nearby.

At Nether Alderley near Macclesfield, Cheshire, was a cross actually shrouded by a thorn. A local history of 1903 confidently states: "The cross is embraced with a thorn tree that is probably the Glastonbury Thorn of the Stanley memoirs, and a successor to the staff of Joseph of Arimathea, a slip from the famous tree that blossomed at the Nativity." The Stanleys, Lords of the Manor of Alderley, were churchmen who displayed great tolerance towards non-conformists—not even, apparently, resenting the latters' reputed destruction of the revered Glastonbury Thorn.

A famous old thorn tree on the green at Chiddingfold, Surrey, is said to be 500 years old. The base of the tree has become tunnelled with age so that the two remaining sides have a curious knock-kneed appearance. The tree was mentioned on an old map many centuries ago. There is no evidence of historic associations except that thorn trees in England seldom receive the careful preservational treatment given to this specimen unless there is such good reason. Also a wall has been built around the old bole as a further protection.

In the small town of Houghton-le-Spring, Durham, there is a thorn known widely as the Gilpin Thorn. This tree was planted by Bernard Gilpin, Rector of the Parish from 1557 to 1584, in the Rectory grounds, now a public park. Gilpin was known as the Apostle of the North, and was revered throughout the countryside for his good works and kindness to the poor. He visited Glastonbury and took cuttings from the "original" Glastonbury Thorn. The old tree, struck from one of these snippets, is still in the grounds today, supported by three props, but only one limb bears foliage.

There are many examples of thorns in Britain associated with

The Mitre Oak at Hartlebury, Worcestershire, before it was "topped".

pilgrimages, though they are not all of the Glastonbury variety. Some do not flower both in December *and* at the end of May, and others are noteworthy only for obscure associations with boundary and gospel-tree traditions. In Ireland, however, certain individual trees are widely revered, and not necessarily because of a Glastonbury ancestry.

A whitethorn tree is still preserved in the middle of Manastereven Forest in Co. Kildare. In times of persecution Mass was said here, and for this purpose the present iron cross was attached to the tree. Twenty-five square yards of clearance was given to the tree, when a new plantation was made, the space being surrounded by a Lawson's cypress hedge, and there is an adjoining path leading to the sacred place. Another Mass tree, a plain hawthorn, is at the convent at Mullinavat, in Kilkenny, and is again remembered as a site for prayer during the persecutions of the late eighteenth century.

At Clareen, in Offaly, seven miles from Roscrea, is a whitethorn associated with the old monastic settlement of Seir Kieran, now in ruins. The tree must have healing or religious import, as witness the fact that, in recent times, a main road was realigned so as not to disturb the tree, in deference to local belief that some catastrophe might occur if it were harmed. Local opposition was again responsible for the preservation of a whitethorn on the Ballintra–Rossnowlagh Road in Donegal in 1968. Thousands of pounds of public money were expended on realigning the road and by-passing the tree, known locally as the Fairy Tree.

Two ash trees at Ballyquin Cross, Mullinavat, in Kilkenny, are conventional resting places for funeral processions and are known as "Coffin Trees". Near Castlepollard, Westmeath, is an ash associated with St. Fechin, who founded the monastery at Fore. Local people maintain that it never produces leaves, yet has remained alive for several hundred years. They say, also, that its timber will not burn.

An ancient sycamore tree stands beside the main Dublin to Limerick Road, about three miles on the Dublin side of Mountrath. On the upper side of one of its limbs is a cavity which holds rainwater, hence the local name of the "Well in the Tree". The belief is that, when the original holy well in a nearby field was filled in, it reappeared miraculously in the tree. Six years ago, plans to widen the road had to be abandoned because of objections to the removal of the tree, and a new highway was finally constructed to avoid interfering with it. The "Well in the Tree" has been associated in local folklore with St. Fintan, who founded a monastery here in the sixth century.

Of unknown specie is another tree beside St. Patrick's Well at Miskaun Glebe, in Co. Leitrim. St. Patrick is supposed to have celebrated Mass at the foot of this tree, which has a hole at its base, always filled with water, no matter what the season. The water is supposed to cure warts and other skin ailments.

In 1968, I received the following information from Mr. M. Macrae of Kyle, Ross-shire, who quotes from the *Life and Times of the Reverend Lachlan Mackenzie, of Locharron, Ross-shire* (1754–1819):

"In warning the people of Locharron of the preciousness of Gospel truth and the great privilege of sitting under the ministry of such as declared the 'whole counsel of God', he stated that as a proof that he had never delivered to the people but what he received from the Holy Spirit, two trees would grow, one on each side of the spot where his pulpit stood, and that nowhere else would there be found precisely the same kind of tree; that when they grew up and their branches intertwined above the pulpit, they would fall to the ground; that would be a sign that the apostacy of the latter days had already begun.

"All this occurred as foretold . . . the trees grew, nobody knew how, as two witnesses to the truth of the doctrine delivered by the man of God to the people, and when their branches intertwined they fell over on to the ground, where they lie in a decaying state, but still there."

The two trees shrank to bush size, and are still there, although nearly dead. Since 1968, vandals have uprooted the two trees, from which it was said that berries and cuttings would never seed or strike. The mystery of the identification of the species, as fore-shadowed by the reverend gentleman, remained, but the prophecy fructified after the church became a roofless ruin. The abandoned pulpit was overgrown by the two mysterious trees which still defied identification. From the various descriptions received, they exhibited the wood of the elder, the berry of the mountain ash, and a leaf somewhere between that of hawthorn and the beam tree. I received two pieces of the dead wood from Locharron, and their appearance seemed similar to that of the buddleia!

A certain Lady Anne Grimston is said to have inadvertently en-sured that trees would grow from her grave. A professed atheist, she declared that it was as likely that she would survive death as that a tree would grow from her grave. On her death-bed she uttered the ominous words: "If there is a God in Heaven may seven trees grow from my grave!" A little unconvincingly, she requested that a heavy stone be placed over her resting-place. She was buried in Tewin churchyard, Hertfordshire. The large grave, surrounded by railings, is now cracked and lifted by several trees, and embedded in their trunks.

A very large ash tree at Torberry Hill near West Harting, Hants, stands near the site of an Iron Age encampment. Known as the Trysting Tree, it measures 24 ft. in circumference at 4 ft. from the ground, but has a hollow centre 2 ft. 6 in. across. Surprisingly, it sup-ports a full crown and seems to be in good health. By tradition it was the site of meetings, and was also possibly a "court" tree. If we accept that ash trees can live for several hundred years (though they have not the longevity of oak) the tradition that the Hundred Court used to be held beneath the tree is fairly acceptable—though more likely it marks the site of a predecessor, probably an oak, a more usual witness of trystings. The position of this tree in relation to the adjoining mounds may signify that its predecessors may have marked the site of pagan religious ceremonies rather than the legal ones of later ages.

On the whole the Christian missionaries were sympathetic to the groves and solitary trees associated with the pagan religions, and the simple connotations of the "Tree of Life" concept were accommodated by the new theology. Indeed, churches and monasteries were purposely founded near sacred groves, and priests of the new order saw to it that their trees were preserved. The first Archbishop of Canterbury, St. Augustine, sent by Pope Gregory in A.D. 597 to convert Britain to Christianity, left in his zealous wake a number of preaching sites, especially in the West Midlands, which were identified by trees, or had commemorative trees planted there by his converts.

There is little doubt that the tree was an effective pulpit. Augustine did not discredit the worship of nature in the minds of his listeners. Rather would he subtly merge his teaching and the practices of the new religion with their not entirely dissimilar beliefs in many aspects.

A Severn village near the Wrekin is named Cressage. In mediaeval times it was known as Cristesache, or Christ's Oak, and it is reasonable to assume that an oak once grew in that village and was venerated for some long-forgotten circumstance. A ruined and hollow oak, having a younger tree growing up through its 20 ft. girth chimney-like bole, is said to be the last relic of an old Royal Forest and is also claimed to be the tree under which St. Augustine preached in the year A.D. 598. A curious story relating to Dean Swift is connected with the tree: during a thunderstorm, the Dean and two travellers— a man and woman—sheltered beneath the oak. The elopers, as they turned out to be, requested the Dean to unite them in matrimony there and then, which he did. For good measure he composed for them a certificate of the occasion, unfortunately effected in rather bad verse.

Another oak, at Bridgnorth, known as the Quatford Oak, was reputed to have been a meeting place between Augustine and the Celtic Bishops of the older faith in A.D. 597.

In Worcestershire many trees marked traditional sites of Augustine's preaching places. The Rock Oak at Rock once claimed witness to the first meeting between the bishops of the two early churches, the Celtic and the later Roman, in an attempt to reconcile their differences. But more important deliberations appear to have taken

Ancient yew at Much Marcle, Shropshire.

Glastonbury Thorn, St. John's Church, Glastonbury.

place at the Mitre Oak at Hartlebury, which (although its authenticity is questionable) can still be seen, though only as a ruined trunk, at Crossway Green, near the village of Hartlebury. Other opinions are that the tree was a boundary mark of the Bishop of Worcester's estate at Hartlebury Castle.

The circumference of the Mitre Oak at its base in 1958 was 24 ft. and its height 60–70 ft. The year before, a woman who passed regularly beneath the tree was nearly struck by a falling branch, and this led to examinations of the decaying giant by various local and county councillors. Prolonged correspondence reporting on the condition of the tree passed between all the authorities concerned. Finally it was resolved to remove the head of the tree completely, as its bole was completely hollow and unable to support large branches at the main fork. Mindful of the Mitre Oak's historic interest, some members of the councils wanted the bole left as high as possible; others with less interest in the traditions wanted it down altogether, or cut off at a height of 4 ft. The compromise was struck at 20 ft., and a contractor was employed to carry out the work.

Dr. Booker, Vicar of Dudley, published a poem dedicated to this oak; two of the stanzas run:

Not Boscobel's famed tree, that saved a king,
When, for his life, on wide-stretch'd bloody wing,
*   Grim vengeance hover'd near,*
In grandeur thee transcended in thy prime;
And, like that tree, all sanctified by time,
Thou to thy lovely province art most dear.

Witness of generations banish'd long,
If thou wert gifted with historic tongue,
*   How might we, listening, learn*
The chronicles of yeomen, who have stood
Beneath thee, in the circumnambient wood,
To mark the antler'd roebuck, 'mid the fern.

The name Mitre Oak is no doubt derived from the headgear worn by bishops. The Venerable Bede mentions an oak near the borders of England and Wales where such a bishops' meeting took place but gives no place name, possibly because no hamlet then existed. The Rock Oak, nearer to the boundary, may have been the oak in question. There is, however, little doubt that the tree marks one of the boundaries of the Manor of Hartlebury, which was granted to

H

Above, *Remnants of Gospel Oak, Polstead.*
Below, *Trysting Tree, West Harting.*

the bishops of Worcester by the King of Mercia in A.D. 670. It has also lent its name to a new public house not far away—a mark of the brewery's flair for publicity.

At Stanford Bishop, Herefordshire, is a large yew some 22 ft. in girth which may also have had associations with St. Augustine. Standing on a tump, which no doubt made a convenient rostrum, the yew (quite possibly the original tree) is said to have given shelter to his chair. This chair is even more legendary than the yew, for it was claimed to have been discovered by Dr. James Johnston while rummaging in a lumber room of the church tower in early Victorian times. Closer examination revealed that the oak chair, then very dilapidated, did have features of craftsmanship that could have qualified it for a seventh-century dating. The rails and boards, except for the back-board, were fixed by oak pegs and fitted into slots in the posts. But the most remarkable feature is the seat, which is hinged as a box lid. The hinges were round pieces of wood, which the Romans called cardines, common during the occupation.

Bede recorded that Augustine was haughty and dictatorial, and refused to rise from his chair on the arrival of the British Bishops, showing prejudice and a lack of Christian humility. Was this seat made for Augustine? The historic chair (if such it was) was lost for 1,200 years, until discovered by James Johnston, from whom it was acquired by Canterbury Museum.

Another large yew, with a seat for seven persons in its hollow interior, is in the churchyard at Much Marcle, Herefordshire. Although no specific legends or traditions are known about the tree, it ranks in impressiveness with the Crowhurst yews, but is little known.

The murder of Thomas à Becket, Archbishop of Canterbury in Henry II's reign, promoted and sustained the cult of St. Thomas the Martyr for several centuries following the assassination. Becket had often preached in the open air during his earlier career, and it has been held in long tradition that one sermon was delivered under a yew tree in the churchyard of the village of Tudeley-cum-Capel, near Tonbridge, Kent. The tree still survives close to St. Thomas à Becket church. The girth suggests that the existence of the yew in the martyr's day cannot be discounted, and for this reason preservation and treatment to the tree has been arranged. In addition, a "Yew of Commemoration" is to be planted close by.

In the grounds of Ormiston Hall, East Lothian, is an ancient yew at one time used as a meeting place by George Wishart and John Knox, the Protestant reformers during the reign of Mary, Queen of

Scots. Here they preached their sermons to the Scots who bore sour allegiance to France. With the prevailing corruption of the Church in Scotland at that time adding weight to their impassioned oratory, the two preachers no doubt contributed to the successful Union of Scotland and England, thus ending the internecine strife for the first time since Edward I's reign.

According to the most reliable sources, the evergreen or holm oak was introduced into the British Isles some time before 1580. Certainly it was to be found growing on many monastic sites when Henry VIII's henchman, Thomas Cromwell, was dismantling the Roman Church in Britain and destroying its establishments. With its Mediterranean origins the ilex or holm oak symbolized the Papacy to the reformers and so gained ill repute. A large ilex oak then grew in the Vatican Gardens, and was described by Pliny as being older than Rome itself. Outside the main gate of Minster-in-Sheppey Abbey, grew such a tree at the time of the Reformation and, although many similar trees were destroyed in the purges of 1536, a holm oak of more mature stature still grows on this very site. Reputed to be the only oak of its kind on the Isle of Sheppey, tradition says it is the original tree. Until it is felled and ring-counted no one can dispute the claim.

In the grounds of an hotel at the end of the esplanade at Sheerness is a mulberry popularly supposed to have been planted by Anne Boleyn when she visited the island before her marriage with Henry VIII. If true, then the introductory date of the mulberry to Britain was earlier than is generally supposed. Anne Boleyn was beheaded in 1536. First records of the distribution of the black mulberry in this country merely state "in the middle of the 16th century". The white mulberry followed later, in 1596.

Other sources of information confirm that mulberries were being planted in the early sixteenth century. In Beaufort Street, Chelsea, on grounds of the Convent of Adoration Reparatrice, once part of Sir Thomas More's estate, is a mulberry reported to have been planted by More himself. He was executed in 1535, after refusing to take the oath of Supremacy when Chancellor to Henry VIII. Hence it appears likely that the black mulberry, which is of Caucasian and Persian origin, was established in this country well before this date. As late as 1964, More's tree was providing fruit for the sisters of the convent.

The decline of the church during the eighteenth century gave rise to strong emotions and frustrations among the poorer classes, who anticipated a return to the troubles that wracked the country as a

Wesley's Preaching Tree, Stony Stratford.

result of the religious upheavals of the two preceding centuries. John Wesley's life spanned nearly the whole of the eighteenth century, and from about 1736 onward he renounced the church practices of his day. With great fervour and skilled organization he held the greatest number of open-air revivalist meetings ever known. Like Augustine more than a thousand years earlier, he addressed his congregations near trees in conspicuous positions. Wesley had a unique gift of gathering together all the gossamer threads of folklore and half-comprehended beliefs into the web of Christian theology without its trappings of anachronistic dogma, thus making direct appeals to the hearts of his listeners with phenomenal success.

Many of his "pulpit" trees have been recorded up and down the country, though only a few now remain. The best known is at Stony Stratford. It is a pollarded elm, fenced around to protect it from passing traffic, and to prevent children from climbing its still flourishing branches. Its age is approximately three hundred years. Wesley's Elm at Portsmouth, a straight, vigorous tree, stands by the side of the

Old London Road at Hilsea. It is protected by a fence and has a plaque with the legend:

> John Wesley (1703–1791). Near this plaque stood a massive elm beneath which John Wesley preached during his ministry. This elm died eventually and in the centre of the shell the young elm now growing was planted in the year 1909.

The habit of this elm resembles that of the Cornish variety, which is usually fastigiate and tapers regularly to its tip. Though not of great girth, it has a purposeful, clean and distinctly safe appearance, unlike the common elm.

And in Cornwall, another of "Wesley's trees" stands at a junction of country lanes near Camborne. This actually is a Cornish elm. It can best be approached along the road between Troon and the Pendarves Estate, on a minor road just off the Helston to Camborne main route.

Not far from Tarporley, Cheshire, is an ancient pear tree which stands in an orchard at Alpraham—yet another of Wesley's preaching trees. Its owner is a member of the Methodist Church.

In the village of Lorton, Cumberland, is a yew tree reputed to be the site where Wesley preached when he visited the Lake District on horseback. In May, 1968, the Methodists from the local Circuit gathered there to hear a service conducted by the chairman of the District of Carlisle Methodists. Some records state that George Fox, the founder of the Society of Friends, also preached under this yew during the latter part of the previous century.

In old age, Wesley visited a favourite ash tree at Winchelsea, Sussex. An extract from his journal reads: "Thursday, 7th October, 1790. I went over to that poor skeleton of ancient Winchelsea. It is beautifully situated on the top of a steep hill, and was regularly built, broad streets crossing each other and encompassing a very large square in the midst of which was a large church, now in ruins. I stood under a large tree on the side of it, and called to most of the inhabitants of the town. 'The Kingdom of Heaven is at hand. Repent, and believe in the Gospel!'" His ash tree died some years ago, but another ash has been planted on the site. It stands on a green verge at the side of the street to the west of the churchyard. The site and tree are protected by an iron railing. An inscription records: "Under an ash tree that stood on the site of this one John Wesley ended his great open-air ministry on October 7th, 1790." John Wesley died the following year.

Chapter Six

Healing and the Occult

There is inevitably some blurring of the edges in attempting to differentiate between the classifications of trees associated with the themes of worship and its attendant theologies and those with themes of veneration—in the secular sense of respect for the physical attributes of trees and for their rôles as catalysts in the practice of the occult arts. Clearly there is a common link—one might almost call it an umbilical cord—that of animism, or the attribution of a living and intelligent spirit to natural objects.

In the case of trees accredited with healing properties no doubt these assets were discovered empirically. For example, the quinine-like effects from drinking water which had been trapped in the hollow of an oak tree, thus becoming a dilute solution of tannic acid—the thirsty victim of a fever from a wound, or from one of the endemic diseases, might well benefit from such a dosage. News of the discovery would soon get around, leading to other experiments with the same medicine for other diseases. Nothing succeeds like success; hence, as we shall see later, certain trees became a veritable pharmacopoeia.

The oak, being an indigenous tree and very widespread throughout the British Isles, not surprisingly has gathered unto itself a richly varied mythology from a whole gamut of successive peoples—Celts, Druids, Romans, Anglo-Saxons, Normans and continuing throughout the Middle Ages almost up to the present day. It was one of the Seven Noble Trees of Irish tradition. The destruction of any of the others—the apple, alder, birch, holly and willow—rendered the miscreants liable to suffer the fine of a cow, or some such economically crippling penalty. When St. Columcille founded a church at Derry he had no compunction about burning down a hamlet and thus risking the king's wrath, in a campaign of literally obliterating the works of man from his chosen site; yet he scrupulously preserved the oak wood from which the religious settlement then took its name.

The first Norse invaders knew the oak as the thunder tree, thus sacred to Thor. Though the oak appears always to have been the tree most commonly struck by lightning it was, because of its associations with Thor, believed to give protection to shelterers, even though the tree itself was struck. Indeed, oaks known to have been struck were often visited from far and wide by souvenir-hunters who took away pieces to be attached to their buildings as a form of protection. By

a slight extension to this belief the oak was similarly prized as a ward against witchcraft. The Venerable Bede told of St. Augustine preaching before King Ethelbert in the Isle of Thanet and being advised by the king always to preach under an oak tree as a protection against evil sorceries. Marriages were frequently celebrated under "Marriage Oaks", until finally forbidden by the usurping Christian Church. Even so, the practice of dancing three times around an oak tree after church weddings was indulged in for many centuries. As a corollary to this custom a sobering drink made from an infusion of crushed acorns used to be generally dispensed to the company after the ceremony.

Indeed, the lore of the oak tree was so much a part of the warp and weft of the human story that we find Aubrey, in his *Natural History of Wiltshire*, telling us that "When an oake is felling, it gives a kind of shrieke or groanes that may be heard a mile off, as if it were the genius of the oake lamenting". Conservationists will endorse this!

But how does one approach the more ambivalent legends of the yew? On the one hand, its symbolism of death; on the other of fertility: perhaps, again, it is an echo of that dualism eternally around man—life and death, day and night, good and evil—an endless cycle. Its "death" aspect probably arises from its poisonous effect on cattle and other ruminants, coupled with a certain funereal appearance (or is that a phobia induced by its mythology?). True, it is invariably found in churchyards and graveyards, but that may not be so much for apt appearance as because it had acquired an exorcistic usage against the Devil and his works. Some authorities claim that it was sited in churchyards for the very practical reason that there it was protected against the browsing compulsions of cattle, for their sakes. But why grow it at all in such profusion, despite its usefulness in the making of longbows and other weapons? After all, imported French yew was a much better proposition for longbows; indeed, all imports had perforce to include a quota of yew.

Regarding the occult practices associated with yew there is one choice example that must surely rank with the Philosopher's Stone, having a top rating in wish-fulfilment. It comes from the Scottish Highlands, from the tortuous annals of clan warfare; namely that if a clansman were to take a piece of churchyard yew in his left hand before confronting an enemy to denounce or threaten him, then the latter would hear nothing of what was said, though all around could hear every word. The point of this being that the denouncer could swear afterwards—and be able to produce witnesses—that he had given clear warning of his intentions and so be able to claim exoneration from the charge of a treacherous attack. Clearly, there must have been a snag somewhere—or perhaps it worked only in Gaelic? —or the embassies of the world would have beaten a path to the door of the Highlands wider than the Pass of Glencoe!

The time-honoured healing properties of many trees have curiously anthropomorphic connotations. For instance, the fibrous, hairlike growths under the bark and on the roots of yews, being thought to resemble the "hair of a virgin", invoked fertility legends. Perhaps as a projection of this, there is at least one echo, as we shall see later, in Christian mythology where an actual incident concerning a young girl and a yew tree gave rise to pilgrimages for the Intercession of the Virgin Mary.

In a similar way, the resilient properties of the ash, a tree whose timber has been valued for centuries for its use in the making of tool-shafts, weapons and all implements that had to be subjected to severe and prolonged strains, have for long been put to use in the healing of ruptures—probably because of the analogy of these qualities with the ability of human muscles to knit themselves together again after injury due to strain.

The leaves and the timber of ash, kept indoors, were believed to protect the occupants of the dwelling from the machinations of witchcraft—the immemorial bane of our forefathers. It was also said that snakes detested the ash and so pieces of it were carried about the person as a talisman. It even had its uses in midwifery, at least in Devonshire, where newborn babies were bathed in water heated over ash faggots, from the belief that this procedure actually happened at the birth of Christ. From midwifery to white witchcraft, perhaps the oldest cult of healing, losing nothing by the ambitious claims of its practitioners and garbled hearsay. Thus warts were cured by the curious permutation of sticking a pin into each wart, then each pin into ash, then back again into the wart, in this shrewd way transferring the affliction to the tree and also inoculating the sufferer (perhaps a better word than "patient") against recurrence. Vaccination is only a shade less esoteric!

Since all body fluids are said to be antiseptic there is something almost acceptably pharmaceutical about the mediaeval cure for ulcerated ears—by applying a wad of wool soaked in an infusion of ash-keys boiled in the patient's urine. Ash-keys had a significance other than in medicine in that it was believed that a failure in the ash-key crop foreshadowed a death in the royal family "within a year". At least one authentic case is recorded as "proof"—the ash-key crop failed in 1648 and Charles I died in 1649.

Unlike the yew and the ash, the apple is not notable for its longevity and hence does not seem to have many of the dark undertones that go with them. Nevertheless, its roots go deep down into the soil of mythology, although with more sanguine connotations of healing and fertility, possibly because of the spontaneous appeal of its blossoming and popular fruitfulness. Wild apples, or crab apples, grew widely in Europe and were seriously cultivated in Roman times as a supplementary crop to the ubiquitous olive. It followed that

Roman law, whose writ, of course, ran throughout the Empire, made early provision for its protection, with severe penalties for those anti-social enough as to cut it down. Centuries later, in Ireland, the severity of punishment was almost Mosaic in demanding a "life for a life"—in practice, the forfeit of cattle, the age-old deterrent, as exemplified in the early poem, *The Triads of Ireland*. The Norse gods prized it for its gift of eternal youth, epitomized by Idun, the goddess of youth and renewal. Conversely, there was a widespread belief that the malfunctioning of apple trees—for instance, a second flowering while fruiting—meant an early death in the owner's family. As the classical emblem of youth and renewal the apple naturally rated high in Greek mythology as the representation of sensual love, being awarded by the famous Judgment of Paris, Prince of the House of Troy and the handsomest living human, to the goddess Aphrodite. As everyone knows, Helen, the *femme fatale* of the ancient world, was promised to Paris as a bribe by Aphrodite, who was unscrupulously determined to be the "Miss Universe" of her day.

Love and desire being synonymous in mythology with guilt leering from the wings, as it were, no doubt a projection of pre-Biblical legend is implied by the Serpent's temptation of Adam in Eden with this fruit of the Tree of Knowledge of Good and Evil. More pragmatically, perhaps, the reputation of the apple for healing is an empirical one, as so often with other medicines, both ancient and modern. King Arthur's grievous wound was treated in the Vale of Avalon, the Apple Vale of Celtic myth. And is there not a "Paradise" in the Glastonbury Avalon? Though maybe that's squeezing the pips of the analogy a little too hard.

One cannot end the saga of the apple without saluting Somerest, the land not only of Arthur but of Joseph of Arimathea and of this fruit of Paradise. Apple wassailing, the ancient salutation, is still a part of Somerset folklore on Twelfth Night, although its association with Epiphany must be a curiously oblique one. On this night, farmers and their womenfolk process to the apple orchard at dusk, carrying firearms, kettles and cider. The lowest twigs of the apple trees are pulled down and dipped into the cider pails, the assembled community bowing three times, then raising themselves with great effort, as if bearing heavy loads, thus miming a heavy fruit crop for the coming season. Shotguns are fired through the tree branches and kettles and kitchenware noisily banged, to drive away the demons of ill-luck and to arouse the tree spirits. "Hail to thee, old apple tree!" goes the wassailing chorus. And the occasion is rounded off at the

Tree of Knowledge of Good and Evil.

Adam vnd Eua jm Paradeyß.

local pub, which is entered by the back door and left by the front door, after all have drunk to the health of the house.

Much could be written on the subject of trees and their parts used as talismans, either to protect from disease or to exorcize the powers of evil. In many cases the origin of the legend is evident from the physical characteristics of the tree in question. For instance, the aspen, or poplar—incidentally, traditionally said to be the tree from which the Cross was fashioned—botanically known as *Populus Tremula*, from the tremulous behaviour of its leaves when disturbed, was popularly believed to yield a cure for the ague, a lock of the patient's hair being pinned to the tree in the belief that the "shivering disease" would thus be induced to leave the patient for a more appropriate host.

In the case of the bay tree the practice of hanging sprigs of it over doorways to offset the plague is more obscure, but, possibly, its strong aromatic scent was thought to be therapeutic. Withering of the leaves usually was taken to be an omen of death, although, conversely, sprigs of fresh bay were placed under pillows to encourage pleasant dreams!

Of the many witchcraft associations with trees perhaps that of the birch is best known. Birch trees were felled and set up in farmyards on Mayday for the dual purpose of dancing around and for protecting cattle from the malefactions of witches. Besom brooms made from birch branches were associated with the traditional chores of housewives and their daughters—and, as a corollary, with those unfortunates suspected of witchcraft. It was considered unlucky to make besoms in May, or during the twelve days of Christmas. In some parts a besom which was inadvertently walked over by a girl signified that she would conceive out of wedlock. It followed, therefore, that a favourite joke of the village youths was laying down besom brooms, or birch branches, across the paths of their girl friends. In Wales, a birch besom would be set aslant the open door of the bride's future home. In front of witnesses, the groom then had to leap over the besom and into the house, followed similarly by his bride. The art was in avoiding touching the doorposts or the besom; failure meant that the ceremony had to be repeated until successful. The expression "Jumped over a besom" still can be heard in North Wales, and means, of course, that the person referred to has been married.

The elder tree had particularly sinister connotations which may have derived from the strong belief that it was the tree from which Judas Iscariot hanged himself. Thus, to crown a man with a wreath of elder twigs was a mark of degradation. It was never used for fuel, for fear of ill-luck. Naturally, it was thought to be a favourite tree with witches, who were said to transform themselves into elder trees to escape detection. When the tree was ceremoniously cut down on Midsummer Eve blood was believed to flow from it. There is a story told in Northants that a father cut a stick of elder for his young son. To their horror, blood began to drip from it. On their way home they met a local woman suspected of witchcraft; her arm chanced to be freshly bandaged and blood stains could be seen. The coincidence was only too pointed, and the poor woman was shortly denounced as a proven witch.

Had it not been for the saving grace of its medicinal properties, the elder would no doubt long ago have been eradicated; but it probably survived because it was famed for the cures of quinsies, sore throats, erysipelas, rheumatism, snake bites, rabies, warts and fits. Perhaps it was that witchcraft was synonymous with all these unpleasantries and so healing of them was clearly a case of the hair of the dog . . . Most efficacious was the juice of an elder that had seeded in the fork of a willow, although the niceties of this conjunction are unclear; maybe, like the Philosopher's Stone, it was an undisputed panacea because it had never been put to the test.

Like the elder in certain medicinal respects, the willow is now chiefly remembered in folk medicine as a cure for rheumatism and kindred diseases associated with damp places, the reason possibly being that the willow was partial to damp sites and hence, like the poplar and the "shivering disease", was the tree that obviously was the authority on diseases of dampness. Curiously enough, salicin, an extract from willow bark, is today used in the treatment of rheumatic fever. Is there significance in the fact that this, and other modern medicines, are used for similar purposes and are derived from the same botanical sources as those of folk medicine? Is there within our mysterious human psyche an archetypal instinct for the sources of healing in the same context as the teachings of mediaeval alchemists, who were acknowledged and valued for their sound psychology by Dr. Jung and his school? Is there, in fact, anything new under the sun? Jung would probably have thought not.

There is, too, the ancient and still respectable practice of water-divining by the use of hazel twigs—although willow, birch and other tree branches are used with equal success by those gifted with this baffling power. Whatever may be the strictures of empirical science on the claims of diviners the degree of success in prediction is at least as high as those who predict the precise times and positions of comets.

Mention of psychiatrists and human symbolism will no doubt illumine for the indoctrinated the analogies of maypoles, figurative stumps of trees, and many other fertility symbols, with the phallic symbolism beloved of Freudians. To these might be added the widespread customs involving hazel nuts. In Devon, brides were presented with bags of the nuts as they came out of the church. In France, the bridal pair were showered with the nuts as they knelt at the altar— possibly the origin of confetti-throwing. "Going-a-nutting" is an age-old euphemism for love-making.

Since trees manifested remarkable properties it naturally followed that they could only possess them through supernatural agencies, and so the animistic links with an appropriate god or nature spirit would be assumed unquestioningly. Similarly, coincidental happenings would result in certain trees becoming invested with prophetic qualities; as, for instance, the shedding of a limb on the death of a member of the owner's family, which would perpetuate a legend for succeeding or surviving members of the family in question. There are numerous examples. Often a very human reaction was to chain up suspect limbs so as to "suspend", if not forestall, other prophecies of doom.

In Christian times, when graphic festivals began to take place to re-enact the major events of the Christian Calendar, certain trees were focal points of the rituals. The portrayal of the Crucifixion, for instance, often utilized a prominent tree, having spreading limbs, to signify the Cross. The origins of many surviving ceremonies involving trees are now obscure, but certain features strongly suggest fertility rites, sometimes transmogrifying into the Celebration of Easter.

Prominent trees, especially if in isolated and forbidding settings, often had reputations as the meeting-places of witches. A tree is actually ascribed to the apochryphal rendezvous of the witches of Macbeth, despite the ambiguity of Shakespeare's stage directions— "a desert place". But it is probable that he, faithful always to the conventions of folklore, would have held no objection. And, for that matter, is there not plenty of precedent for such a licence in the present day personification of the Sherlock Holmes legend? How many tourists in London have been able to resist a pilgrimage to Baker Street, or have followed the journeys of David Copperfield or Mr. Pickwick; or how many pilgrims over the centuries have reverently progressed along the Stations of the Cross? A sense of drama has always been an attribute of the human psyche and, not unnaturally, the inherent drama of trees has often been linked with real, or imagined, events of tragedy or with the schemings of sinister beings.

In a different key are the origins of curious fables involving the antics of clowning rustics who traded on the gullibility of their superiors and so diverted a threatened invasion of their rights and privacy. The delectable story of the Wise Men of Gotham and the "Cuckoo Tree" is a classic case, as will be seen later, the locust-like progress of King John's hunting entourage being shrewdly sent off at a tangent.

One should not overlook the special place in Celtic folklore of the rowan, or Mountain Ash. It has particular relevance to the travail of these people, perhaps because of its hardy vitality and persistence in thriving in the dour soil of mountain fastnesses. It is also accredited with an important part in Druid ceremonials. Like the hawthorn it is possible that the small, red, bunched berries of the rowan suggested drops of blood, evocative of Christ's Agony, hence it was frequently invoked in early Christian times against the powers of evil as personified by the Devil.

Lewis Spence, in his fascinating *The Fairy Tradition in Britain*, cites examples of fairy associations with trees, especially on Dartmoor and in Wales, Ireland and Scotland, the last strongholds of the native Celts, Erse and Gaels of these islands. Even in England the old folk rhyme still endures:

Fairy folk
Are in old oaks.

As Sir James Frazer said in *The Magic Art*, the general idea of fairies and trees is one with the ancient conception that spirits of the dead often take up their abode in trees, there to await re-incarnation. There is much in Irish and Scottish folklore that supports this belief —a form of ancestor worship—as W. B. Yeats and Lady Wilde have separately and vividly recorded.

In the Hebrides it is said that a fairy came out of a certain tree once a year and distributed the "milk of wisdom" to the local women, although, regrettably, the tenets or the terms of this much-prized wisdom is unspecified.

While it is not now possible to identify any tree, or trees, having attested local traditions of fairy activities, W. Henderson, in his *Folklore of the Northern Counties of England*, cited one such tree in the park of Sir Robert Vaughan in Wales, an oak tree known locally as "the Elf's Hollow Tree". Ancient hawthorns were often considered to be sacred to fairies; indeed, no countryman would cut down such a tree for fear of being struck dead. In Scotland there used to be many isolated rows of trees, thickly planted, which were locally regarded as sacred. They were known as "Bell" trees, from the Gaelic *Bile*, a tree. No one dare deface or interfere with them lest the sacrilege bring unthinkable misfortune on the vandal. It is possible these purposeful plantations were a form of funerary memorial to distinguished members of local clans, again no doubt symbolizing a form of ancestor-worship, one of the oldest and most universal of religions.

Because of a sad lack of "authentic" examples of fairy trees we must, therefore, remain content with the immortal testimony to fairies of Sir James Barrie. Fortunately, it has all been anthologized in wood, for us and for posterity. A legion of fairy folk and animals were carved on a tree stump which originally stood in the old Richmond Deer Park, in 1922, by a wood carver named Ivor Innis, with the permission of the then Minister of Works and Buildings, the stump being later transferred to the Children's Playground in Kensington Gardens. Mr. Innis added to the carvings about 1945, making of the whole a marvellous evocation of the fairy kingdom. Alas! this unique work fell into disrepair for years. But there is a happy ending to the story. In 1963, Mr. Spike Milligan, noting this neglect, volunteered to restore it. The Ministry magnanimously agreed to let Mr. Milligan have his way—even collaborating to the extent of rigging up a plastic shelter for him. And so, over a period of two years, between his many other preoccupations, he spent six months on the labour of love, and so gave it back to us once more, epitomizing by his devotion the magic spell of trees and their immortal denizens.

Mr. Milligan informs me that there is another tree similarly carved by Ivor Innis, at Rustington, Sussex. Also, yet another, known as the Elfin Oak, in the grounds of a villa at Cannes, by the same inspired carver. The idea seems also to have spread to Melbourne, Australia, where there is another Elfin Oak, carved by a New Zealand sculptress, Ola Cohn.

And so, briefed by this rather wide-ranging survey, let us pass on to more particular examples of trees and their legends of healing and the occult.

The fig tree, whose lineage is as ancient and fundamental as the olive in the economy of Mediterranean civilization, was not introduced into these islands until Henry VIII's time. Cardinal Pole is reputed to have planted the first fig tree in the grounds of the archi-

Madonna and Thorn,
Ballyhaunis, Co. Roscommon.

episcopal palace in Lambeth in 1548. On the other hand there is the legend of the fig tree which grows from the wall of St. Newlyn East Church, Cornwall, attributed to St. Newlina, who is alleged to have placed a stick of fig wood in the earth on the site where the parish church now stands—a parallel legend to that of Joseph of Arimathea and the Holy Thorn. The root appears to grow out of the stonework itself, for no bole or roots can be seen suggesting any contact with the soil. A local rhyme of unknown source runs:

In ancient days Newlina came
The Saint who gave this place its name.
Her staff she planted and she prayed
Let here a church to God be made.
This fig tree is her staff folks say
Destroy it not in any way.
Upon it lays a dreadful curse,
Who plucks a leaf will need a hearse.

It is said that four Cornishmen at different times defied the curse by pruning the fig when it became overgrown and liable to break. All of them suffered early retributions. One story is that a few weeks after one of these operations the culprit pruner's leg was broken while tree-felling in the area, putting him out of work for three months. The legend dies hard, for local people can still be heard muttering darkly about their fig tree, "Where do 'e come from? Where do 'e go?"

The most remarkable collection of fig trees is at West Tarring in Sussex, most of which were planted in 1745. Several are said to have been established by Thomas à Becket in the twelfth century, another contradiction of the "official" date of introduction. A garden here and another at Sompting have been, it is said, on rare occasions, visited by the Deccafico, or Italian Fig Eater, a bird which feeds upon the ripened fruit. This species of bird was said to have visited no other part of England.

In the last century figs were much prized for their "medicinal virtues", which were surprisingly versatile. One textbook recommends the "milk that issues from the leaves or branches when they are broken off, should be dropped upon warts to remove them". As an encore it advocates a decoction of the leaves for the cure of leprosy, also to "clear the face of scurvy and the body from scurf, scabs and running sores". A syrup made from such a decoction is guaranteed to "allay bloody fluxes as well as being good for coughs, hoarseness,

I

Interior of Wistman's Wood, Two Bridges, Dartmoor.

*The Fig Tree growing from stonework of
St. Newlyn East Church, Cornwall.*

shortness of breath and all diseases of the lungs; also dropsy and falling sickness, and to promote the suppuration of boils." Curiously enough, no mention is made of its undoubted aperient qualities.

There is a tradition in Cornwall that those who buried treasure always planted a hawthorn tree over it. John Rolle, an ancestor of Lord Clinton, lived at Dobel's Thorn, St. Giles-in-the-Heath, between Boynton, Devon and Launceston. He dreamed several times that if he went to London Bridge he would become rich. He finally did visit London Bridge, and met a man who also had dreamed of wealth in the form of a crock of gold—at Doble's Cross, under a thorn bush in a corner of a field called Four Acres! Mr. Rolle accordingly returned home and duly found the treasure. On the tree he is said to have found the inscription: "Under me lie three." On investigating this intriguing information he found three pots of gold hidden under the roots. This rewarding faith is said to have founded the Rolle estate, on which Exmouth was built.

The legend is similar to that of the "Pedlar of Swaffham", in Norfolk. A certain wealthy citizen named John Chapman dreamed that if he went to London he would hear on London Bridge something to his advantage. He went there and was approached by a stranger who asked him what he was about. He retold his dream, upon which he was advised to return home and dig up the hawthorn on his own land, under which gold would be found. What mars the legend is that the story grew out of the inscription on the town's wooden sign by the fountain representing a carved figure of the Pedlar of Swaffham, feather in hat, staff in hand and with his dog at his feet. The caption reads as follows: "Ye tinker of Swaffham who did by a dream find a great treasure." Obviously John Chapman was no tinker, unless there was a namesake.

The churchyard at Stoke Gabriel, Totnes, Devon, has an imposing old yew, in good condition, with some fertility legends invested in it. For instance, if you are male, and walk backwards around it, or female and walk forwards, fertility is assured. Another superstition promises that wishes come true if you walk around the yew seven times. Certainly the area beneath the tree is weed free, possibly indicating the large numbers of the credulous regularly performing these rites. The yew is a female, 45 ft. in height, 17 ft. in girth.

An Old Boy of Blundells School, Tiverton, tells of an oak he and his schoolfriends used to visit fifty years ago. It was situated at the bottom of Newt's Hill, not far from the school, and stood at the junction of three country roads. It was rumoured that if one walked around the oak tree three times, then touched it, a relative would die. So far as records go, none had the courage to put the legend to the test. The oak became known as Newt's Tree or Kind Hearts and Coronets! Its origin is intriguing, but possibly it was not so much domestic as a garbled version of the spells of witches, since witch-burning was often carried out at the junction of lanes and tracks in remote areas.

The treatment meted out to witches and all their kindred of the evil eye was possibly akin to that dealt out to the alleged reanimated bodies of vampires and certain kinds of criminals in parts of south-east Europe. In the latter cases an oak stake used to be driven through their hearts, so as to end forever any possibility of reincarnation or remote controlled magic. Any coincidental oak tree growing from the spot later would no doubt be accepted either as a token of the stake itself, or as a memorial of the ending of a scourge.

Many trees still surviving on grassy islands, or stumps at cross-roads are often the local objects of legends or superstitions. Most of the tales vary considerably, but there is a common factor—a warning against evil, with a prescribed antidote, should it befall. In some instances a tree is preserved as a centrepiece at cross-roads to represent the arms of the Cross. Occasionally this occurs on parish boundaries, marking the site of the "bounds" landmark or perhaps of a preaching tree as mentioned earlier.

There is a legend that a witch was buried in the churchyard at Clavering in Essex, and that at his death he asked that an acorn be buried with him. Not an oak, however, but an oddly shaped ash of no great height grew from the grave, splitting the tombstone and disrupting the iron railings around it. The date on the tombstone is 1776.

The traditional place of the meeting of the witches in Shakespeare's *Macbeth* was Birnham Wood and the position of an ancient oak, until recently the last survivor of the original wood, is sited rather less than half a mile below the bridge spanning the Tay at Dunkeld on the south bank. In Renfrewshire, at Kilmacolm is a solitary oak in a field on the right of the bridge of Weir-St.-Fillian's Church Road, known as the Warlock's Tree, said to mark a one-time meeting place of witches and warlocks.

The fall of a branch or of a whole tree was believed to foretell death or misfortune, especially where the original planting of a tree could be traced to a family ancestor. The fortunes and disasters of families were commonly thought to be foreshadowed by the corres-

Stoke Gabriel Churchyard Yew.

ponding wellbeing of, or accidents befalling a cherished tree. At Greenhill Court, Herefordshire, was the Prophet Elm, which "foretold" the death of members of the Eckley family whenever it shed a branch. At Hinton-on-the Green, Worcestershire, an elm, if it should fall, was supposed to give presage to a drop in the number of male children to be born in the parish. One lime in an avenue at Cuckfield Park, Sussex, is said to shed a bough on the approaching death of a member of the owner's family. A more challenging story is of an oak with a twist in the trunk at Dunsford in Devonshire which, it is claimed, will untwist if at any time a Fulford ceases to own the property on which the tree stands.

A cedar at Bretby, Derbyshire, has its main branches chained and braced to prevent the collapse of any part of the tree. At one time this tree belonged to the Caernarvon family, and prophesied the death of a member of that family should a major branch fall. The last fall of a limb is said to have taken place on the death of Lord Caernarvon after his discovery of the tomb of Tutenkhamen.

There is an interesting fable told of the Cuckoo Bush at Gotham in Nottinghamshire. From the time of King John is traced a superstition to the effect that the ground the monarch passed over would become a public right of way. The Wise Men of Gotham, as they are now styled, knowing that John's royal passages often resulted in the setting up of hunting lodges, and fearing a forcible confiscation of their land, attempted to deflect the passage of his entourage. Failing to do so, some feigned madness by trying to drown an eel in a pail of water while others dragged their wagons to a position beside a wood "in order to shade the trees from the sun". More energetically, if obscurely, others began to roll their cheeses towards Nottingham. Another contingent joined hands around a bush in which, they said, a cuckoo perched, and would thus be kept there by them to ensure a perpetual summer. John and his escort, fearful of staying among fools, left them in peace. An inn nearby, the Cuckoo Bush, is all that remains to perpetuate the story.

The Darley Oak at Linkinhorne, Cornwall, was a notable hollow tree measuring 36 ft. in circumference. Still standing in 1958, in full health, it had seven stone steps inside, which seems to imply that it was used as a look-out post. Many stories have been told of tea-parties held inside its shell. But the main fame of the tree is attributed to the story of a lad who hid there from a press-gang in the eighteenth century.

Another oak which stands opposite the Golden Grove public house at Chertsey, Surrey, was fitted with steps which lead to a platform at the top of the main trunk. No doubt, another "look-out" tree, it fronts a house where conductor and composer George Smart used to live. Since once a part of Chertsey Abbey, now gone, was here sited and known as Monk's Grove, it is probable that the oak was planted by the monks and later used as a preaching tree.

Hoxne, Suffolk, was the scene of the martyrdom of St. Edmund in the ninth century. The site of his capture by the Danes is marked on a small brick bridge over a stream below the parish church. Nearby, it is said, stood the oak tree to which St. Edmund was tied, scourged, pierced with arrows and beheaded. A stone cross marks the site. An address by the Reverend Lord Arthur Hervey, President of the Institute of Archaeology on a visit by members of the Institute to Bury St. Edmunds on July 7th, 1854, included: "And here I cannot help adverting to a most singular tradition, to which I give implicit credence. At Hoxne was an old oak tree which had always been known as St. Edmunds Oak. The common tradition was that it was the identical oak to which King Edmund was tied some 1,000 years ago when he was shot by the arrows of the Danes. Some seven or eight years ago this venerable tree split from extreme old age, and its very centre was exposed to view. In it was found an arrow-head.

This remarkable fact, coupled with the previous tradition, makes me believe that this was the very tree to which he was bound in the Forest of Hoxne." The arrow-head was for some years preserved at Hengrave Hall, but its location is not now known.

In Great Packington Park, probably the most beautiful park in North Warwickshire, is a stone monument telling of a more recent tragedy with a humbler moral. It abuts on an oak tree which still survives, and was set up as a memorial to William Cawssey, a farrier from London who sheltered under the tree and was struck by lightning. The monument was erected during the later years of the eighteenth century, a period when pillars, obelisks and memorials proliferated, often at the slightest of pretexts—at the drop of a farrier, as it were. The following message is inscribed on the stonework:

"On Thursday, September 11, MDCCLXXXIX, William Cawssey of London, Farrier, was on this spot struck by lightning. To commemorate this awful event, as well as to warn others from exposing themselves to the same danger by taking shelter under trees in thunderstorms, this monument is erected."

The inhabitants of the town of Carmarthen in South Wales have for centuries cherished a superstition concerning an old, dead oak stump, now carefully preserved in concrete and protected by railings. Great concern was felt by the inhabitants when road improvements threatened the removal of this monument, which stood in the middle of the highway, the road to Abergwili, because, according to mythology, Merlin, the ancient sage and sorcerer, predicted:

"When the oak falls down
Then sink the town."

and

"When Merlin's oak shall tumble down
Then shall fall Carmarthen town."

From the twelfth century onwards, Merlin the Magician prophesied England's destiny, but no one will tempt providence to this day by interfering with his oak. Merlin predicted that the town would become flooded on Lammas Day and for many years the populace of Carmarthen would desert the town on that day. That practice ceased to take place, but the oak still receives the highest regard. Carmarthen is reputed to have been Merlin's birthplace. At the Battle of Agincourt, his emblem was on the banner borne by the fighting men from Carmarthenshire, whose archery probably won the day for Henry V.

According to reports quoted by Arthur Mee in his *King's England* of 1947, a strange ritual used to be carried out on November 5th under a hollow oak now filled with concrete on the village square at Shebbear, in Devonshire. Beneath the tree was a large boulder, not of local origin, weighing about a ton. After sunset a number of men rang a peal of bells in the church, then came to the square to turn over the stone with staves and crowbars. They then returned to the church and rang the bells again. All this, despite the fact that no one seemed to know the origin of the custom, nor how the stone came to be under the oak, reputed to be over a thousand years old. It may be interesting to speculate that the custom derives from ancient pageantry or allegory of the Crucifixion and the moving of the Stone from the Tomb, with its undertones of the Resurrection.

Perhaps the most mysterious collection of ancient and gnarled oaks is in Wistman's Wood, on Crockerne Tor, Dartmoor. At one time hundreds of oaks, very old and yet of little girth, were crammed among the low blocks of granite that abounded on the hill-site which is about 1,400 ft. above sea level. A section of one tree from the wood was taken to Kew Gardens in 1868, where it was found to measure only 7 in. in diameter yet showed 163 years by the ring count. This means that growth was only an inch in diameter in 47 years, whereas the average growth in oaks is $\frac{1}{3}$ in. increase in diameter a year.

Wistman's Wood is really a remnant of the old Forest of Dartmoor, at one time the haunt of wolves—for which reason it was probably burned down in mediæval times. In the surrounding bogs on the moor, sometimes embedded 20 ft. below ground, have been found great trunks of oak, showing incontestable evidence of grander prim-æval forests and a more congenial climate.

Their stunted, lineal descendants may have been the remains of the groves where Druids performed their rites and held the solemn courts of their judicature. The priests preferred high places giving them a clear view of the majesty of the heavens, for they were philosophers as well as astronomers. There is also strong presumptive evidence that the Moor was a chosen spot for the ancient worship of the Dumnonii, a Celtic tribe which took up residence in Cornwall and Devon before 55 B.C.

King John made Dartmoor into a Royal Forest, and the royal hunt continued until the days of Elizabeth I. The wild waste of the Moor became the reputed haunt of fairies and pixies, and no part of

England is so steeped in such lore as this area. Pixies, as every dweller on the Moor knows, especially delighted in playing practical jokes on farmers and dairymaids. After nightfall, no traveller would approach an oak wood lest he be led astray, tripped and intimidated by small bands of these tormentors; even his horse would be set upon and the hairs on its tail pulled. The only remedy in such cases was to turn a part of the clothing, which at once dispelled them.

William Campden, an antiquary of the Tudor Period, recounted a strange legend of a priest in Yorkshire, who having murdered a virgin who had refused his addresses, cut off her head and hid it in a yew tree. The tree became an object of veneration and pilgrimage, the devotees plucking and taking away branches, believing that the hair-like veins and filaments found between the bark and wood were the hairs of the Holy Virgin. The name of the village, Houton, was later changed to Halifax, signifying "holy hair". The rich offerings brought by the pilgrims, and the constant trafficking and ancillary trading, as so often elsewhere, were the nucleus of the now famous town of that name. The phenomenon of fibrous hair roots in old yews is, however, quite common. There are two ways in which they can be formed: one, previously referred to, from the falling berries germinating in the humus of their decaying trunks, later rooting as saplings and showing a cross section of matted rootlings which become exposed when the humus falls away or is disturbed; the second way by a dormant bud being abnormally accelerated in growth by the accumulating humus and so becoming in time an independent part or "sucker" of the parent tree. Thus have yews immortalized themselves *in situ* for centuries in this curiously incestual manner, at the same time making nonsense of attempts to ring-count their ages.

Some legends about trees make quaint reading. For instance, the yew in Worfield Churchyard, Bridgnorth, Cheshire, has a seat under it made from timbers from the demolition of the belfry fifty years ago, to encourage, no doubt, the perpetuation of the local belief that to sit under the tree's shade is a sure cure for indigestion. In another case, a holly tree stands on the top of Hydon Ball, a small hill at Hambledon, Surrey, about which it is said that the tree turns around when the church clock strikes 12. Many visitors have attended in hopes of witnessing the "miracle". The more observant of the disappointed pilgrims may have noticed when the pregnant moment arrived that there is no church clock!

At Chilham Castle, near Canterbury—which, by the way, possesses perhaps the finest and straightest hornbeam trees in Britain—

are about three acres of mixed beech and ash which have been a heronry since time immemorial and is mentioned in Domesday Book. Herons, unwelcome birds in many parts, especially near fisheries, are kindly thought of at Chilham Castle for there is an old belief that "if the herons do not arrive on Lady Day each year the occupier of the castle will die." They have, so far, always kept the appointment on the crucial day.

Only two miles from the site of the Monmouth Ash, where the luckless Duke was captured in 1685, is the Remedy Oak. It stands on a grass verge at a road junction, at Woodlands, near Verwood, Dorset. Of great age, it is now a majestic ruin, little more than a half cylinder of a bole, with several heavy branches balanced precariously from the upper rim. A new plaque placed on the tree by the direction of the late Lady Shaftesbury reads:

"According to tradition, King Edward VI sat under this tree and touched for King's Evil."

There has been much controversy about the significance of "King's Evil", or scrofula. Many think it could be an echo of the once prevalent belief in the magical powers of the "priest-king". There are many precedents, as can be discovered in Fraser's evocative accounts in *The Golden Bough*. We should note that as possibly the oak was accredited with curative powers, probably from the tried properties of the tannic acid chiefly from its bark, these attributions, blessed by the royal touch, were naturally believed to have enhanced efficacy. All parts of sessile and pedunculate oaks contain astringent acid; indeed, the bark of either species can yield a substitute for quinine. Decoctions of bark were used in the dressings of sores, and for diseases of the throat. Further, it was believed that those closely concerned with the handling of oak and its derivative tannin were immune to scrofula. In addition, pigs throve healthily on the oak-mast, especially from the sessile variety, and the finest quality bacon and pork was obtained from swine put out to "oak pannage".

Scrofula was, until a century ago, a generic diagnosis for glandular swellings of the throat and chest—probably tonsilitis or maybe even a form of tuberculosis. In passing, is it too far fetched to infer that "Scrofula" was derived from *"scrofa"*, a sow—with the latter's swollen and pendulous jowls?

A year before his death, in 1552, the young King Edward VI, when only fifteen years of age, visited Somerset and Dorset, dispensing his therapy at the roadside. This oak is commemorative today of that historic ceremony. Doubtless the prime oak's sheltering canopy would have lent its own special aura to the occasion. Oaks therefore received unquestioned veneration—a quality undoubtedly respected by royalty for the not inconsiderable merits that rubbed off on to them, and so was a factor in their preservation.

It is revealing that between 1660 and 1682, over 90,000 people, mostly children, were touched by Charles II, the popularly restored king, probably reimbued by his people with the time-honoured powers. With the last of the Stuarts the custom died, and with it the age-old concept of the priest-king invested with divine powers of healing.

Less dramatically, the astringent properties of the bark were also made use of in the treatment of sore throats, for removing obstructions of the liver and for alleviating the spasms of gravel. It is said that Galen used the bruised leaves for healing wounds. Some country people used to collect the water found in hollow places in old oaks as a cure for scabs, the itch and bathing ruptures.

The common ash is the second important indigenous tree in Britain, and, though not so long lived as the oak, its haunts and inherent grandeur give it a special charm. In Teutonic mythology it holds a conspicuous place. Under the shade of an enormous ash tree, the crown of which reached to Heaven and the roots to the infernal regions, the gods held court. On the topmost branches was perched an eagle who watched earthly affairs, assisted by a squirrel, who employed his time climbing and descending, examining and reporting on what was passing below. More rationally, Dioscorides the physician stated that the juice of the ash was an antidote against adder bite, which, however, has never been proven.

But we need not go back too far in time to find superstitions and cures respecting the ash, most of which are based on its legendary properties as an antidote against poisons. In many parts of England, even as late as the nineteenth century, country people believed that if they split young ash trees and passed young children through the aperture it was a cure for rupture. If a hole was bored in an ash branch and a shrew mouse imprisoned within it, that branch would cure cattle of lameness and cramp, afflictions thought to be caused by the machinations of the poor shrew mouse. In Scotland, at the birth of a child, the midwife would put one end of a stick of ash into the fire, collect the oozing sap from the other end and administer the liquid to the baby as its first spoonful of food.

Gilbert White quotes in his *History of Selborne* an example in the middle of his village where a row of pollard ashes could clearly be seen to have been cloven, but had healed over. He said that wedges were used to keep the young and flexible trees well open at the splits. Ailing children were stripped naked and pushed through the apertures under the persuasion that such treatment would cure them of rickets. These ceremonies took place at three o'clock in the morning, and the passing of the children through the clefts carried out three times on three consecutive mornings. The breaches in the trees were carefully closed and bound together, then plastered over with loam. It was believed that if the severed parts of the trees healed and the tissues of the cambial area knitted then the cures would be effective; if not, the operation would be a failure.

Ash trees thus used as surgeries were preserved with great care, for it was thought that if, during the lifetime of the patients, the trees were felled or injured, either the affliction would return or the patient would die simultaneously with the tree. White thought the practice was a superstitious ceremony derived from the Saxons before their conversion to Christianity. With the inability of medicine to relieve deformities and crippling diseases, it is not surprising that cures of this nature were resorted to, and even less surprising, in the light of certain recent re-appraisals of faith-healing, that many successes are on record. It seems largely to have been a case of infusing the powdered leaves in boiling water and using the liquid as a purgative. Occasionally, a distillation from soaked bark was drunk daily as a cure for dropsy or obesity.

Near Beaminster, Dorset, is the small village of Mapperton. Less than a mile away stands the Posy Tree, a sycamore, reputed to be about 350 years old. At one time it was pollarded back to its trunk, and allowed to put on a fresh head of shoots. Probably for this reason it still stands, for although Dorset is a county with many fine sycamores the species is inclined to break up in old age from the weight of heavy branches. This hollow tree must have been a young healthy seedling at the time of the Great Plague, when it received its distinctive name. The plaque on the tree records its history:

The Posy Tree

In 1665, when the Great Plague reached its peak, the parishioners gathered under this tree holding posies of flowers and herbs to ward off the disease when the dead were carried down this lane to a mass grave.

There is little doubt that the floral and herbal aids were more in the nature of deodorants than antiseptics.

The rowan, or Mountain Ash, is not allied to the common ash. Of the genus sorbus its specific Latin name *aucuparia* refers to the long established use of its berries as a bait by bird-catchers, *auceps* being Latin for fowler; the tree sometimes being known as Fowler's Service Tree. Given footing in a rocky crag and sufficient soil into which its roots can adventure, or overshadowing smaller trees and shrubs which will shelter but not shroud it, the rowan can flourish and stand out starkly brilliant against the contrasting backgrounds of pines of limestone cliffs. The blood-red berries, the white cluster of flowers and the silver bark glistening in shafts of sunlight or moonlight may have singled it out both for uses in the black arts of witches and also for the reciprocal function of exorcism of witchcraft—an interesting study in the duality of opinion. We are also told that the Druids also highly esteemed the tree—at least, if archaeologists will allow our informants the harmless fiction that the frequent proximity of rowan trees to stone circles is a sure sign that the Druid votaries of the latter actually incorporated rowan trees in their priestly ceremonies.

In remoter parts of Britain today there are those who still hang parts of rowan from doorways, cowsheds and other outbuildings. Some secretly carry a small sprig on their clothing to ward off the dire effects of witchcraft and the vagaries of luck. The tree is planted profusely in small gardens in Scottish villages, and for similar reasons in many of the grounds of the older houses both in town and country all over the British Isles. A century ago, at Strathspey, farmers would make their cattle pass through a hoop made of rowan, and, as an added precaution against unspecified evil, step through it themselves.

There is an interesting and controversial line in Shakespeare's *Macbeth*: the sailor's wife, being ordered by a witch to bring some chestnuts, answers: "Aroint thee, witch!" Perhaps this is a garbled colloquialism for "A rowan tree, witch!" At one time the rowan was as common a sight as yew in Welsh churchyards. This may possibly be a throw-back to Celtic beliefs, with faint echoes of Druidism, rather than for exorcistic usages against witchcraft.

The Sweet Bay is a member of the Laurel family and a native of Southern Europe and North Africa, and was introduced into Britain about the time of the later Renaissance. It was renowned as a flavouring in cookery but also had medicinal properties. An infusion of crushed bay leaves and berries was thought to help digestion and widely used in making fomentations. It was considered by the

Romans to be an emblem of victory, victorious generals being crowned with it on triumphal processions. The common soldier always carried a sprig of it, and even dispatches announcing victories in battle were wrapped in sprays of bay. The aromatic odour of the leaves was considered to dispel contagion and during one pestilence the Emperor Claudius shifted his court to Laurentine, celebrated for its bay trees. Superstitious Greeks would, at crisis times, keep a bay leaf in their mouths for the whole period to protect themselves from misfortune, while diviners, known as Daphnephagi (*daphne* being the Greek for laurel), chewed bay leaves in the belief that it inspired in them the spirit of prophecy.

During the Middle Ages it was customary to place wreaths of berried laurel on the heads of poets of distinction, hence the title Poet Laureate. Students who had taken their degrees at universities were likewise called bachelors, from the French *bachelier*, a word derived from the Latin *baccalaureus*, meaning laurel berry. It is interesting to note that such students were not expected to marry, lest their marital duties should distract them from the pursuit of learning. Single men therefore "looked to their laurels"—and are to this day "bachelors".

The walnut is of eastern origin, and was known to the Greeks as Caryon, from *kara*, a head, because its strong odour was thought to cause headache. Or could it have been because of a striking resemblance between the shelled nut and the human brain! The Romans called it *Juglans Regia*, or Jupiter's mast, since it was as superior to other woods in the making of masts as Jupiter was to lesser, or upstart, gods. Walnuts were prized as food, but more particularly for their numerous medicinal properties, especially as an antidote to poison and against rabies. In English folklore the profuse flowering of the walnut heralds a good harvest, the reverse is the case when there is an abundance of lush foliage and few blossoms.

John Evelyn stated that the husks and leaves of walnut, macerated in warm water, formed a mixture which, when poured on to bowling greens and grass lawns, killed the worms without endangering the grass. He said that anglers would scatter the crushed concoction around the ground to force worms to come to the surface when they required fresh bait. The unripe fruit and its juice was used as a laxative, and the vinegar in which walnuts were pickled was a useful gargle.

By mid-Victorian times, the medicinal properties of the walnut had almost become the panacea for all ailments, as can be seen from the following extract from *The New Family Herbal*, by M. Robinson,

M.D. Published about 1870, it was probably a universal family standby. In the preface, the learned doctor puts in a vociferous plug for his book by roundly disparaging such works as *Culpeper's Herbal*, dismissing them as "entirely useless [for] the government of herbs by the sun, moon and planets has been explored by modern science". Of the walnut tree he says, "The husk and shell and peel of the kernels are sudorific [sweat inducing], and used to expel the tape-worm. The juice of the green husks boiled with honey is an excellent gargle for a sore mouth and wounds, gangrene and carbuncles. The kernels burned will stay women's courses, being taken in red wine. Beaten with rue and wine they relieve the quinsy. The kernels, taken inwardly, are good for colic and expel wind. The young kernels taken before they are half ripe and preserved with sugar, are good to strengthen weak stomachs. The distilled water of the green husks, before half ripe, cools the heat of agues and is a very cooling application to fresh wounds, quickly healing them . . ." And so on. The careful recipes and confident claims invest it with authority, but one wonders if the human guinea-pigs were inclined to announce a cure as a psychological reaction to the prospect of continued treatment.

The Rev. J. Collinson, in his *History of Somersetshire* (1791), mentions that there grew in the Glastonbury Abbey churchyard, on the north side of St. Joseph's Chapel, a miraculous walnut tree, which never budded before the feast of St. Barnabas (June 11th). On that one day only would it leaf. He added that the tree was sought after by the credulous, and that Queen Anne, King James and nobility of the realm, gave sums of money for cuttings from it. The "miraculous" nature of the tree was probably due to its being of a late variety, called by the French *Noyer de la St. Jean*.

A woman, a spaniel, and a walnut tree,
The more you beat them, the better they be.

So runs the old adage, implying that the tree thrives best if the nut is roughly struck off the stalks rather than picked—a difficult operation if a tree is of great height. The theory was that the tips of the branches were broken, causing the production of new spur shoots below the damaged parts, which would fruit the following year. The practice of beating the branches was probably peculiar to France because the majority of the trees were not enclosed, the fruit being thus collected by passers-by. No doubt the torn tips of branches *would* encourage new shoots to bear, but that would surely represent poor pruning, the jagged parts being open to decay and frost.

"Interruptions" of the normal functioning of trees, and especially of those species grown for fruiting purposes, are common practice. The barren fruit tree which has been damaged deliberately, ringed with wire or slightly charred by fire will suddenly come into bearing. This is because the partial ringing resulting from the removal of a section of bark and cambium from the bole will often reduce the vigour of the foliage, thus causing a concentration of the tree's vitality towards fruit growth. But the longer-term result is usually a permanent set-back to the welfare of the tree.

Although not strictly relevant in this chapter, one cannot end the saga of the walnut without reference to the quality of its timber. This is always in great demand not only for furniture making but also for veneering. High prices are offered by merchants for sound boles of trees over 6 ft. in circumference. Very few avenues and groves of the tree remain in Britain today, though several outstanding single specimens still stand when the tree is preserved for its amenity value. A walnut at Gayhurst, Newport Pagnell, Buckinghamshire, which was measured by Henry Elwes in 1906 as being 17 ft. in girth, was recently sought after by timber merchants with an offer of £1,500. But the Planning Officer of Bucks County Council stepped in to save the tree by placing a Preservation Order on it. Later, the County Council bought the tree and the site at a cost of £1,600 and fenced it round—a commendable act which one hopes will be a precedent for similar cases.

While on the subject of nuts perhaps it is forgiveable to end it with the following anecdote concerning a walnut tree at the northern end of the main street in the town of Rushden, Northants. It is described as a "walnut which bears nuts all the year round". The nuts referred to are normally classified as ironmongery since they are threaded on to steel rods used as braces, to ensure that the branches are safely supported!

At Mottisfont, near Stockbridge, Hants, is the Oakley Oak, which stands near the River Test, opposite Oakley Farm, near Mottisfont Abbey. The girth of the bole is $31\frac{1}{2}$ ft. and twenty persons could once stand inside the hollow. Traditionally, it is more than seven centuries old, and has given rise to an amusing legend, concerning a cow which gave birth to a calf within its shell. Aside from the long history of fertility rites which the location and the legend might conjure up, the local lore has it that this is the setting for the popular story of the "cow that jumped over the moon". The cow, tilting at the moon as it appeared from behind the tree, fell inside the hollowed oak, caus-

Above, *Remedy Oak, Woodlands, Dorset.*
Below, *Tortworth Chestnut, Tortworth, Glos.*

ing premature birth of its calf. The famous cavity is now almost occluded, aptly enshrining this quixotic legend.

And now to relate an even stranger story concerning a chestnut tree. The testimonies of the persons involved in the events can be vouched for in their fullest integrity, but, for reasons of privacy—readily appreciated by many others caught up in the ballyhoo of over-publicity—it has been requested that names and location should be suppressed.

During the 1939–45 war, a certain Mrs. X bought a Georgian property in Yorkshire she had long wanted. Later, she viewed the overgrown garden and an old horse-chestnut tree with its mass of creamy flowers; the tree was well known and her neighbours asked if they could collect the conkers later in the year, as they had always done. Time passed and eventually Mrs. X and her family moved into the house. A friend called one morning and asked to see the "old chestnut tree". The visitor, an ex-army officer, acquainted with the tree since his youth and a trained observer, returned to the house asking why the chestnut had been felled. The new owner went into into the garden, and there, instead of a chestnut, stood a gaunt sycamore some thirty-five feet in height!

The gist of the account was immediately passed to the Forestry Commission officials for comment, but the invitation to inspect the site of such a metamorphosis was declined.

Some years later the history of the phenomenon was again reported to the Commission officials for comment, and the expected reply was received: "Postulation of supernatural happenings, i.e. those breaking the physical laws of the universe on the grounds of the patchwork memories and ideas of people inclined to think that these things have occurred is absurd. None has yet manifested itself in any remotely vigorous conditions of observations."

But statements from the "witnesses" were never taken by the Commission's representatives. Surely the witnesses, among them children, could not be ignored, fantastic as the statements may have appeared to be? Added to this, during the days that followed the change-over from horse-chestnut to sycamore, a doctor and a delivery-man asked the whereabouts of the tree and remarked on the straggly nature of the usurping sycamore. And could the chestnut have been cut down without the knowledge of the next-door neighbours? But there the affair must perforce be left.

K

Tilford Oak.

Royal Associations

All would agree that trees are the monarchs of the vegetable kingdom. There is also an unchanging hierarchy among them: an indigenous nobility of ancient lineage—the oak, the elm, the chestnut, the ash, and all; a middle-class of mixed origins dominated by the territorial clans of the conifers; and an amorphous population of lower orders, busily absorbed in procreation and keeping up with the Joneses. In short, a familiar and recognizable pattern. Woven into this living tapestry are ubiquitous punctuations of yews, draped in their sombre cassocks and seeming deep in a hierophantic plotting or listening eternally like confessors. In insular competition with the latter is a proliferation of sturdy undenominationals, the hawthorns and the hollies.

There are also settled immigrants from alien lands; some that languish in our harsher climate and others that have prospered and overspilled their original ghettoes. Here and there are the ambassadorial types, haughty, aloof and privileged—the towering dark-complexioned cedars, inhospitable Chile pines, Japanese cedars called Cryptomeria because of their foreign habit of wrapping their seeds in scales, and the antipodean eucalypts. There are even geological aboriginals such as the gingkos, tourist trophies from a lost corner of prehistoric China, looking as if they were still dreaming of steamy heats and improbable creatures that died long ago to be slowly entombed by the dust of their microscopic contemporaries.

But we are here concerned solely with the royal attributes of trees with more familiar names. As in mythology mountains are linked with the classic adventures of gods so in history and legend the regal bearing of our oaks, elms, chestnuts and their like has become inevitably associated with the Iliad of kings and queens, princes and courtiers. Indeed, so instinctive is the analogy that it would be in the worst of tastes to couple their larger-than-life passions and dynastic ambitions with lesser symbols than the monarchs of our forests. Who, for instance, would countenance the story that the ricochet of an arrow from, say, an alder or a birch caused the death of King Rufus? Although it would appear improbable that Walter Tyrell, or the charcoal-burners who traditionally found the slain king, put it on record that the arrow glanced off an oak, nevertheless, in accounts that differ in pertinent ways, all concur in the insistence that it was an oak tree. In short, the analogy lends the story credibility. Or again, who could bear the thought of Good Queen Bess making clandestine love with a favoured courtier were it not dignified by the precincts of an oak tree? Or the seduction of a king by a beautiful widow under a holly bush when a royal oak was available? And is there not a stark Medean poetry in the symbolic slaughtering of her oak trees by the relatives of Lady Jane Grey, berserk with grief on the day of her Machiavellian execution?

In lighter context is the story of the well-intentioned but accident-prone James I with his introduction into this country of the wrong variety of mulberry tree, in a Gilbertian enterprise to cash in on the silk-making habits of cocooning larvae. The many royal favourites who accepted his gifts of mulberry trees must have darkly pondered the fable of the Emperor's new clothes.

Legend has had many kinds of bed-fellows, some noble and tragic, others bizarre to the point of unbelief. At Cranbourne in Windsor Great Forest stands the great shell of the Conqueror's Oak, parts of which are still alive and in leaf every spring. Some 27 ft. in circumference, it is now barely 25 ft. in height, the main stem having collapsed about a century ago. Traditionally, William the Conqueror held this oak very dear. That being so, it would not be exaggerating to suppose that its age might be 1,200 years, assuming it was in its prime in the days of his regal sport of hunting. Another oak, a great pollard at Forest Gate, girthing 37 ft., once contended with the Cranbourne tree for the title of Conqueror's Oak. It was, however, a wreck by the turn of this century, and has since been removed. The Park and Forest are full of ancient trees bearing regal titles. A beech and three oaks near Highstanding Hill were respectively named after four Queens: Adelaide, Anne, Charlotte and Victoria. The Prince Consort Memorial Oak, planted by Queen Victoria to commemorate the place where her husband ended his last day's hunting, still flourishes.

Among these dignified veterans are younger trees, a group of sixty oaks planted to represent the original territories of the British Empire, growing in positions corresponding to their relative geographical situations on the globe. Henry Elwes mentioned many well-grown straight oaks, over 100 ft. in height, near the Prince Consort's Chapel in the Cowpond Grove. One of these was 10 ft. in girth in 1908. Fifty years before, an offer of £100 had been made for this tree, for the making of a ship's keel. Elwes predicted it would become the finest timber oak in the forest. Other veteran oaks have sprung from acorns planted by Lord Burleigh, when he had the future of England's shipbuilding in mind. Accompanying Queen Elizabeth I on walks in the Great Park, he would beg leave to plant fallen acorns in strategic places.

It is difficult to find a tree, or indeed a corner of the great Crown Estate at Windsor, where history has not been glamoured by the royal touch. On the site of the present Castle itself, Merlin is said to have reared a magic fortress, and no doubt in its great hall, decorated with trophies of war and chase, Arthur's symbolic Round Table would have stood. In its beginnings it was the stronghold of Saxon kings. In later centuries notable improvements were made to the fabric by William of Wykeham, the fourteenth-century founder of Winchester School, also by Edward IV, Henry VII and Elizabeth I. Its surrounding green belt, the noblest park of kings, is lyricized by Alexander Pope in *Windsor Forest*:

Thy forests, Windsor! and thy green retreats,
At once the Monarch's and the Muses's seats,
Invite my lays. Be present sylvan maids!
Unlock your springs, and open all your shades.

The circumstances of the death of William Rufus, the heir to the Conqueror, are debated to this day. At Canterton Glen, near Stoney Cross in the New Forest, Rufus, or the Red King, thus nicknamed for his flaming hair and beard, was murdered, or accidentally killed, by an arrow from Walter Tyrell's bow. On the site stood an oak tree which became famous as the Rufus Oak. Its memory was perpetuated by the Rufus Stone in the middle of the eighteenth century.

Many predictions and pre-visions of Rufus's death were claimed. One of these ran as follows: "The day before the king died, he dreamed he was bled by a surgeon, and that the stream of blood reached to heaven, clouded the light, and intercepted the sun. The following morning, a monk told Robert Fitz Hamon, one of the principal nobility, that he had dreamed a strange dream about the king, in which Rufus had seized a crucifix, gnawed the arms and torn away the legs of the Saviour. The dream was related to Rufus,

Parliament Oak, Sherwood Forest. From a painting about 1900.

who accused the monk of "dreaming for money", yet he was moved by the premonition, hesitating to go out to the hunt with his friends. After consuming more than his average quota of wine, the king ventured into the forest with a few attendants, among them Walter Tyrell, who had been induced to come from France at his invitation. Tyrell remained with the king while the others dispersed on a private chase. Towards sunset a stag appeared and the king let fly with an arrow, slightly wounding the animal which limped on into the dense cover. Rufus, closely followed by Tyrell, ran after it, shading his eyes

Tortworth Chestnut. Modern photo.

from the rays of the dying sun. As they ran, Tyrell startled another stag. Impulsively, he released his arrow at it the moment it crossed Rufus's path. The fatal shaft pierced the king's breast and was thrust through his body by his fall. Tyrell, shocked by the implications of such an unwitnessed event, panicked, leapt on his horse, and fled the scene, pursued only by the hounds of conscience. William Rufus's body was placed on a cart by local peasants, who had little cause to mourn their unpopular king, and driven to Winchester. It is said that the trail of the bizarre cortège was sustained by his blood. There are many other versions of his death, mainly conflicting.

It was six and a half centuries before a private nobleman thought to raise a stone to inform the subjects of the realm where and how their second Norman king died. The stone commemorated an oak which, it is alleged, was the cause of an arrow glancing off and striking Rufus. There are other and similar precedents for the legend that the tree forthwith began to leaf at Christmas, continuing to do so thereafter until its death. There is perhaps a special significance in this alleged Christmas leafing. The year 1100 was believed to herald the end of the world. Further, despite the obloquy of the Church on these matters, there still persisted strong pagan adherence to fertility rites and symbols. It is said that Rufus, who was known to be ostracized by the Church, subscribed to many of these dark beliefs and that with his knowledge and inevitable connivance he, the priest-king, was marked for sacrifice in an effort to appease the gods and to ensure the survival of his subjects. Even his red hair lent authenticity to the fateful necessity. Be that as it may, his black tomb in Winchester Cathedral bears no name or insignia in that royal burial place and is clearly a political compromise by a reluctant Church.

The Parliament Oak at Clipston, Sherwood Forest, was formerly on the boundary of Clipston Park. In 1896, then a senile wreck, it surprisingly bore a large crop of acorns. There may be some truth in the story that King John, while hunting in the Royal Forest of Sherwood, was informed of a Welsh revolt and hastily summoned a Parliament to meet beneath the tree. Another account relates that Edward I, on his way to Scotland in 1290, ordered a Parliament to meet at Clipston at the same spot. The tree was still alive at the turn of this century, when it girthed nearly 29 ft.

The Great Tortworth Chestnut stands splendidly in a paddock adjacent to Tortworth Church, between Falfield and Wotton-under-Edge, Gloucestershire. It is about a hundred yards from a quiet road and marked on Ordnance Survey maps as the Torthworth Chestnut. This famous tree has received the attentions of writers and arboriculturists throughout the centuries and their descriptions and eulogies have changed little. Foresters have mocked at the assertions of its age, but few of its pilgrims have failed to be impressed by it. To assess its age by measuring its gargantuan, twisted bole is an impossibility, for it consists of a huge, gnarled, twenty-foot high trunk from which great heavy laterals radiate, some still held upwards, others reaching the ground where they have become layered and rooted, producing complete secondary trees. The appearance now is of a forest of sweet chestnuts emanating from one root, thus perpetuating the matriarch.

There are repeated references to this tree in historical records, namely that the Tortworth Chestnut was of some stature in King Stephen's reign in the twelfth century, and that it was a "tort" tree, that is to say a tree where courts were held and laws were enforced.

Queen's Oak at Potterspury, Northamptonshire. Meeting of Edward IV and Elizabeth Woodville beneath tree. A very old postcard.

It has also been suggested that King John and the Barons from this area had preliminary talks under it for the drafting of Magna Carta. In the confirmation of a grant made by Henry II to the monks of Flexeley, the tithe of "Chestnuts in the Forest of Dean" was secured to the monastery. From this information it is apparent that the sweet, or Spanish chestnut was well established by mediaeval times, and, granting that this tree was a large specimen in the thirteenth century, it is reasonable to suppose that the species was indigenous in Saxon times. Possibly the Roman legionaries, fresh from the Mediterranean provinces, introduced the trees accidentally by carelessly dropping the chestnuts which formed an important part of their diet. In suitable circumstances the "litter" would thus regenerate. Kent, parts of Sussex, Surrey, Gloucestershire and Herefordshire, being most frequented and settled by the Romans, all reveal signs of original chestnut establishment.

Two hundred years ago, the bole mass, plus the timber resulting from the surrounding colony of the sweet chestnut, was estimated at 2,000 cubic feet of mixed material. The bole itself is extremely difficult to measure, varying from 80 ft., by draping the tape around the base, to about 50 ft. at 10 ft. from the ground. The whole "forest" of chestnuts in this amazing community is guarded by railings. The debris from the tree is never removed, nor the ground interfered with —doubtless the reason for its continued good health and wellbeing.

This example of seeming immortality and perpetuation of vegetation is quite remarkable, and it appears that for centuries very little change has occurred in the profile of the chestnut. In view of the amount of disbelief and scoffing the estimated age of the tree has received, the following letter extracted from an issue of the *Gentleman's Magazine* in 1762 is worth recording:

"I submit the following calculations of the age of a celebrated chestnut tree, which, in all probability, is the oldest, if not the largest tree in England, being 52 ft. round, to be transmitted by your means to posterity.

"This eminent tree is the property of the Rt. Hon. Lord Dacre at Tortsworth, *alias* Tamworth, Gloucestershire.

"I may with reason fix its rising from the nut in the reign of King Egbert, A.D. 800. From this date, to attain to such maturity and magnitude as to be a signal tree for a boundary or landmark, called by way of distinction the Great Chestnut-Tree at Tamworth, in the reign of King Stephen, I cannot allow less age than 335 years, which brings it down to the first year of King Stephen, A.D. 1135; from this date we are certain of its age by record to the present year, 1762. In all 962 years.

"Mr. Evelyn, in his fifth edition, has this remarkable passage relating to this tree, viz: 'Boundaries to great parishes and gentlemen's estates, famous for which is that great chestnut at Tamworth, in Gloucestershire, which has continued a signal boundary to that manor in King Stephen's time, as it stands on record.'

"If any regard is to be paid to the three periods given to oak and chestnut, viz., three hundred years growing, three hundred years standing, three hundred years decaying, it favours my conjecture that this stately old chestnut tree is very little, possibly more, than a thousand years old; and yet such vigour remains, it bare Nuts A.D. 1759; from them young trees are raised."

Four years later, in the same magazine, a Mr. P. Collinson wrote:

"The extraordinary size and antiquity of the chestnut tree at Tortsworth, now the seat of the Lord Ducie, mentioned in your faithful register excited my curiosity to see it, and I have been for some years trying to procure a drawing of it from its noble owner, but without success. I have at last met with an ingenious young man, John Player, of Stoke, who, at my request has attempted to give a sketch of it, as well as the nature of its situation between three walls would admit; I hope the following particular account of it will prove acceptable to the admirers of trees:

"The old chestnut has a very singular situation, for it stands in the angles of three gardens, the walls having been built up to it, or against it, which undoubtedly, has been a great check to its growth and occasion of decay. These walls stand to the cardinal points of the compass in the form of the letter T inverted, the tree being in the angles of the head, as expressed by a dotted circle. In the garden to the North East the side measures 18 ft. To the West it measures 18 ft. To the South East it measures 14 ft.

"Five feet from the ground it measures 50 ft. round. Three feet from the ground it measures 52 ft. round. The body is about 10 ft. to the fork. Then it divides into two great limbs, about 8 ft. long each, but on the North East side there appears to have been several large limbs cut off many years ago. This dismembering seems to have contributed much to the decay on that side; on the North West it is still sound. The largest part of the tree is living and very fruitful, having on it a great quantity of nuts, seemingly like the true Spanish kind. As the nuts fall their growth is encouraged by the weeds that are under it. Many young trees are come up and surround the old one. The solid contents of this venerable tree, according to the customary manner of measuring, is 1,965 feet of timber, but its true geometrical contents are much more."

Tradition claims an oak tree as being the actual site of the first meeting between the lovely widow of Sir John Gray, a noted Lancastrian leader at the time of the Wars of the Roses, and the youthful King Edward IV. There the lady, better known as Elizabeth Woodville, waited for Edward when he was hunting in the neighbourhood of her mother's estate at Grafton, Northants. Beneath the shelter of its great branches this fascinating woman appealed to the monarch, holding her fatherless boys by the hands. With the king beguiled, she threw herself at his feet and pleaded for the return of part of the forfeited inheritance of her children. The king was impressed by her beauty and soon bewitched by her grace, modesty and sweetness. He became a suitor, and the oak their trysting place. The Queen's Oak, as it became known, was the scene of many a meeting between Elizabeth and the enamoured Edward. It stood directly between Grafton Castle and Whittlebury Forest and thus was a convenient rendezvous under the pretext of a hunting foray. The king's ardent advances were gently repulsed by the lady, who made it clear that consummation of his infatuation could be only at the price of marriage.

On one occasion Elizabeth made a memorable reply: "My liege, I know I am not good enough to be your queen, but I am far too good to become your mistress." Deservedly, she prevailed and they

Meavy Oak, Devon. Photographed before recent "surgery" and renewal of props across road.

were married at Grafton Regis, near Stony Stratford, on May 1st, 1464. The peasant poet Bloomfield immortalized the clandestine meeting place at the oak in these words:

> *Genius of the forest shades,*
> *Lend thy powers, and lend thine ear,*
> *A stranger trod thy lonely glades*
> *Amidst thy dark and bounding deer.*

The Royal Oak at Meavy, Devon, was traditionally said to be

known to King John and his followers in the chase. The predecessor of the Royal Oak Inn is thought to have been originally church property at the time of Domesday, and used by priests or neighbouring monks. Later, John may have used it as a hunting lodge. The inn, as it became, is now owned by the parish and helps to pay the Church rates. Standing by the lych gate of St. Peter's Church, built in A.D. 1122, and alongside the village cross, the old oak was supported by strong timbers spanning *across* the road into the churchyard. It was also used as a Gospel Oak, and may have been originally a preaching place whilst the church was being built. The remains of Sir Francis Drake's Mansion are near the Church.

An engraving was made of the Meavy Oak in 1833 together with a recent photograph for comparison. With the original print was a description of the tree: "It is stagheaded and about 50 ft. in height; the trunk, which is 27 ft. in circumference (no height given or position of measurement), is hollow, and has held nine persons at one time. This oak is supposed to have existed at the time of King John."

Early in 1970 some concern arose for the oak's safety; the wooden props which supported it across the road were found to be badly decayed, and alarming fungal brackets appeared at the base of the tree. However, the best tree surgeons available were called in to examine the threat to Meavy's most important village feature, resulting in a scheme for its preservation. This consisted of cleaning out the hollow, exposing and treating the fungus-attacked areas, relieving the deadweight overhang on the propped side, ending with a general tidying-up of the branches and removal of deadwood. The wooden supports were replaced with steel rods of $2\frac{1}{2}$ in. diameter, threaded through the tree about two-thirds of the way up the main structure; the bases of the rods being set into concrete stands to prevent them from sinking with the weight of the leaning tree.

As there was little money in the Parish Council's coffers, the cost of the work, approximately £100, was to be met by public subscription, and if by chance a surplus occurred the bonus was to be used for planting and future maintenance of trees in the parish. How important this old Gospel Oak is to Meavy is reflected by the decision to ensure the conservation without knowing whether funds would be forthcoming or not. History thus leaves its legacy to small villages without concern for cost.

Bradgate Park, near Newtown Linford, Leicestershire, once the home of the nine-days' queen whom we know as Lady Jane Grey, was given to the people of Leicestershire in 1928, "to be preserved in its natural state". When this modest and studious sixteen-year-old girl, inveigled into an unwanted royal entanglement, was condemned to die on the scaffold at the Tower on a February morning in 1554, a seemingly wanton yet symbolic act was performed at the park where she had spent her childhood. Many of the oaks in her thous-and-acre playground were "beheaded" on the same day as the martyred girl. Some of the old pollarded oaks there today are tradi-tionally claimed to be the same trees—indeed those on one of the slopes at the entrance to the park appear ancient and stunted, yet still alive, girthing more than 12 ft. at breast height. The height of the trees is insignificant, perhaps 40 ft. at most and giving an appear-ance of a reluctance towards antiquity, yet still bearing their im-memorial scars.

Trees with Queen Elizabeth I connotations are legion. The pity is that so many of them are apocryphal, for they so aptly fit the glamor-ous image of this once-for-all monarch. Even so, her passionate patri-otism, coupled with her love of the chase, have immortalized many trees with the patina of her memory. The first examples are in the London area.

For instance, an elm still stands, though now only 12 ft. in height, in Half Moon Lane, London S.E.15. It was well known in Chaucer-ian times, which means that it was a notable tree before 1340. It may be the oldest trunk of a living elm extant in these islands. A drawing of the tree in full vigour was made in 1875 and appeared in a book by William Harnett Blanch, entitled *Ye Parish of Camerwell*, pub-lished by E. W. Allen, London.

Alleyn's name is famous in this area in connection with Alleyn's School, Dulwich College, and Dulwich Village. At present the elm sports twigs and leaves, demonstrating that it still draws nourish-ment through its gnarled layers of sapwood and cambium. The bole is split in several places and the shattered carcase is bound together by a chain.

Another famous oak gave name to a London suburb. At One Tree Hill, Camberwell, stood the Honour Oak, under which it has been said Queen Elizabeth dined on one occasion during the last year of her life. A correspondent informs me that the remnants of this tree may still exist, and that its original title was The Oake of Honour, the name being bestowed upon it by the Queen. Clearly its name and the occasion imply much significance from Elizabeth's personal in-terest, the circumstances of which I have been unable to trace.

Dead since the 1870s, Queen Elizabeth's Oak in Greenwich Park,

S.E.10, now a mere shell, still stands, covered with ivy. During the monarch's reign it was flourishing, and it is recorded that she "danced below the bows of this tree". Elizabeth was born in Greenwich and spent much time walking in the park during the years following the spectacular eclipse and death of her ill-fated mother, Anne Boleyn. In her later years she would recall resting in the oak's "cool darkness". With age, the tree became hollow and for three centuries afterwards offenders against park regulations were locked up in it. It is still fenced around as it was when used as a lock-up. The area is today used as a bird sanctuary.

The best-known relic marking an important event in Elizabeth's life is the decaying stump of an old oak in Hatfield Park, Herts., where she stayed regularly during the years of her ostracism. Reading her Greek Testament beneath this tree, on November 17th, 1558, she was informed of the death of her sister Queen Mary, and thus the tidings of her accession to the throne.

In the park of Gorhambury, Hertfordshire, still stands an oak under which it is said that Queen Bess was caught in the act of kissing the Earl of Leicester, one of her favourites. It is still known as the Kiss Oak. On another occasion, in the company of the Earl of Leicester, Elizabeth rode to the village of Aldworth, Berkshire, to visit the churchyard's great yew tree, which today girths 28 ft. There may have been an ulterior motive for her journey, for she asked to inspect the genealogical documents of the De La Beche family, whose ancestors dated back to the days of the Conqueror. These were unlocked from the chest hidden in a recess in the walls of the church and handed to Elizabeth. They were never seen again. Another apocryphal story? Or did Elizabeth, an insecure Tudor, still inhibited by the see-saw politics and intrigues of her day, genuinely fear the claims of another dynasty?

Part of another old oak still remains at Huntingfield in Suffolk, on an estate which Henry VIII settled upon Anne of Cleves, his "Flander's mare", after pensioning her off. Queen Elizabeth visited her cousin Baron Hunsdon here. The oak has borne the name Queen's Oak ever since the day she shot a buck with an arrow from the cover of its 33 ft. girthed bole. A description of the tree was given by a Mr. D. Barker, of Heveningham Hall, in 1836: "It is between 1,000 and 1,100 years old according to an historical document in my possession. At this time some parts of the tree are in great vigour, having healthy arms 10 ft. in circumference, and one even larger. The boughs cover a space of 78 yards, but the trunk has long since gone to decay, it being quite hollow." The Hall itself, which stood within "two bow-shots" of the tree, is worthy of comment. Hunting-field Hall was remarkable for being built around six massive oaks (whether alive or not is not known), which originally supported the roof. Upon these tree-trunks the foresters and yeomen of the guard used to hang their "nets, crossbows, hunting-poles, saddles, calivers and bills". In 1772 the roots of the trees had decayed so much that the structure had to be supported by extra logs and masonry. No trace of the Hall now remains, the ruins having been taken down towards the end of the eighteenth century.

A great oak still survives at Northiam, Sussex. The large limbs are secured to the main trunk by heavy chains. Miss W. L. Davies, who has written a history of the village, has kindly sent me the following account of the tree:

"The Queen Elizabeth Oak or Northiam Oak. In 1573 Queen Elizabeth I passed through Northiam on her way to Rye. On Tuesday, 11th August, she stopped to dine under the oak tree on the village green, her meal being supplied by George Bishop and his family from the bakehouse of Hayes Farm. She left behind her a pair of shoes which, it is claimed, are today in the possession of the Trewen family. The tree stands on the north-west corner of the green. Its age is not known, but it must have been of considerable size in 1573, and in view of the very great age to which oaks live this particular one would possibly have started as an acorn in the time of Alfred the Great." The Queen had possibly removed her shoes because they pinched her feet. The Trewens had treasured the shoes and preserved them at Brickwall Manor until they moved away some years ago. This tree was reported in the *Gentleman's Magazine* in 1816 as having been partially blown down in a storm in that year.

The Panshanger Oak, in the now built-up Panshanger Park, Hertingfordbury, Herts, was traditionally planted by Queen Elizabeth I. J. C. Loudon wrote in 1844: "The Great Oak at Panshanger, growing on the estate of Earl Cowper, is a fine specimen of an oak in its prime. Though upwards of 250 years old, and though it appears to have been called the Great Oak for more than a century, it appears even now scarcely to have reached its meridian; the waving lightness of its feathery branches, dipping down to the very ground, the straightness of its stem, and the redundancy of its foliage, give it a character the opposite of antiquity."

In 1789, Gilbert White journeyed from Selborne to see the tree. Sir Winston Churchill remarked that it was the "finest and most

stately oak growing in the South-east of England". In 1953 a preservation order was placed on the tree by Hertfordshire County
Council. Nearby is an oak planted by Churchill which is descended
from the Panshanger Oak, being one of its many regenerated acorns
which have been planted in many parts of the country. The girth
of the tree is now 20 ft.

A pear tree planted by the unfortunate Mary, Queen of Scots, in
the garden of Queen Mary's House, Jedburgh, Roxburghshire,
flourished for nearly four hundred years, finally being blown down
in a gale early in this century. But Queen Mary, the grandmother of
our present queen, replaced it with another from Sandringham on
November 24th, 1934. Today it is known as Our Queen Mary's Tree.

Black as well as white mulberry trees appear to have been established in Britain during the latter half of the sixteenth century. The
black mulberry is supposed to have been a native of Persia; the white
variety is said to come from China. The widespread popularity of
silk prompted James I in 1605 to promote the cultivation of silkworms, which meant the planting of mulberry trees. In the grounds
of Charlton House S.E.7, is an old wreck of a tree known as the
Charlton Mulberry, surrounded by railings. A plaque attached
reads: "The first mulberry tree planted in England in the year 1608
by order of King James I." The details are incorrect, for Dr. William
Turner, the sixteenth-century botanist, is accredited with the honour
of establishing the first trees at Syon House, Middlesex. Cardinal
Pole may have made the same claim for another at Lambeth
Palace in 1555. Maybe James I merely directed that seeds from the
Syon House trees (or those at Lambeth Palace) should be propa-
gated and extensively transplanted to meet the fashionable demand.
James offered free seed to all his cronies.

Poor King James! Like so many of his good intentions, the scheme
misfired, for it was not the variety the fastidious little grub fancied
as a diet. Because of his ill-starred political preoccupations the *faux
pas* was overcome by more pressing events and so never corrected.
No doubt the vested interests of the silk industry, if not a party to the
original misleading advice to James, certainly did not bestir themselves to plant the particular variety to which silkworms were partial,
so the *status quo* of the import-export business remained undisturbed.
Or was it the English climate the pampered worms really objected to?

Even so, the mulberry did open a new and exciting chapter in the
English pharmacopoeia, as will be seen from the following extract
from an early Victorian medical book:

Devil's Stone Oak, Shebbear, Devon.

The Prince of Orange's Oak, Teigngrace, Devon.

Remnants of Gospel Oak, Polstead.

"The ripe berries by reason of their sweetness and slippery moisture, open the body, especially when they are dried. They are good to stay fluxes and profuse menstruation. The bark of the root kills tapeworm, and a syrup of the juice of the berries cures inflammation or sores of the mouth, throat and palate, when it is fallen down. The leaves beaten with vinegar are good for burns. A decoction made of the bark and leaves is good to wash the mouth and teeth when they ache. The leaves of mulberries applied are said to stay bleeding at the mouth or nose, or the bleeding of the piles, or of a wound."

So perhaps after all James I was a greater benefactor than he ever knew, for who would not rather have a remedy for such maladies than wear cheaper silk from home-grown mulberries?

The late Reverend Lonsdale Ragg, in an article in *The Tree Lover* in 1943, relates a legend concerning mulberry trees in the reign of the second King James:

"It is a fact of history that King James II and his queen, Mary of Medina, visited Bath in 1687, the year before their son was born (June 10th, 1688). Local tradition says that the queen, anxious for an heir, took the sacred waters of St. Winifride's Well, and that the royal pair, attributing the queen's long deferred fertility to those hallowed waters, made a present to Bath in the year of the birth of that heir, an event which was to be the signal of the end of the Stewart kingship.

"The present is said to have taken the form of a number of mulberry seedlings, which would show James following in the footsteps of his grandfather, James I. Just eighty years earlier in 1608 and 1609, the first King James' propaganda for the planting of mulberry trees, with the hope of starting an English silk industry, was at its height. If this legend is true we ought to be able to verify the existence of some survivors, mulberries now 255 years old, in the neighbourhood of the site of the well. That the well was on what is now known as Sion Hill is attested by the presence on the lower slopes of that hill, or rather on the approach to it, of a property called 'St. Winifrid's'.

"An enquiry at Kew as to the probable girth of a mulberry 255 years old evoked the reply from Mr. Bean that it would vary from 7 to 9 ft. at 4 ft. 6 in. from the ground, but that would very much depend on the nature of the soil and climatic conditions. There are four such trees still living on Sion Hill which, from their dimensions, might claim to be some of King James' seedlings (or cuttings), and a fifth hard by in Landsdown Crescent might also be classed with them, though it only measures 6 ft. 7 in. below the fork.

"The most massive of these is at Lyde House, although badly damaged in the air-raids of April 1942. At Sion Cottage there is a second one of unusually upright growth, also a third tree farther down Sion Hill, and yet a fourth in an adjacent garden. Two other large mulberries existed in the neighbourhood within living memory; one died and the other was cut down."

The occupant of Sion Cottage, Major W. F. F. Thurstan, informs me that the second mulberry still thrives, and that one or two of the other trees still exist.

Until a century ago, an elm stood at the entrance to Spring Gardens, between the Mall and Whitehall in London. Planted by the Duke of Gloucester, brother of Charles I, it was pointed out and re-marked upon by that unlucky monarch while being escorted by his guards on the morning of his execution. Perhaps the tree recalled the memory of happier days at Hampton Court, where his leisure hours were often spent beneath an elm which became known as King Charles' Swing, being a curiously shaped tree with a gigantic lower branch which refused to conform with the general shape of an elm and uncharacteristically continued to defy gravity and gales.

A notable oak tree stands at Teigngrace, Devon. At breast height the circumference is nearly 30 ft. It marks the site where the Prince of Orange, later William III, rested on the day after his landing at Brixham, on November 5th, 1688 at the head of his formidable force of Protestant troops from Orange. Traditionally, the oak was about eighty years old at that time, and in full vigour.

William III's successor, Queen Anne, encouraged the planting of commemorative trees. One of her now impressive legacies is the avenue of limes at Ashridge Park, Hertfordshire, which she had planted in memory of her children. Unfortunately, during an era arrogantly dubbed the "Age of Reason", the practice grew of apply-ing to Parliament for local and private enclosures. The common lands of immemorial tenure were ruthlessly expropriated in return for paltry compensations. A new fashion, of questionable taste, for the formal shaping or "topiary" of trees became popular. The Arlington or Harlington Yew, which stood in the churchyard of the village of that name in the early eighteenth century, was ravaged into the most grotesque shapes. The tree was nearly 60 ft. in height and its bole was surrounded by a seat. Ten feet above this began a large, circular canopy, formed by the lower branches of the yew, which was topped by circular balls of foliage at equal distances.

Above this was another and smaller canopy, and above that a pyramid, 20 ft. high, capped by a globe which in turn supported a cock. In 1729 the poet John Saxy rhymed execrably:

> *A weathercock, who gaped to crow it,*
> *This world is mine, and all below it.*

In 1788, during George III's reign, the tree was allowed to revert to its natural habit, perhaps in reaction from the alien culture brought back across the channel by the francophile milords on their package "Grand Tours", thus heralding the new movement of Gothick follies and sentimental naturalism. The long-suffering and unhappy George III found solace on his rare visits to the Royal Forests, though it is doubtful if he enjoyed the sport of hunting. Occasionally he contrived to give the slip to his court on such expeditions. Once, during a chase between Lyndhurst and Lymington, he gave the last rites to a dying gypsy woman, at the request of a child who had searched the neighbouring villages in vain for a parson. He died in 1820, having been the longest reigning monarch in our history. An avenue of beeches was planted and dedicated to his memory at Stanstead Park, Sussex, on the day of his death.

During Queen Victoria's long reign, numerous commemorative plantings were made wherever she had visited. The Wellingtonia, or Big Tree from the Sierra Nevada, was one of her favourites, so called in honour of the distinguished and famed general, the victor of Waterloo, who died in 1852, not long after the tree was discovered in the New World despite the more apposite claims of the original name, Washingtonia. At Arreton Manor, on the Isle of Wight, she planted a conifer, recorded as *"chamaecyparis optusa conisca"*, during a visit in the year of her Diamond Jubilee. This tree, now 50 ft. high, with a bole circumference of 6 ft., is possibly *chamaecyparis obtusa*, the Japanese Hinoki Cypress. I sent a sample of the foliage to Kew for identification and was informed that it was "almost certainly" *cupressus sempervirens*, the Mediterranean Cypress: the *"conica"* or *"conisca"* description, in their opinion, could neither be confirmed nor justified.

The line of trees in Salisbury market square were planted in 1887 to celebrate the Golden Jubilee of Queen Victoria's reign. A tree known as Queen Victoria's Oak, of which few people are aware, stands only 150 yards from the Queen's Arms Inn, near the A287 from Farnham to Odiham, Hampshire, on a minor road almost opposite the inn. When visiting Aldershot the Queen would be driven to this spot under the oak to enjoy the magnificent views of the Hampshire countryside.

Few of the remaining trees connected with Victoria's official visits or ceremonies have plaques still on them, but at Auchmore, Killin, in Scotland, there is an exception, and the wording in the cast-iron at the base of the tree reads:

SEQUOIA WELLINGTONIA
PLANTED BY HER MAJESTY QUEEN VICTORIA
10TH SEPTEMBER, 1842

At first sight, especially to the uninitiated, this record may be unquestioned. The visit of the Queen took place, as did the later planting, but *Wellingtonia* had not been introduced into these islands by that date, which I have confirmed is wrong. The ceremony must have taken place some time after 1852. The height of the tree is 131 ft. and its girth 22 ft. 9 in.

At Brislington, Bristol, at the rear of a disused cinema, stands an oak planted to commemorate the wedding of the Prince of Wales, Queen Victoria's heir, later to become Edward VII, to Princess Alexandra of Denmark on March 10th, 1863. The decrepit cinema is shortly to be demolished. The oak, 9 ft. in girth and 50 ft. in height, appears strangely ill at ease in its undistinguished environment. Let us hope that, in the future development of the district, this noble oak with its commemorative trust may be spared, to grace the iconoclastic logic of our ephemeral age.

Chapter Eight

Myth and Memorium

Unlike the Georgian "follies" built by competing eccentrics as an expression of the exaggerated rhetoric of that age, trees do not seem to have been planted as an act of self-glorification. Most human beings naturally wish to see with their own eyes and approve of their memorials in their lifetime rather than that a dubious posterity should be entrusted to perpetuate the homage currently considered to be owing them. Hence, "memorial" trees have tended to be planted either by a person's admirers, by heirs and assigns, or, in certain cases, to focus the point of a cautionary tale.

Most trees outlive us; a few endure for no more than the human span. But it is perhaps salutary to remember that even those of the briefest spans, unlike so many of our race, usually leave the world of Nature better for their having been. Nevertheless, despite the unhappy anomaly, there has always been an affinity between men and trees, or at least on the part of men—not unlike that between the mahout and his elephant. More explicitly, perhaps, the relationship might be defined as being exploitive and authoritative on the one hand and permissive, in the Pavlovian sense, on the other.

But since man is the only one of God's creatures endowed with the biographic urge, the long record of his associations with trees is inevitably one-sided, little being told of his ravages or mutilations save by the silent witnesses of dismembered skeletons or sandy deserts. Those who care enough to digress and read of the latter are referred to the writings of Richard St. Barbe Baker or the late Rachel Carson, among others. Suffice it here to recall a few of the episodes of men against the backcloth of trees, in which our petty dramas of comedy or tragedy have occasionally taken on a borrowed gloss of dignity or purpose from the continuity of life and memory manifested by trees.

That popular archetypal outlaw of mediaeval times, Robin Hood, would no doubt have dealt out rough justice to the anonymous

Frenchman who asserted that "when men take up their abode in forests they relapse into a state of barbarism", and in its execution doubtless proving the point! The pros and cons of Robin's existence have been propounded throughout the centuries but, recently, information has emerged confirming that a certain "Robert Hood" did actually flourish at the turn of the thirteenth century, and much as we all would have him be—leader of a band of "Meinie" or merry men, crack bowmen in the evil days of Norman forest laws, champion of the oppressed; a Raffles of a seamier age.

In the fourteenth century Langland wrote his *Piers Plowman*, showing that legends of the forest hero were then popular with the peasantry. These lines are spoken by a character named Sloth:

"I kan not perfittly my paternoster as the prest it sayeth,
But I kan rymes of Robyn Hode and Randolf, Earl of Chester."

A century later the outlaw's memory was again honoured. In the reign of Edward IV, Sir John Paston, complaining of the ingratitude of his servants, mentioned one who had promised never to desert him: "I have kepyd him all this three yer to pleye Seynt Jorge, and Robyn Hode and the Shryf of Notyngham, and now when I wolde have good horse he is gone into Bernysdale, and I without a keeper."

In the middle of the sixteenth century Bishop Latimer considered Robin Hood no myth. In a sermon preached to Edward VI, he told the tale of a journey he had taken from Derby to London, during which he had decided to preach in the church of a certain town in Nottinghamshire. He had sent word ahead of his impending arrival, but, on the appointed day, he found the church locked and the town seemingly empty. Only one parishioner turned up, to inform the Bishop that it was "Robin Hoode's daye, a busy daye, too busy a daye to listen to a bishop".

The writer Washington Irving was a firm believer in Robin's authenticity. On an antiquarian ramble in Sherwood Forest he visited the Pilgrim Oak, with its connotations of the popular outlaw, which stood in front of the gates of Newstead Park. He wrote of this mouldering monument: "It is a venerable tree of great size, overshadowing a wide area of the road. Under its shade the rustics of the neighbourhood have been accustomed to assemble on certain holidays and celebrate their rural festivals. This custom had been handed down from father to son for several generations, until the oak had acquired a kind of sacred character. The 'old' Lord Byron, who later came to the estate, and in whose eyes nothing was sacred, laid his desolating hand on the groves and forests of Newstead, and doomed likewise this traditional tree to the axe. Fortunately the good people of Nottingham heard of the danger to their favourite oak and hastened to ransom it from destruction. They afterwards made a present of it to the poet, and the Pilgrim Oak continued as a rural gathering place for generations."

In the nineteenth century the Reverend Joseph Hunter, F.S.A., historian and antiquarian, wrote that "neither is Robin Hood a mere poetic conception, a beautiful abstraction of the life of a jovial free-booter living in the woods, nor one of those fanciful beings, creatures of the popular mind springing in the very infancy of the northern civilization, one among the personages of the early mythology of the Teutonic people, but a person who had a veritable existence quite within historic time, a man of like feelings and passions as we are. Not, however, a Saxon struggling against the Norman power in the first and second reigns of the House of Anjou, nor one of the Exhere-dati of the reign of King Henry III, but one of the Contrariantes of the reign of King Edward II, and living in the early years of the third, and fixed in the decennary period, 1285 to 1295, that he was born in a family of some station and respectability seated in Wake-field." Hunter goes on to claim that Hood supported the Earl of Lancaster, and after the baron's fall retreated into the depths of Barnsdale and the Forest of Sherwood, accompanied by numerous comrades. They lived well by deer poaching, and prosperously by a form of blackmailing akin to a protection racket on travellers along the Berwick to London Road. Their ubiquitous leader became the respected champion of the "rights" of the middle and lower order, a self-appointed Ombudsman of his times.

But despite the strongly and widely persisting legends, Robin Hood is not found mentioned in any contemporary chronicles. Only in ballad and folklore has he echoed down through the centuries for us, mostly from thirteenth-century sources but occasionally from as late as the sixteenth century. There are three single ballads in manu-script form which cannot be later than fourteenth century: *The Tale of Robin Hood and the Monk*; *Robin Hood and the Potter*; *Robin and Gandelyn*. More important is a poem printed by Winkyn de Worde about 1495 entitled *The Lytell Geste of Robyn Hood*, in the form of a life story. According to this authority, he continued to live in the greenwood for twenty-two years, and met his death by the treachery of a nun.

The Forest of Sherwood once stretched from Mansfield to Notting-

The Major Oak, Edwinstowe, Sherwood Forest. Photo of painting from J. Rodgers, Sherwood Forest.

ham, and was about ten miles wide. Its poor sandy soil was unsuitable for farming, but deep-rooting oaks, many very large, survived in parts of the forest. Once an impressive Royal Forest, it has long since been partitioned and desecrated by private landowners and the various Enclosure Acts. More than twenty square miles of the area have been "renewed" by planting with pines and larches, and the few private estates remaining contain in total no more than a few thousand acres of hardwoods, chiefly oak, sycamore, ash and Spanish chestnut. Fortunately, those spirited times which bequeathed us the tales of Friar Tuck, Allin o' the Dale, Will Scarlet and the seven-foot tall Little John, are still remembered by tree associations.

The Major Oak, in Sherwood Forest near Edwinstowe, was the object of popular pilgrimage until recently. Officialdom has now "enclosed" the tree, thus keeping us all at a safe and official distance from the largest surviving oak in the forest. Measuring over 30 ft. in circumference and 60 ft. in height, this patriarch takes its name from a noted antiquary, Major Hayman Rooke, who resided in the neighbourhood a hundred and eighty years ago.

Like others of its greenwood brethren, the Major Oak has had its limbs battered by the storms of a thousand winters, stunting its noble proportions to those of a pollarded dwarf. Surviving branches are supported by iron stays and props and although the main bole has been hollow for centuries, the tree is still alive. About 1860 the inhabitants of Edwinstowe knew the tree by its earlier name, The Cockpen Tree. At one time this part of the forest was famous for a breed of game cocks, and the Major's hollow trunk was their roosting place.

A few years before the production of his play *The Foresters*, Lord Tennyson, accompanied by his son, visited Sherwood Forest. The setting of the play was Sherwood, and Tennyson must have had the Major Oak in mind when writing this passage:

> Robin Hood: Where lies that cask of wine whereof we plundered the Norman Prelate?
> Little John: In that Oak where twelve can stand inside nor touch each other.

Major Rooke discovered the brand-mark of King John some eighteen inches beneath the bark of one of the Sherwood oaks, about a foot from the tree's centre. This came to light when felling and sawing of some of the old trees in Birkland was being carried out. Within the trunk of one was found cut lettering. In one section was original lettering and in an adjacent part the reversed letters in relief, formed by the layers of new wood which had covered the depressions. In another tree he found the carving of a crown, with "W.M." for William and Mary. In a third, "I" with a crown, which could represent King John. The tree with the "W.M." insignia was felled in 1785, when the letters were found to be nine inches from the outside of the bark of the oak and 3 ft. 3 in. from the centre. The letter "I" was eighteen inches beneath the surface and about a foot from the centre.

To the north-west and not far from Edwinstowe stood one of the finest oaks of the forest, named Simon Foster, after a villager who, availing himself of a commoner's privileges, was accustomed to herd his stock during the night under the shelter of this tree. Its bole at the base resembled a spiral column, rising massive and tall from an immense root system which gripped the ground in all directions.

Dividing the estates of Thoresby and Welbeck and at the western extremity of the Broad Drive was an oak, known as the Centre Tree, which was notable as a landmark. Though only about a hundred and forty years old at the turn of this century it was then a fine spreading specimen—although a mere stripling compared to some of its ancient neighbours. Half a mile from the Centre Tree and to the west stood the Shambles Oak, or Robin Hood's Larder, a tree reputed to have been a storehouse for the outlaw's dried venison and other titbits of the chase.

In the palmier days of private ownership, the Thoresby estate of Lord Manvers maintained gates and boundary posts by painting them with a distinctive red, as opposed to those of the Duke of Portland, of Welbeck Abbey, which were painted white. The region is known, not surprisingly, as the Dukeries.

A description of some of the most notable oaks on the Welbeck estate was published by Major Hayman Rooke in 1790. The first of these was known as the Duke's Walkingstick. It rose to a height of 111 ft. and had a circumference of 14 ft. at 3 ft. from the ground. A Mr. Mearns, the estate gardener, claimed that this oak was cut down shortly after Mr. Rooke's publication and that it had had an absolutely straight trunk, clear of side branches to a height of 70 ft., before forming a small rounded head of foliage. Henry Elwes visited the estate early in this century and mentions the tree as if it were still standing. What he may have seen was the Young Walkingstick, another tree which was 95 ft. high by only 5 ft. in girth in Rooke's time, a younger facsimile of the felled original. This means that the tree had grown in girth by 9 ft. in a hundred and sixteen years—an extremely fast expansion rate for the species, but not entirely unprecedented if given ideal circumstances. Elwes also mentioned the Two Porters, oaks so-called because they grew opposite each other at a gateway in the park, the first measuring in 1903 25½ ft. in girth, the second 23 ft., both trees having expanded over 2 ft. in a century.

The most remarkable of other celebrities was the Greendale Oak, now but a vestige today, which Evelyn described as having a larger girth than the renowned Major Oak. In 1724, the Duke of Portland made an after-dinner wager, claiming that he had a tree in his park with a bole big enough to take a coach and six. The wager taken, a tunnel was indeed cut through the trunk to a height of 10 ft. 3 in., 6 ft. 3 in. wide. The circumference of the trunk just above the top of the arch was 35 ft. 3 in. The top branches of the oak had to be reduced to allow for the weakened architecture of the main strut, but even this lunacy did not kill the tree. It continued to shoot forth foliage long after the Duke won his infamous wager by driving his coach and six through the hole. It is no mitigation that the expedient coachman cut his coat to the cloth by using a purpose-made coach and the thinnest horses available.

Sherwood's oaks have supplied the needs of many of our ship-builders since Tudor days up to the hearts-of-oak of Nelson's campaigns. Small wonder that little of the original forest remains. In the seventeenth century thousands of oaks were felled without regard for regeneration. High wages and profits paid to woodmen feeding the shipyards via the proximity of two navigable rivers, the Trent and Idle, encouraged indiscriminate extraction. The few historic shells of oaks remaining were probably fortuitously spared because of unsuitability for shipbuilding. Still tenaciously clinging to life they now preserve for us a last tenuous link with a grimly romantic past.

One of the glories of the Dukeries at Clumber Park is "Duke's Drive", a magnificent avenue of lime trees three miles long, two rows on each side, in the shape of a crescent. In 1770 the site was a barren waste and used as a rabbit warren, before being thus laid out by the Duke of Newcastle when he built Clumber House.

Another forest containing some interesting relics of oaks is Salcey, on the borders of Northants and Buckinghamshire. At Piddington is the Church Path Oak, upon which a wooden plaque tells us that William Henry, the Sixth Duke of Grafton, was accustomed to sit under the tree on his way to and from Piddington Church. The Duke's son and heir, the Earl of Euston, was Warden of the Forest.

The great Salcey Forest Oak, in the final stages of decay, stood at Hartwell, about four miles south of the Church Path oak. It was reputed to be over a thousand years old a century ago. It was then hollow, with two sound sides, giving an archway 14 ft. high, comparable with the Greendale Oak. In girth it was 47 ft., but only 33 ft. high. In the early nineteenth century the huge ruin was known as Tom Keeper's Stable, because a manger was built inside the hollow and a horse stabled there. Ten people at a time have sat inside comfortably.

Another interesting tree is the Milking Oak, so called because its great spread gave shelter from sun and rain when milking was done out of doors. The girth of trunk at 4 ft. from the ground is 20 ft. 9 in. and the circumference of a large branch 2 ft. from the trunk is 10 ft. 3 in. This branch extends some 25 ft. in length, giving shade and shelter not only from its foliage but from the bulk of its timber. Other large oaks in this area are the Piddington Oak, which stands on a bridle-riding near Hanslope, and the Two Sisters, an oak with two large trunks rising from one root system.

Greendale Oak, Sherwood Forest, c. 1910 painting. Coach and six driven through aperture for a bet!

A well-known oak is associated with the rebel Robert Kett, a tanner from Heathersett, Norfolk, who led an uprising against the enclosure of common and waste lands in July 1549. Known as Kett's Oak, and marked by an attached plaque—"Kett's Oak 1549"—it stands at the side of the Heathersett to Norwich road, close to Wymondham, and is solidly propped and banded with steel; its hollow trunk is topped up with concrete and bitumen in a somewhat haphazard fashion. This tree is close to the site of the former residence of Kett and his brother William, and is reputedly the oak under which both pledged to reform the State and Church. Like most spontaneous uprisings of the peasantry, Kett's Rebellion, or the "Norfolk Commotion" as it was known locally, was soon harshly put down by the establishment. Although several other oaks in Norfolk have had alleged Kett connections in their day, this is the only survivor. Its height is only about 20 ft., but the circumference of the trunk is 16 ft. The hollow trunk was first banded with iron about 1884, when it was known as the Oak of Reformation. In 1933, Norfolk County Council horticultural experts examined the tree and had various treatments carried out to preserve it. It was sprayed against caterpillar infestation, fed with a mulch of sulphate of potash and finally enclosed with railings. This dumpy old relic surprisingly appears in full vigour today, although experiencing most difficult conditions on a little green verge very close to dense and fast-moving traffic.

Another "Kett's Oak", which stood on Mousehold Heath, Norwich, the scene of the battle between Kett's followers and the organized landlords, under which Robert Kett was ceremoniously seated and dubbed King of Norfolk by his supporters, has now vanished. The last oak recalling one of the origins of this "democratic" movement was at Ryston, near Downham, in West Norfolk. Elwes mentions this tree as a trysting-place of the Norfolk rebels in 1547, not 1549, and points out that the brothers and "other governors" selected large oak trees under which their Courts sat to administer "justice" and curb disorders. The Courts apparently did not regard sheep-stealing as an evil, for the following inscription was left on the tree, graphically conjuring up the climate of the times.

Mr. Prat, your shepe are very fat
and we thank you for that
we have left you the skinnes
to buy your lady pinnes
and you must thank us for that.

The dimensions of the tree in 1906 were, at ground level, 49 ft. 6 in. and at 3 ft. from the ground 26 ft. 6 in. In Elwes' time the tree was sound and alive. No information has been forthcoming of its existence today. This Kett's Oak was marked on a seventeenth-century map and was a noted landmark.

Approximately two and a half miles from Hexham, Northumberland, on the Slaley to Blanchland road, is the "Holly Bush", as it is locally called. This tree is not a holly but no doubt grows from the stump of an old holly tree. It has no plaque, or other identification, except that it stands on a sharp bend at the side of the road. It is reputed to be the site where the Earl of Derwentwater and his sweetheart, Dorothy Forster, would leave notes for each other—their *poste restante* during the first Jacobite uprising, during which the Earl and the Forster family collaborated to arouse Catholic forces against the Protestant Hanoverian George I. The records of this intrigue are not definitive, but the year 1715 is generally accepted as the probable date of the affair, for shortly after that the Earl surrendered to the royalist troops at the Battle of Preston. He was later beheaded.

In Battersea Park, London, there is a turkey oak (*Quercus Cerris*), planted by Sir John Crastor shortly before the Second World War to commemorate the memory of Grace Darling, the heroine who achieved immortality on a stormy night in 1838, when she rowed with her father from Longstone Lighthouse at Bamborough, Northumberland, to rescue the surviving crew of a ship battered to a wreck on the offshore rocks. Grace Darling died of tuberculosis only four years after the event, but her exploit has been recorded on plaques attached to many trees on the East Coast. Sir Charles Trevelyan sent the first commemorative trees to Battersea Park, and a programme for planting in ports was arranged by the Grace Darling League and the Green Cross Society. Both Societies have now been disbanded, but the original distribution plan for the commemorative trees can still be seen in the Grace Darling Museum in Bamborough, which was established by the Grace Darling Memorial Committee and the Royal Lifeboat Institution in 1938.

Toddington Manor in Bedfordshire now belongs to one of the large animal-feed firms, but in the seventeenth century it was the property of the Westworth family, who had close associations with the ill-fated Duke of Monmouth. It seems a far cry from the Somerset and Dorset escapades, but here is yet another Monmouth tree associated with this luckless man. The tree, in an avenue of oaks, was hollow, and into it climbed one of the Duke's men being pursued by James's troops. He was shot and killed, whilst in the tree, but the Duke, hiding elsewhere, escaped. Henrietta Wentworth, a close friend of the Duke, named the tree Haunted Oak. It should, however, be said that no one is now sure which is the one in the story. Toddington Manor was the refuge of Monmouth at the time of the discovery of the Rye House Plot. It was here also that the Duke's affairs of heart and state were later to crystallize, first, in the planning of the abortive Rebellion of 1685, causing his subsequent capture and execution, and finally in his lover's languishing heartbreak and death at the Manor a year later.

Mr. Daniel Day was born in 1682 at St. Mary Overy, Essex, the son of an affluent brewer. A worthy and eccentric character, he was both a manufacturer of pumps and a block-maker in Wapping, where he was highly esteemed. He instigated a popular festival in the nearby Hainault Forest which became known as the Fairlop Fair, held annually on the first Friday in July. The focal point of the Festival was the grandest old oak in the forest, the Fairlop Oak. This tree was situated four miles from Wanstead Hall, three from Ilford and two from Chigwell, and ten miles from the outskirts of London. Day, or "Good Day", as he was dubbed by his companions, used to invite friends once a year to dine with him on beans and bacon beneath the tree. The annual barbecue soon began to attract sightseers to the spot, and inevitably, about 1725, the occasion grew into a popular Annual Fair. Undismayed, Mr. Day rose to the situation by distributing free sacks of beans and proportionate quantities of bacon to the revellers. These supplies he had stored from the dawn of the Fair Day in the hollow of a massive tree, soon to become known as the Fairlop Oak, which measured 36 ft. around its trunk at 3 ft. from the ground. The short bole of the oak threw out eleven huge leading branches on all sides, some measuring 12 ft. in girth, and its gigantic natural cover cast a shadow an acre or more in area. Beneath the spread of branches in a circuit of over 300 ft. various stalls were set up, none being allowed beyond the spread of the outermost twigs, a shrewd condition possibly insisted upon by the expectant beneficiaries of this prodigal host! By the middle of the eighteenth century many of the boughs had suffered from the enthusiastic barbecues, not to mention the damage from climbing revellers and vandals. Several branches fell in 1766, the year before Mr. Day died, aged 84. He was laid to rest in Barking Churchyard, in a coffin made from parts of large limbs, torn off in a storm. Some years after the patron's death further signs of decay were evident, no doubt due to

Prince of Orange Oak, Teigngrace, Devon.

the effect of the numerous fires lit underneath it. Also, its many wounds, unprotected from the weather, had contributed to a general deterioration and the ground beneath had become compacted by the annual crowds to an almost impervious surface.

Those who continued the rather haphazard administration of the fair for long after Day's death, along with the Hainault Archery Society who held their meetings under it, voted to "rest" the tree. Accordingly, a fence was erected five feet high around the compacted area and a notice fixed to one of the oak's limbs: "All good foresters are requested not to hurt this old tree, a plaster having been applied lately to his wounds."

Perhaps the publicity given to the sufferings of the Fairlop Oak prompted the first studies in tree surgery, for in 1789 William Forsyth, a gardener to George III at the Royal Gardens, Kensington, published a treatise entitled *General Observations on the Diseases, Defects and Injuries of all kinds of Fruit and Forest Trees*. He claimed he had discovered a remedy which had never failed to cure the ailments of trees, whatever their nature, by the application of a special plaster to injured parts. The plaster was "of a soft and healing nature; it was absorbent and adhesive and resisted the force of washing rain, the contraction of nipping frosts, and the effects of hot sun or drying winds. It also excluded the pernicious influence of a changeable atmosphere." Approached by the Crown Commissioners for information on the cost of this panacea, Mr. Forsyth replied that the prime cost of the "balsam" would not be more than sixpence per tree, the profit element, he added, being a matter solely for the Commissioners' discretion! It turned out that the secret potion, which was indeed applied to the sores of the Fairlop Oak in due course, was composed as follows:

"One bushel of cow-dung, half a bushel of lime rubbish of old buildings (that from the ceilings of old rooms is preferable), half a bushel of wood ashes and a sixteenth part of a bushel of pit or river sand; the three last articles to be sifted fine before mixed. Work all well together with a spade, and afterwards with a wooden beater, until the stuff is very smooth, like the fine plaster used for ceilings or rooms. Then prepare the tree properly by cutting all the dead, decayed and injured parts, till you get back to healthy wood, rounding off the edges with a draw knife. Then lay the plaster on one-eighth of an inch thick.

"Take a quantity of dry powder of wood ashes, mixed with a

M

False Acacia, Bradford-on-Avon churchyard.

sixth part of the same quantity of the ashes of burnt bones; put it into a box, with holes in the top, and shake the powder on to the surface of the plaster, then let it remain for half-an-hour to absorb the moisture. Apply more powder rubbing it on gently with the hand, repeating the application of the powder till the whole plaster becomes a dry, smooth surface."

As for Forsyth's reward for his magnanimity, he not only received free publicity from the findings of the Committee of both Houses of Parliament, but, from his later launching of the remedy after this auspicious start, he netted handsome profits. There was certainly money in his muck! Unhappily his ministrations to the Fairlop Oak were disappointingly ineffectual. Gypsies began to set up encampments in the hollow tree. More seriously, one evening in 1805 a party of drunken cricketers lit a disastrous bonfire under the wilting branches. Two hours after the sportsmen had left, the oak was discovered to be on fire. All through that night local people with chains of water-buckets tried desperately to save their landmark. The following morning the fire was still blazing, but the wind had died, so that by mid-day the smouldering trunk was finally damped down.

Fairlop Oak.

The remnants stood for another fifteen years until extremely high winds in February, 1820, completely smashed the greater part of the crown, leaving only the squat shell of the bole standing. Thus ended a thousand-year reign in Hainault Forest. The remains were grubbed up by a local builder and from parts of the still sound wood a handsome pulpit and reading-desk were constructed and installed in New Church, St. Pancras.

The end of the Fairlop Oak, and its associations with the rights of commoners in the forests around London, had in it a kind of premonition of the sad events which followed. Hainault and Epping forests became mostly enclosed by the lords of neighbouring manors. Thousands of acres of trees were rooted up, the rights of tenants being bought or exchanged for portions of land. One vast enclosure was made by a certain Mr. Maitland, Lord of the Manor of Loughton, and a rector of that parish. He was sufficiently benevolent or conscience stricken to leave some nine acres of woodland for the recreation of his parishioners.

The inhabitants of Loughton had always had the right to lop trees for firewood in Epping Forest from November 11th, St. Martin's Day, until St. George's Day, April 23rd, a grant dating back to the first Elizabeth. A condition was that the commoners must establish their rights by cutting off branches at midnight on November 10th. It therefore became customary for the loppers to meet at Staples Hill in the forest just before midnight. This was inaugurated by the building of a bonfire, followed by suitable refreshment, before starting a couple of hours' pruning at the appointed time. They then returned home. Maitland, however, sought to trick the locals into failing in their midnight tryst on one particular St. Martin's night. He invited them to a feast the evening before the ritual lopping began and generously soaking them with liquor in the hope that they would be unfit for their labours. Towards midnight, one man who had either held his drink well or had rumbled Maitland's plan, left the orgy with his two sons and exercised his and, by proxy, the sodden company's rights by commencing lopping at the witching hour. When they returned to the party, the thwarted Mr. Maitland vented his spite by ejecting his parishioners forthwith from their expropriated land. In 1866, on the eve of the annual lopping ceremony, a man named John Willingale, a professional firewood merchant who sold wood during the winter to his neighbours, broke into Maitland's own enclosure and started to lop the trees. He was convicted of trespass and sent to prison with his two sons, who had aided and abetted him, but one of the sons caught pneumonia in prison and died. This emotionally-charged incident nearly caused a revolt in Loughton and the East of London. Willingale the elder obtained help from the Commons Society and a lawsuit began, both in his name and on behalf of the people of Loughton, claiming lopping rights in their part of the forest and demanding an injunction to prevent Maitland from making further enclosures and de-foresting more woodland. A thousand pounds was raised by public appeal to support the lawsuit. Maitland, to his undying discredit, intrigued and pressurized to prevent Willingale senior from finding local employment. Failing in this, he later offered him an inducement of five hundred pounds to leave the district. Willingale refused the bribe. The suit dragged on for four years, until the death of Willingale. But his stand had at least obtained publicity and a breathing space for the forest rights for four crucial years. It halted many enclosure-bent landowners all over the country, lest Maitland's case should be a precedent for their own designs. But the legal wrangle dragged on for many years and was not satisfactorily settled until 1882, twenty-two years after the first enclosures. Finally, the Forest of Epping was handed over to the public, judgement having been delivered against seventeen Lords of the Manors who had combined in an expensive enterprise to fight the case. The total expenses ran to over £200,000, some of which comprised compensation to the cottagers who benefited from the lopping rights. As for the Loughtonians, they received £7,000 compensation for the eventual withdrawal of their privilege to extract firewood. But they decided to accept only £1,000 of this amount towards defraying expenses and to spend the remainder on a village hall at Loughton to be used as a reading-room and meeting-place, a truly magnanimous gesture in view of the long drawn-out agony of the lawsuit. The hall was named appropriately Lopper's Hall, and although the Lord Mayor of London was invited to perform the opening ceremony, Maitland, their arch-enemy, had the impertinence to invite himself to the proceedings, offering a prayer for the blessing of the hall as his opening gambit!

Whereas the hornbeam tree in Epping Forest supplied the favourite fuel-wood to the natives of Essex, the beech of the Chilterns, especially in the area of Burnham, was equally acceptable to the people of the Buckinghamshire chalkland. The famous group known as Burnham Beeches is on land once owned by Burnham Abbey, and all the woods here had remained in private possession from the Dissolution until 1880, when the Corporation of London bought the area for public use. Just north of Slough are the old pollarded beeches which have repeatedly reproduced branches from their short boles, despite constant hacking from fuel collectors and craftsmen in the local furniture trade.

Opinions have always been divided as to the origin of the beech-woods of Buckinghamshire. Some say they were planted by land-owners after enclosures following many years of sheep-grazing by the commoners. Other authorities declare that the beech has always dominated the Chilterns, is truly native, for, if it were not so, the old and gnarled trunks could never have survived constant decapitation of their life-giving canopies. Some years before the First World War a "Committee" condemned to death many of these old grey-boled, dragon-like pollards. Unaccountably, no one appeared to be aware of the decision, so no protest was raised against the Committee's recommendations. But the Committee members all died, and the trees lived on. During the Second World War when the main area of the beeches was requisitioned as a military transport park, by some miracle, or the good offices of a tree-loving Commandant, only ten out of the sixteen hundred ancient trees died.

These old beechwoods hold memories of Mendelssohn, who is said to have derived inspiration for some of his music from the sound of the wind in the treetops. Bearing in mind the onomatopoeia of his Scottish Symphony, this is an agreeable and acceptable idea. The poet Thomas Gray often stayed at the Grove, Burnham. He wrote to Walpole of the "revered vegetables that, like most other ancient people, are always dreaming out their stories to the wind". Three miles away is Stoke Poges, and there, of course, is the churchyard with the sentry yews mentioned in his famous "Elegy".

Some experts consider that the Burnham trees are less ancient than popular tradition would have it. The maximum estimate of age for several individual trees is five hundred years. Most of the pollards are, however, rotten and hollow, so exact dating by annular ring count is not possible. But among the trees blown down during the last twenty years there have been a few from whose sound wood a ring count was taken and an estimate made of the remaining distance to the supposed pith, allowing for larger ring growth in earlier years. These calculations assumed ages ranging from two hundred and eighty-five to three hundred and eighty years. The assessors reck-oned that the beeches were first pollarded at an average age of thirty-five years, say three hundred years ago. The evidence also implied that lopping was carried out every twelve years. But it ceased about a century ago, when coal became plentiful and cheaper than wood as a fuel. Many of the pollards were said to be compound trees where two or three stems had married. One beech trunk measured 8 ft. diameter in one direction and 3 ft. the other. Despite the virtues of coal, Queen Victoria invariably had her charcoal supplied from Burnham Beeches, from where it was specially transported to Balmoral.

There is no mystery about the origin of the great beech circle on Chanctonbury Hill, between Steyning and Washington, which rises to a height of eight hundred feet. Between these two Sussex towns lies the village of Wiston, where Charles Goring, the planter of the Chanctonbury Ring beeches, lived. As a schoolboy his daydream was to plant trees over the whole top and northern slopes of the Downs above his home. He achieved the first part of his ambition while still a lad, plodding up and down a well-worn path to the top of this small area at the western end of the South Downs. It is said that he toiled back and forth with his seedlings long after the famous Ring was established, week after week, month after month, lugging up bottles and cans of water to refresh the roots of his young plantation. Thus a bare shoulder of the Downs was transformed into a beechen wood. Unfortunately, Charles Goring attempted to write verse towards the close of his life in commemoration of his achievements. But, in charity, let us merely comment that tree planting has more of posterity than his rhyming. He died at eighty-five years of age, a rare individual who had watched over the gradual metamorphosis of an environment through his own patience and husbandry. It is sad that the undoubted value of his landscapings has never received universal acclaim.

Visitors can still see Goring's now mature beeches from the churchyard in Washington where he is buried. His grave was placed under the wreck of an old split yew.

Colonel A. Tuck, of Monteagle House, Yately, Hampshire, sends information of an old mulberry tree growing close to his property which was planted in 1540, the date of completion of the building, shortly after the Dissolution of the Monasteries. Again we have a contradiction in the supposed introductory date of the mulberry. Henry VIII had the property built as a farmhouse in his Windsor Deer Forest. Later, at the time of the Gunpowder Plot, it was probably given to Tresham, one of the plotters and a kinsman of Lord Monteagle. Monteagle himself may have received it as a reward for uncovering the plot, most likely from the hand of James I. At this time the mulberry would have been a mere youngster of about sixty-five years. Its fruit was impartially enjoyed later both by Royalists and Roundheads, not to mention a certain renegade Parson Darley who used the house as a base for his activity as a highwayman in the eighteenth century. Although the tree's main branches split badly about a hundred and fifty years ago, it still flourishes and produces mulberries annually. Its girth is 7½ ft. and height 24 ft.

In the centre of the village of Aston-on-Clun, in the parish of Hopesay, Shropshire, at the centre of the meeting of five roads, stands a black poplar which has become known as the Arbor Tree. No one knows why it is so-called. It is accredited with a strange mixture of tradition, making sense only as yet another example of that arch symbiosis of the pagan fertility rites and the marriage consummation embodied in the Christian ethic. An estimate of its age is two hundred and sixty years; it has become hollow in the last sixty. An assessment of over two centuries for a poplar could be doubted. Some are inclined to believe it is a second planting; others that the original Arbor Tree was an oak, replaced in error at its death by the wrong species.

The following may sound confusing: a tree in the middle of a village, close to a public house—rather a common sight in the quieter hamlets of England. The striking feature, on occasion, is that it is decorated by flags and bunting of many colours, giving the impression that some sort of perpetual carnival is taking place. Four separate theories are offered by local people for this phenomenon:

1. That the tree commemorates the marriage of a lady born in 1712. By this we may suppose that it was planted at the time of the ceremony. The branches were decorated with flags annually on May 29th. The Marston family of Oaker House nearby initiated the ceremony, which included bequests to the poor of the village.

2. That the tree is bedecked with flags every May 29th in commemoration of Miss Marston of Oaker House. The flags stay on the tree throughout the year. The late R. J. T. Marston was expected to spend a pound in hospitality at the nearby inn on each occasion. Estate workers climbed the tree to tie on the flags and were paid for the work. The earliest records of the custom date from 1786.

3. That the tree was dressed to clinch an agreement between two hitherto feuding local gentry.

4. That the ceremony celebrated the birth of an heir to the Marston family.

There are more variations on the theme, most pointing to a fertility rite, as suggested above, with the corollary of renewal by procreation.

May 29th is also Oak Apple Day. Was the Marston marriage purposely arranged on that day? On Oak Apple Day 1660, Charles II restored the old customs discredited by the Puritans and the date is still a firm fixture in many parts of England to celebrate the escape of the monarch from his adversaries at the Battle of Worcester. Possibly an original oak did die and the poplar in error or by a forgotten design supplanted a *robur caroli*. Or maybe the initial tree really was a poplar. If so, the change is puzzling for it is difficult to trace any significance the poplar can claim in terms of fertility connotations.

The Arbor Tree is still rather desultorily decorated on the occasion of a local marriage. The parish council still a trifle disinterestedly maintains the ceremony, until recently relying on voluntary subscriptions for the upkeep of the tree and the annual renewal of the decor. Local records mention that the original Marston bride left money in her will to perpetuate the old observances on the occasion of a Marston marriage. Significantly, it is also known as the Bride's Tree. It stands by the side of the Craven Arms Hotel; map reference SO 393817.

In private grounds at Melbury Park, Dorset, stands the unique, exceptionally burred oak, well known as Billy Wilkins. The now retired head gardener, Mr. W. Lee, writes saying that the first Lord Ilchester was knighted by Charles I beneath the tree. I have not found out who Billy Wilkins was, or how the tree became so named. Elwes measured the tree early in this century and found it to be 35 ft. in girth at 5 ft. from the ground, but only 50 ft. high. He considered the tree to be eight hundred years old at that time—yet it still bore a good crop of acorns. It has changed little since its first recording two centuries ago, although Loudon thought its age little more than three hundred years in his time, i.e. about 1840. Melbury Park contains many interesting trees, and is an arboretum in its own right. A permit is required from the estate's agent by those who wish to enjoy the sight of some fine and varied trees.

Holwood Park, Keston, in the London Borough of Bromley, is now the headquarters of the Seismograph Service. Perhaps it is fitting that, close by, on a public path leading from Keston to Downe

Road, are the remains of an old hollow oak, supported by straps and with a young oak planted within the shell. Under this tree William Wilberforce used to sit, meditating endlessly on his ambition to abolish slavery, which was destined to shake the establishment of his day. A stone seat beside the tree was erected in 1862 by Earl Stanhope, bearing an inscription taken from Wilberforce's Diary of 1786:

> "I well remember after a conversation with Mr. Pitt in the open air at the foot of an old tree at Holwood, just above the steep descent into the Vale of Keston, I resolved to give notice on a fit occasion in the House of Commons of my intention to bring forward the abolition of the slave trade."

The controversial William Cobbett (1763–1835), politician and agriculturist, radical and reformer, writer and rural rider, predicted that the false acacia (*robinia* or *pseudo-acacia*) would rival the oak for structural qualities. Between 1820 and 1825 he imported vast quantities of the tree's seed from America, filled his own garden with thousands of saplings and sold nearly a million of his well-publicized "sensational discoveries" to gullible landowners. Ironically, nurserymen had stocks on their hands during the time of Cobbett's pronouncement which they could not sell, but Cobbett, a natural entrepreneur, relieved them of their unsaleable plants. Needless to say, this echo of the Stuartian myth of the mulberry faded when the acacia wood failed to match the unassailable qualities of oak. Cobbett probably undermined the prestige of oak as a plantation tree for some years, though he made good profits for himself in the short term. Hardly any trace of the prophet's arboricultural fantasy remain today, save for a few isolated specimens near large manor houses, surviving merely for their ornamental value. Those with girths of 10–12 ft. remaining today are possibly scions of Cobbett's original parcels of American seed.

Cobbett, however, still had the grace to acknowledge the beauty and proportions of the native oak. On one of his rural rides he passed through Tilford, Surrey. He descended from his horse and admired Novel's Oak, or the Tilford Oak, as it is now called. In his day it was probably about a hundred and seventy years old. Although the tree has been lopped rather severely at the top, this may have contributed to its present state of health by easing the strain on the heavy leading branches, any one of which could have been broken off in the many vicissitudes of its life to allow the inroads of decay so often seen in ancient trees. Its girth today is 26 ft. 4 in. In Cobbett's day it was doubtless 16–17 ft. in girth. Close by the tree is a stone seat with a plaque attached to the supporting brickwork and quoting Cobbett as saying "by far the finest tree that I ever saw in my life". The plaque also claims a possible age of eight hundred years, which must be doubted. Only thirty yards from the oak is another planted in 1901, which already measures 8 ft. 5 in. in girth. Another named the Jubilee Tree, a hundred yards away, is 8 ft. 1 in. (planted in 1897), while King George V's tree at the top of the green, planted in 1911, is over 6 ft. in girth. Because these oaks are all in the same soil and situation they assume the habits of the old tree, so we may more realistically calculate that the Tilford Oak is no more than three hundred and twenty years old. But it would be folly to estimate all oaks by these standards on other types of soil and in varying climatic conditions. As we have already seen in the case of the Wistman Wood stunted oaks, and of many of the ancient pollarded oaks, these, for many reasons, remain static or produce only tiny ring growth, are often completely hollow and have little foliage to help them produce the wood cells for normal growth.

At Farnham in the Castle grounds are some fine Cedars of Lebanon which were grown from seed brought personally by Bishop North and his wife from the Lebanon at the end of the eighteenth century. Farnham Castle was the seat of the Bishops of Winchester from 1128 until 1928, and subsequently of the Bishops of Guildford until 1956. The property is now occupied by the Overseas Service College.

John Evelyn, although a lover of peace and patron of all the arts, inherited the fortunes of his family founded on his grandfather's gunpowder-making business. He was born and brought up at Wotton in Surrey, where he planted many trees. After marrying a child of twelve years of age, he qualified for the Bar. Then he became a Royalist soldier for a few glorious days, after which time he travelled and studied on the Continent. Returning to England he made Sayes Court, in Deptford, his home for the next forty years, purchased an adjoining hundred acres which he landscaped and planted rather sparsely. All that remained in 1691 were a few phillyrea and holly trees. His pride and joy was a holly hedge four hundred feet long and nine feet high, five feet in width. In 1698, the house and grounds were temporarily let to Peter the Great and his rather outlandish Russian entourage, who indulged in the curious habit of wheeling their royal master over the flower borders and through the orna-mental hedges in a wheelbarrow. Still alive, but dishevelled, is a black mulberry tree supposedly planted by the Czar during his period of "observing shipbuilding methods". The tree is well protected by a circular railing. Not a good specimen, it appears to have fallen and split apart at some time but has nevertheless produced new shoots from its base and extended its still-living branches to form an irregular shape. Some say it was planted by Evelyn himself, others that Peter the Great placed it there to compensate Evelyn for the havoc caused by his barbarous tenants.

The black mulberry has been moved twice from its original site, once in 1884 and again in 1913. In both cases the transplantings were necessary because of development and landscaping changes. In 1954 the parish council of Abinger Hammer, Surrey, requested cuttings from the tree, because of the parish's associations with the Evelyn family. In 1962, the John Evelyn Society obtained snippets from the original tree for planting at Wimbledon House, where Evelyn had laid out the gardens.

Shakespeare is said to have planted a mulberry in the garden of his house at Stratford-on-Avon. After Sir John Clopton rebuilt the house in 1702 he took great pains to preserve the tree, but when a bad-tempered parson named Gastrell bought the property in 1756, inquisitive sightseers asking to see the tree, and climbing his wall when refused admission, enraged him so much that he demolished the mulberry tree and sold it for firewood—object warning to those who would visit historic monuments without prior permission of the owner. Cuttings from the tree were given to friends both by Shakespeare and Sir John Clopton. On a lawn near the church at Abington, Northamptonshire, David Garrick planted a rooted cutting from the Stratford tree in 1778, thus forming a tangible link between the great dramatist and perhaps his greatest interpreter.

Popular though the mulberry had become as a tree for dedications and commemorations, it originally merely epitomized a whim, reflecting a social snobbery which absurdly mushroomed from a *faux pas* of James I in promoting the wrong kind of mulberry for a hoped-for silk industry. Yet, in mitigation, let us not forget that James was one of the first to pronounce on the dangers of smoking, a habit he detested and attacked in his treatise, *A Counterblast to Smoking, 1604*. A counterblast against Sir Walter Raleigh may have been an added reason for his repugnance of the "Stygian smoke of the pit that is bottomless", for not only was Raleigh responsible for the introduction of the weed to Britain but James considered him a threat to the monarchy and one who was always engaged in conspiracy against him. In 1584, Elizabeth had commissioned Raleigh to discover unknown countries in the New World, resulting in the colonization of Virginia together with the importation of the fragrant tobacco plant. In 1588, he was granted a wardenship of Youghal, near Cork, Ireland. A yew tree here under which he smoked and popularized tobacco among the local inhabitants is traditionally believed to mark the spot where this new and controversial habit was sparked off in the British Isles.

John Hatchett (1763–1806) was one of the foremost coach-builders in London. He employed over two hundred men at Long Acre and exported coaches as far as Poland, Russia, and, astonishingly, India. When thirty-five years of age he built a country house, named Belle Vue House, by the Thames at Chelsea for his wife and only son. In 1776 he planted a weeping willow overhanging the river at the end of the fine garden laid out beyond the house. He lived there for several years before moving first to Long Acre and then to Hammersmith, where he again cultivated a garden, this time of twenty-six acres. After his death in 1806, his son Charles returned to the Chelsea home, which was on the site of what is now 92 Cheyne Walk. Charles continued to maintain the garden for twenty-five years, and during this time the willow became famous as one of the best known landmarks of the river on this reach and an individual specimen tree of its kind. Until the time of the construction of the Chelsea Embankment in 1870, wayfarers passed along the riverside by way of Lindsay Row, which separated the house from the garden. John Hatchett's willow was inevitably destroyed during the buttressing and building of the new embankment, but the tree in its original setting was photographed by a certain James Hedderley. It would then have been nearly a hundred years old, past its prime but thriving, and by now the property of the poet, painter and writer William Bell Scott (1811–1890). On a map of Chelsea, dated c. 1838, the little square garden of Belle Vue is marked and portrays an enormous tree called The Willow.

From Hatchett's one-time garden the local authorities have created a small public garden and in a corner of it, well protected, is another young willow. The London County Council, as it then was, had no knowledge of the well-known willow tree, hence the younger one was never intended to commemorate it. By the side of the newcomer stands an old crooked mulberry tree which may have been a survivor from the original garden, perhaps struck from a cutting of Sir Thomas More's tree in Beaufort Street.

An interesting Hertfordshire tree is the Oxhey or Grimstone Oak at Oxhey Place, planted by Lady Elizabeth Grimston in 1711. Although no legends or historical importance are attached to this tree, it has remarkably survived the passing of several mansions on the site and been in the ownership of many important persons. When Lady Elizabeth gave the tree a place near the chapel on the estate, the manor house, built in 1688, boasted one hundred windows on each side in accordance with the "keeping-up-with-the-Jones" custom of those days. The edifice was pulled down by the Hon. William Bucknall, the second son of Viscountess Grimston, in 1799. Next comes a record of demolition and rebuilding in 1866, when the estate was sold to W. H. Smith (Mr. "Pinafore" Smith). He in turn sold to Mr. Thomas Blackwell, of the well known Crosse and Blackwell bottling and canning business. After the Second World War the property passed to the local council and was used as a community centre and clinic. Oxhey Place was burned down in 1954, but the oak, a witness to the vicissitudes of the house, survived due to the providence of a persistent drizzle and favourable wind. An estate developed by the old London County Council is the oak's latest environment. The authorities were sensible enough to ensure its conservation by constructing railings around the trunk, which is remarkably straight to a height of 26 ft., at which point the first branch emerges. The girth of the trunk at breast height is 18 ft. Curiously, the tree has the towering appearance of a lighthouse—perhaps a not inappropriate coincidence.

At the Hirsel, Coldstream, in Scotland, on Sir Alec Douglas-Home's estate by the bank of the River Leet, is an ancient five-hundred-year-old Spanish chestnut overhanging the water. Further on, towards a walled garden, is a tulip tree reputed to be the largest specimen in Britain, 78 ft. in height and 23 ft. in girth. This native of Virginia, U.S.A., is rare in Scotland, although this specimen is admittedly only just over the border. J. C. Loudon, writing in 1838 mentions a tulip tree at the Hirsel as "a low tree, planted one hundred years but only 13 ft. high, with a trunk 4 ft. in diameter and branches 33 ft. in diameter (*sic.*)". Strange measurements—but probably he was referring to the spread of the canopy.

The link between the old world and the new, depicted by this example of the ornamental tulip, is perhaps more momentously underlined by what is perhaps the largest living memorial to a man of world renown. In December, 1963, at the Irish Institute in New York, certain Irish American communities discussed the question of an epitaph to the late President of the U.S.A., John F. Kennedy. They had already pledged themselves to raise a hundred thousand dollars for the provision of a Memorial in Ireland. Committees were set up in many American cities, resulting in substantial additions to this target. They then approached the Irish Government for suggestions, who ultimately proposed that the memorial might take the form of a Park, to include an Arboretum and Forest Garden, which would be dedicated to the memory of the late President. The Americans accepted this project enthusiastically. The cost of founding such a Park and Arboretum, together with its upkeep, will be much in excess of the money already collected, but the Irish Government, keenly interested in the project, has promised to meet the additional expenditure.

The site selected for the Memorial Park is on the lower slopes of Slieve Coillte, an imposing hill rising above the Kennedy ancestral home in Dunganstown. A soil survey has been carried out by the Irish Agricultural Institute and conditions have been found to be suitable. Responsibility for the work is to be shared between the Lands Minister and the Department of Agriculture. The Public Works department have undertaken to design and erect buildings and roads, and also to provide water supplies. About fifty acres will be reserved for a Horticultural College and a hundred and forty acres will be devoted to a Forest Garden, with an extra two hundred and seventy acres to be laid out as an Arboretum. A comprehensive collection of trees and shrubs, suitably labelled and arranged, will be introduced, not only for the advantage and enjoyment of visitors, but also for research and scientific study. It is further hoped that it will stimulate a wider public interest in the appreciation and enlightened use of woodland plants. The main collections of trees have already been established; conifer circuits, hardwood sections demonstrating trees suitable for hedges, roadside and garden plantings, and areas containing Rhododendrons, Azaleas and Ericas. There will also be a special Acer (maple) collection. In the years to come it is hoped that six thousand of all the species envisaged will be planted.

In the Forest Garden plots of single species up to a quarter of an acre will be grown. So ambitious is the concept that it is intended that about two hundred and fifty species will finally be represented. The master plan will be arranged in geographic regions, blocks being allocated to each continent. The North American block, comprising some sixty types, was the first to be completed in 1968.

Twenty-two countries, including Great Britain, are helping to support this grand landscaping project, and while the main object of the Park is educational and scientific it is also being designed to provide for public recreation, with picnicking areas. On the terrace near the reception area is a granite-hewn rock weighing over ten tons. It carries the words:

Ask not what your country can do for you . . .
Ask what you can do for your country.

What more fitting an epitaph than this for John F. Kennedy?

Chapter Nine

Curiosa

Inevitably, in such a harvesting as this of stories of trees and men, one is left in the winnowing with a handful or two of unclassifiables too arrestingly exotic to be swept aside, hence this chapter of eccentrics and non-conformists both among the trees and men. Of the trees, some are definable as "sports"—bizarre mutations caused by exigencies of climate or a collector's zeal for uprooting specimens from a congenial environment and replanting them in an alien one. Others are either living memorials to the rape of men, or outstanding for shape or size or perhaps owing their recording simply as discoveries by observant passers-by, as might apply to an ossified fragment of a primæval tree or the tooth of a dinosaur.

Hollow trees, not surprisingly, have throughout the ages given shelter and refuge not only to individuals but also to nascent social movements, revolutions, or breakaway religious sects. There are cases on record of the insides of large trees having been used for long-term family housing as improbable as that of the old lady who lived in a shoe; or as workshops, storehouses, alehouses, tollbars, lighthouses, hidey-holes by the score, even chapels. Such tales are legion.

Finally, there are accounts of the moving and re-siting of large mature trees that would have intrigued Dean Swift, of armies of men with primitive equipment who successfully moved trees many tons in weight appreciable distances at the bidding of human whims.

At which should we marvel the more—the enduring existence of of our great flora or the precocity of man?

To the east of Fanny's Lane on Bucklebury Common, near Reading, grows a beech tree with a strangely pregnant appearance. Although only 50 ft. in height it is 11 ft. in girth at 2 ft. from the ground. Then comes a bulge 12 ft. 7 in. around, followed by a second bulge of 14 ft. 11 in. The tree is known locally as Merry Tidbury and the reason for its eccentricity is as follows: Charles

Scissors Tree at Dawlish, Devon.

Tidbury, a farmer who lived in the area about a hundred and thirty years ago, was once reeling home to his cottage after celebrating at a local hostelry when he collided with the then young beech; its tip arched across the lane, so Tidbury forthwith grasped the supple obstacle and tied a knot in it, thus bending it upright and out of his way. Surviving the outrage but unable to divorce itself from the Tidbury knot, it remains to this day the equal and the opposite to Alexander's ruthless solution of the Gordian Knot.

Another farmer, Edward Stevenson, of Measham, Burton-on-Trent, gave an ash sapling similar unexpected status about the turn of this century. One day, walking his broad acres, he spied a straight sapling which appeared ideal for use as a walking-stick, but, having no saw, he pulled it out by the roots. Arriving home, he found it too thin for his purpose, so replanted it in his garden. Until two years ago this tree still flourished in perfect shape, and, although not so upright as its history might suggest, it became known as Stevenson's Walking-Stick. (The land on which the tree stood at Iveagh House has recently been sold for development purposes.) The remarkable point of the record is, of course, that ash trees do not tolerate root damage or enjoy changes of environment, let alone the indignity of being discarded as unsuitable for walking-sticks.

There are many deciduous trees colloquially called "walking-sticks". Any tall straight tree which ascends to great height, is straight, clean of branches to say, 60 ft. or more, seems to qualify for the description, and is often preceded by the landowner's name. At Dawlish, Devonshire, in a private garden, is a bay tree with the name of another domestic artefact, the Scissors Tree, so called because at the base of the trunk are two circular grafted branches, free of foliage, which curiously suggest the holes for thumb and first finger of a pair of scissors. There is little doubt that the graft is man-made and graft encouraged, but it is probable that the intention was as fortuitous as that of Tidbury's more dramatic feat.

An elm with an unusual social history once stood on the high road from London to Brighton at Crawley, Sussex. Although it had lost its top in a gale it still stood 70 ft. in height, had a circumference of 55 ft. at shoulder height, and was completely hollow to the top of the trunk. One side of the trunk of the Crawley Elm, as it was known, was open, but a door had been fitted by the Lord of the Manor, for which he held a key. On certain occasions, with the owner's permission, villagers held feasts within the tree's cavity, the floor of which had been paved with bricks. Once a poor woman gave birth to a child

The Hampstead Elm from an old print. Tree lost.

within the tree. She even took up residence there for a time. Another huge elm at Hampstead, London, became a veritable lighthouse and viewpoint. During the sixteenth century it was fitted with a door and had a spiral staircase of forty-two steps which led to a turret 34 ft. in circumference at the top of the trunk, upon which there were seats for twenty sightseers. An engraving of this—"The Great Hollow Elm of Hampstead", by Hollar—appeared in 1653. In the same period several poems extolling this remarkable tree were composed by Robert Codrington and E. Cotes, which were probably sold as broadsheets to visitors to the tree.

At Abbot's Leigh village between Bristol and Portishead in Somerset, an ancient hollow elm stands at the cross-roads. Its buttresses and surface roots are completely exposed above the surrounding road surface yet the branches and twigs radiating and sprouting annually appear completely healthy. The tree is typical of the central focal point of any English village, more so as it is a comfortable, low-spreading pollarded elm, inexpensive to maintain yet sufficiently imposing in character to ensure it place as long as it can survive

amidst the increasing fumes and rumble of heavy traffic. The Hollow Elm was decapitated in a great storm in 1834, which resulted in its present shape. Yet that catastrophe has ensured its present stability, for there remains no great top hamper to threaten its uprooting. The history of the English village and indeed the history of England has accumulated around such trees which can still be seen at cross-roads and on greens. The significance of some of these has already been mentioned.

In the same context, it may be excusable to mention the Chapel Oak at Allonville, about a mile from Yvetôt between Rouen and Le Havre, which doubtless no longer exists. In 1696, the Abbé du Détroit, curate of Allonville, transformed the oak into a living place of worship. Fortunately, a copy of a contemporary engraving still remains for us. The tree was 35 ft. in circumference just above the ground and 25 ft. a little higher up. Although a low tree for its girth, the branches thrown out were enormous and covered an extensive area. The crown was alive, but the trunk was hollow, the latter being wainscoted and the floor paved. The opening in the trunk, from which hung an iron gate, led to a small chamber complete with bed, access to which was by way of a staircase winding around the hollow interior of the trunk.

The crown of the tree was broken off, and over the decaying cavity was erected a pointed roof covered with slates in the form of a steeple and topped by an iron crucifix. The cracks which occurred in parts of the tree's main structure were also slated over. Above the entrance to the chapel was an inscription to the enterprising Abbé, and over the door of the upper chamber a plaque dedicating the whole to "Our Lady of Peace".

An immense dead hollow oak of 36 ft. girth, which for safety's sake had been shorn of its seven great limbs at about 18 ft. from the ground, survived in the village of Bale, Norfolk, until the middle of the nineteenth century. The tree, notorious for obscure and unspecified reasons, was highly prized in the neighbourhood. It is said that twenty persons could stand upright within without touching each other. For one whole summer a cobbler occupied and used the interior both as a home and workshop, and for convenience and privacy adapted part of the shell as a doorway.

Another famously gigantic oak in Norfolk once stood on the Earl of Albemarle's estate at Quiddenham Hall, Winfarthing, near Diss. In 1820 it was 70 ft. in circumference at its buttressed roots, and at shoulder height 40 ft. The shell, which could easily have held thirty

Hollow Elm, Abbots Leigh.

Oak at Bale, Norfolk, now lost.

men, was at one time equipped with a table and chairs, possibly for parish or evangelical meetings. At least one such use is testified to by a brass plate said to have been affixed at one time above the entrance, with an inscription inviting donations to the Bible Society from visitors. The inscription reads as follows:

Ye who this venerable oak survey
Which still survives through many a stormy day,
Deposit here your mite with willing hands,
To spread in foreign climes, through foreign lands,
The sacred volume, so divinely given,
Whose pages teach the narrow way to Heaven.—Doggett.
O send out Thy light and Thy truth.—King David.

    May every subject in my dominions possess a Bible, and be able to read it!—*King George III.*

(Doggett was the tenant of the farm on which the tree stood.)

This tree was said to have been known as the Old Oak at the time of the Norman invasion. Botanists have calculated that an oak 40 ft. in circumference could not be less than thirteen-hundred years old. The Winfarthing Oak, as it was called, did not collapse completely until 1953.

Another hollow oak, now, alas, gone, also renowned for historical associations, was the Henham Hill Oak or Wangford Oak, Wangford, Suffolk, in which Sir John Rous hid and eluded a party of

Winfarthing Oak, Norfolk. Only fell in 1956.

Roundheads. The tree was used by the Rous family of Henham Park
as a summer-house. Luckily it had a door faced with bark, which
fitted perfectly to the outer tissues of the oak so that the strangers
never suspected the hiding-place. During the three days that the
Parliamentary troops remained in the vicinity of the house, searching the premises and bullying Lady Rous to reveal her husband's
whereabouts, she secretly stole out to the tree nightly to keep him
informed and fed.

Hollow trees, especially if ancient, would naturally become objects
of exaggerated lore, particularly if specific events had been enacted
within a short distance. They sometimes harboured other mammals
besides man. At Wedgnock Park in Warwickshire a giant old oak used
to be given a wide berth by wary locals as it often sheltered a bull
which sought refuge in the cool interior on summer days. When disturbed it was in the habit of charging out on the unsuspecting. The
Bull Oak, as it was known, measured 40 ft. at 1 ft. above the ground
and 37 ft. at 6 ft.

Another oak on the north side of the A365 between Melksham and
Devizes, still alive and visible from a lay-by not far away, was known
to shelter cattle pestered by flies. But it is better known for its associations with Oliver Cromwell. A tradition is that he once slept at a
nearby house and had several Royalists hanged from the oak before
breakfast at the time of the Battle of Roundway Down. As one may
expect, there are several versions of the story. A tramp lived for a time

Bull Oak, Wedgrock. Print c. 1830.

in the tree about 1910, which provoked the owner to seal up the entrance.

To meet under a conveniently sited old oak or elm was to country people the same as townees meeting under the clock at the railway station. Some used trees as covered stalls to display their produce and hang their wares from on market days; others for intrigue or the birth of a revolt.

At Prior's Haugh near Jedburgh, in Roxburghshire, Scotland, is the Capon Tree, 21 ft. in circumference at shoulder height. It is a surviving oak from the old Forest of Jed and reputed to be over a thousand years old. No one appears to know the true origin of the word capon. There have been suggestions that it derives from the cowls, or capons of Franciscan monks, who once lived nearby. The Concise Oxford Dictionary defines it as a "castrated edible cock", which doesn't help us in this context. Another interpretation comes from the Scottish word "kep", meaning "meet", which may be closer to the truth, for tradition has it that this was the spot where border clans rallied for action during the troubled days of the sixteenth century. The crown of the tree was, in Loudon's time (1850), fantastically crooked. It had been poorly and unskilfully pruned at some earlier date, but the then Marquess of Lothian, to whom the tree belonged, later took steps for its preservation, to which it owes its survival.

Another survivor of an oak forest stands at the corner of Queen Parade and Victoria Avenue in Harrogate, Yorkshire. It has no particularly interesting features, except perhaps the plaque which reads "This Oak Tree—the Oldest Tree in the Borough, Remaining from the ancient Forest of Knaresborough".

Early in 1970, Burley-in-Wharfedale, in the same county, lost a favourite landmark when a sycamore, known as the Pudding Tree, was considered unsafe and accordingly felled. There is some confusion about the date when huge puddings were served under the canopy of the tree, which stood near the Malt Shovel Hotel in the village. Local historians state that the last puddings were dispensed in 1787, and that an elm was the original tree. But journalists insist that the Great Pudding Festival took place every seven years, and that the ceremonial cooking and eating was carried on throughout most of the nineteenth century. A local Burley-in-Wharfedale councillor is at present researching into the true history of the ceremony. Meanwhile a young sycamore is to be planted to commemorate the decayed tree and dedicate the tradition.

Brewer's Oak, surviving four hundred yards from the Boundless and Brook turning off the A3 road to Hindhead, Surrey, was noted as a meeting place for brewers' draymen. They used to tie their horses to the tree at rest periods, and no doubt these intervals for reminiscence enriched the local annals and immortalized the tree.

At the hamlet of Great Oak, one mile west of Eardisley, Herefordshire, is an oak girthing 30 ft. 4 in. at 5 ft. from the ground, from which the village takes its name. Some fifty years ago the original crown was torn off in a gale, but the tree has recovered to a large extent and recently underwent an overhaul by tree surgeons. Doubtless the Great Oak was an important meeting place in centuries past, but there is little documentation. Probably it was either a court or gospel oak. Herefordshire has many such fine oaks, relics from the old Wyre Forest bordering on Radnorshire. In the neighbouring county of Shropshire, at Cleobury Mortimer, at the junction of the B4202 and A4117 roads, near the western edge of the Wyre Forest, is a notable oak of fine dimensions but having no traditional associations. Known as the Mawley Oak, it has probably taken its title from a landowner. Despite its lack of an authentic story-line it is worth recording, for such a splendid example of English oak is aesthetically pleasing in its own right.

In the grounds of Pennybridge Hall, near Ulverston, Lancashire, can be found an old oak, apparently nameless, under which representatives of the Abbot of St. Mary's Abbey of Furness used to sit to receive the dues of abbey tenants. Recently there were fears that it would have to be removed for road widening purposes, but good taste and reason prevailed and the County Council realigned the road in order to leave the tree undisturbed.

In 1923 Mr. Sidney F. Wicks founded the Rostrum Movement, a club interested to promote the art of public speaking and in defence of the freedom of speech. This organization has now five club branches in Britain and many more in Australia. The central committee is called the Dais. Under a yew tree at Greendale Farm, Mottram St. Andrew, Prestbury, Cheshire, the inaugural meeting was held on 21st July, 1923. Members renew their pledges annually here and new members are sworn in under the tree:

> "I promise to submit myself to the discipline of the Rostrum and to endeavour to advance its ideals and enrich its fellowship. I will defend freedom of speech in the community and will try at all times not to be silent when I ought to speak."

The event is always held on the Saturday nearest to July 21st. Once again we have an example of a tree as witness and host to allegiances and ceremony, and so this yew is suitably acknowledged as a marker tree to commemorate this admirable organization with the aforesaid plaque.

The Beehive Inn in Castlegate, Grantham, is unique in that its sign, a living beech tree, has a hive erected in its main fork containing at times a swarm of Caucasian bees originally imported from the United States. When the beech flowers well the occupants do not have far to travel to collect nectar.

Among the many contorted pines in the Breckland Forest of East Anglia is a snake-like specimen on Barnham Cross Common near Thetford, Norfolk. The trunk of the tree has formed into a loop, and a not so ancient legend credits it with magical powers. Known as the Trysting Pine and often as the Kissing or Wishing Tree, its magic is to be acquired by pulling off a cone, holding it in the right hand and easing the head through the loop of the tree, and making a wish. Enterprising couples today test its reputation by holding hands and kissing through the loop, pledging their hopes in the time-honoured way. As the tree ages, the space inside the loop will lessen, hence, time is of the essence to the contract. No doubt the ritual will continue with appropriate modifications.

Outside the inn at South Leigh, near Witney, Oxfordshire, are three large box trees, possibly planted during Tudor times, for the building itself dates from that age. Large box trees are not common. They do not attain great height or girth of wood, and are invariably topiarized into topical shapes of their period. Not far from this unique anachronism in the old vicarage garden are three large Wellingtonias one hundred years old and as many feet high, from which it is said pilots approaching the R.A.F. Station at Brize Norton take their bearings.

The single Wellingtonia at Wyck Rissington Rectory, near Bourton-on-the-Water, Gloucestershire, is of particular interest, not because of its size but for its date of planting, 1853. In that same year extensions to the Elizabethan rectory were completed, and, as was the custom in the Cotswolds, a commemorative tree was planted to mark the occasion. It is recorded that this planting was certainly Wellingtonia Gigantea, the big tree from the Sierra Nevada, on the west coast of America. The records, as already mentioned, maintain that this species was not discovered until 1853, when Matthew and Lobb, the botanical explorers, sent seed and a few small plants to British nurserymen. Their plants died due to the sea delays of the passage by sail and early consignments of seed were difficult to raise. I have been informed by the Rev. H. S. Cheales, the present incumbent of the Rectory, that this tree was one of a consignment of three sent across in pots on the propeller-driven *Great Britain* steamship during its last transatlantic journey in 1852, and that the faster journey enabled the tender plants to survive the salt-laden air. Thus the Rectory tree was planted by the Rev. H. J. Richmond, grandfather of Lord Fisher, ex-Archbishop of Canterbury. Mr. Richmond stated that the remaining plants were probably sent to Kew and Westonbirt, Gloucestershire, where Robert Holford was establishing his arboretum. Unfortunately, unmindful of the eventual size such a tree would attain, the Mammoth Tree, as it became known, was planted only thirty feet from the house.

In 1875, the rector's son climbed the tree and had to be rescued from the summit by the longest ladder in the district, a forty-feet farm makeshift. At the turn of the century the tree was struck by lightning and the apex fell off, ruining its chances of becoming the tallest of its kind in Britain. However, the Wellingtonia is one of the few conifers able to restore its crown, for it produces new shoots to reform a rounded top. It recovered and by the end of the Second World War its height was again ninety feet. The new rector had nervous nightmares and became considerably alarmed at the prospect of being crushed by the tree falling from the north-west towards the Rectory. He applied to the Diocesan Authority for permission to have it felled, but was refused, it being deemed to be safe. Compromising with authority, the reverend gentleman decided to reduce the danger by cutting off the lower branches—an imprudent act which raised the centre of gravity of the tree, thus making it more dangerous. His operations ended when he performed the classic feat of removing the branch he was standing on and breaking his arm in the inevitable fall. He left the parish shortly afterwards.

In 1950 the Reverend Cheales dreamed of a maze around the base of the tree, and in 1952 the circular hedges became a reality. They are there now—planted, of course! The Wyck Rissington Big Tree is also known as the Centre and symbolizes Eternity. In the churchyard nearby is a yew tree only 9 ft. high and shaped in the form of a cross. Interested visitors, who annually number five thousand, are welcome to enjoy these unique attractions.

Some time before the middle of the nineteenth century, Robert Fortune introduced the Chusan Palm from China to this country and it is not uncommon to find it in our temperate regions, especially the south and west. One would not, however, expect to find a fairly mature example gracing the pavement of a road in Wimborne, Dorset. A moving story can be quoted from the Bournemouth *Evening Echo*, May, 1968, of the West Indian visitor to the town who, seeing a tropical tree standing proudly on the pavement of the link road, promptly knelt in amazed and nostalgic tribute. No mystery really exists, for this exotic was adopted by Wimborne Urban District Council when the building of a link road necessitated taking over part of the walled garden of a private property, where the tree had been sheltered for years. The Parks Department now have a botanic problem—keeping the tree in good health. During the first year's expropriation, the palm was dressed in a skirt consisting of a plastic sheet stuffed with straw acting as a warm blanket and frost protector, and not least to protect its bark from the inquisitive. In summer the shield comes off and is replaced with a metal weldmesh guard.

The Gingko Biloba, or Maidenhair Tree, a native of China and Japan, and once considered a conifer, but since classified as a gymnosperm (it bears ovules not enclosed in an ovary) was introduced into

England about 1754. It is extremely rare in counties north of a line drawn from Fishguard across to Felixstowe. An exception occurs in Cowick Park, near Snaith, West Riding, Yorkshire, and could qualify for the most northern position of the species in England. Neither Loudon nor Elwes mentions an example north of Barton, Suffolk, or Margam Park, Glamorgan, and on a more recent list of gingkos Hertfordshire and Middlesex appear to be the limits to the north. There are no significant trees in Scotland or Ireland.

The Stone Pine, or Umbrella Pine as it is sometimes nick-named, is a native of the Mediterranean. At one time it may have been found in North Africa, but it is certainly not discovered wild there today. Two cones, however, were found in a tomb of the twelfth Dynasty (2200–2400 B.C.), in Egypt, which could point to the trees' existence there over four thousand years ago. The cones are preserved in the museum at Boulac. This half-hardy pine has been successfully established in the more temperate parts of England where it succeeds on sandy soils. Augustus Henry remarked on the outstanding plantation of Stone Pines at Matchams, near Ringwood, Hampshire. They were apparently raised from seed sent by Lord Nelson from the Mediterranean about a hundred and sixty years ago and have grown and flourished alongside the road on otherwise barren heathland. An interesting group of these impressive though unlovely trees can be found on a railway embankment at Bilsdean on the East Lothian border in Scotland, on the margins of the Dunglass estate. They were planted shortly after the railway was cut through from Edinburgh to Berwick-on-Tweed during the 1840s. Elwes and Henry mention six trees growing here in their time, the largest being 30 ft. in height (1908). Such an example of hardiness and survival on this eastern coastline so generally inhospitable to trees makes us wonder why this specimen is not found in more favourable parts of Scotland. The shelter of the railway embankment may have guarded the young trees from the North Sea winds primarily, since when they have become adapted to their alien soil and even borne cones. They are noteworthy for being the only thriving Stone Pines in Scotland of any stature. The kernel of the seed, of which there are about a hundred to each cone, is edible and used as a sweetmeat in Southern Europe. "Stone" merely alludes to the hardness of the thick seed-shell, but is a truer description than that of "Umbrella". The true Umbrella Pine is *Sciadopitys Verticillata*, a Japanese tree, first planted at Kew and Ardkinglas towards the end of the last century. Its popular name in Japan is "Parasol Tree", not because of a so-descriptive crown, but because of its spread of leaves, like the ribs of a parasol or umbrella.

The vagaries of mutation sparked off by alien environment have caused countless improbable associations of tree characteristics, giving nevertheless true non-conformists which leaf "early", leaf "late"; trees which have leaves other than of their own "species" growing upon them. Others defy identity and are natural hybrids contradicting text-book dicta. Again, there are the dwarfs and "spastics" of our orthodox flora, scarcely explicable by botanical laws. But the majority of cases have a simple scientific and rational cause for deviation from the normal. A change of water supply, alteration of ecological circumstances, mechanical interference by man, untempered exposures to unfamiliar sunlight, or even the unpredictable migrations or multiplications of the armies of bacteria in the soil around tree roots might distort or abort normal conservative growth.

A splendid oak at Witley, Surrey, known as the Forrard Oak, is usually in leaf by mid-March. But this sprightly habit should not be taken too seriously as heralding continual good summers by those who swear by the old adage—"oak before ash, we're going to get a splash, ash before oak, we're going to get a soak". The Forrard Oak measures 80 ft. in height and 13 ft. 6 in. in circumference at waist height.

The New Forest once boasted of an oak at Cadenham (now Cadnam), near Lyndhurst, which for over two centuries drew visitors on Old Christmas Day, 5th January, to witness that it had already sported buds and small leaves, which on the following day it had retracted, giving the tree a normal winter appearance again. Around the tree ran a small stream which may have had some mineral content affecting the tree's metabolism. Whatever the cause, there is good reason to believe in the legend, for the Reverend William Gilpin, a naturalist writer of great integrity, examined the oak on the day in question, in 1782, and although he would only admit that swollen buds did appear to be breaking, the following day he engaged the landlord of the local White Hart Inn to collect a sample branch from the oak. He recorded that the buds had expanded into one-inch leaves overnight! J. C. Loudon, in his *Arboretum*, records that an oak raised from the seed of the Cadnam Oak, when planted at Bulstrode, acquired the properties of its parent, and was in leaf, together with perfectly formed flower buds, by December 21st.

Thus Nature has its own "sports", sometimes resulting in twisted or dwarfed offspring and displaying unconservative complexions, from which full advantage has often been taken by nurserymen to

"The Two Lovers". Beech and pine growing together on summit of Critchell Down, Dorset.

perpetuate freak characteristics by cuttings. The sight of hawthorn branches apparently growing from an oak tree is not unusual. Close inspections usually show that such cases occur where hawthorns are encased in oak shells, passing their branches through holes in the outer bark. The variations are innumerable; rowan in willow, birch in elm, hornbeam growing in the fork or hollow of beech, oak in yew, and so on, though some species will be unsatisfactory co-existents, the consequences seldom being satisfactory either to host or migrant. There are even reports of a tree at the Woodrow Inn at Cawston, Norfolk, having part beech, part hornbeam and part oak leaves on all its branches, not isolated, but indiscriminately mixed upon every part of the tree.

Trees of different species often embrace each other. A Scots Pine and a beech grow harmoniously trunk to trunk, each enwrapping the other with its branches, at the edge of a clump of tall beeches on the summit of Critchel Down, Dorset. They are locally spoken of as the Two Lovers. Although they grow on private land a mile from the nearest road, an accessible bridle path passes within a few feet of the trees. The best way to find the path is at the Old Toll House at the top of the hill east of Tarrant Hinton village, where it leaves the A354 Blandford to Salisbury road. The path is marked by a Dorset County Council signpost, "Bridle way to Long Critchel". The Ordnance Grid Reference number is ST962100, the exact location of the trees.

It is not an uncommon sight today to find hitherto open and bare landscape "instantly" furnished with "semi-mature" trees. Although the description is a misnomer, for they are certainly not half-way to maturity, the term applies to youthful specimens of from 18 ft. to 30 ft. in height which will make an instant impact; several firms specialize in supplying these larger plants and a few of them grow trees from the seedling stage until they are large enough to "prepare". This preparation before transplanting to a new situation is a most important and necessary operation. The practice is to dig a small trench around one side of the root system at a distance in keeping with the size of the tree, sever the roots then fill in the channel with good soil or feeding materials in order that a fibrous root-growth will be formed compactly and vigorously. At the same time, the untouched roots on the opposite half of the circle of roots ensure that not too much of a shock is imparted to the remainder of the tree. Perhaps the following year, or even later, the remainder of the roots are treated likewise and allowed to consolidate until the whole system is a fibrous mass of closely-knit and easily transportable roots. When required for planting by local authorities, builders, landscape gardeners and select individuals who can afford prices varying from fifteen pounds to over a hundred pounds for single trees, depending on the size and rarity, special machines lift the trees from their nursery sites without effort, the root-balls are wrapped in materials which prevent the soil and roots from disintegrating, and the whole is carried and carefully planted in newly prepared holes where desired. The trees are watered in, given a bonus of rich topsoil and braced either by guying the root-balls underground or by wire stays radiating in four directions from the trunks to anchors in the ground.

There is no doubt that ugly industrial heaps and hillsides are benefiting enormously from this popular modern exercise, and with all the modern lifting equipment available it is not surprising that the mechanics of the exercise cause little difficulty. Yet the botanical successes are still not one hundred per cent. On alien soil and in hitherto unaccustomed climatic situations, many of the large transplants fail to make much headway and remain static for many years.

However, the business of moving large trees is nothing new, and the results have never been foolproof. They may, on the other hand, have proved foolhardy, as the following account of a hoax meant to be perpetrated in an edition of the Royal Forestry Society's *Journal* was intended to underline:

"Those of your readers who are also students of ancient history will know of the dangers inherent in this exercise in impatience. To them it will be well known that Rameses II was extremely sensitive to criticisms concerning the changes in the skyline taking place in the Lower Nile Delta, and it was to assuage this indignation that he tried to reduce the apparent enormity of his personal pyramid by resorting to the use of instant trees. Bad advice was undoubtedly the trouble. Failure was followed by failure, and an expedition was finally sent as far as the Land of Punt to find suitable species which might succeed (hence the expression 'a punter', for one who relies on luck). However, as was then discovered, no species will put up with this drastic treatment, and by the time Rameses died, a bankrupt and disappointed man, almost the whole of the Sahara Forest [*sic.*] had been stripped of trees in this futile attempt to soften the geometrical harshness of his new buildings." (The contributor to the *Journal* sent a photograph of a section of Egyptian hieroglyphics illustrating the planting of trees.)

Yet even during the latter part of the eighteenth century it became

o

practicable to move quite large trees with the aid of specially built two-wheeled trailers, supplemented by large gangs of men labouring for small wages who prepared and dug around the root systems gingerly. The method became perfected by the incomparable Capability Brown, and was similarly used by Sir Henry Steuart of Allanton, whose treatise on the transplanting of large trees may be found in *The Planter's Guide*, 1828. Sir Henry elevated the art from a rather barbaric practice to one which took into account all the needs and requirements of the living tree.

Those principles are still adhered to today; the preparation of the roots of the trees by stages, the encouragement of a growing fibrous root system before removal, followed by the careful transportation and gentle housing of the protected roots in its new home. Trees growing in dense clumps which were selected for moving were first isolated by thinning the surrounding crop, so that they would adapt over the years to eventual open positions. By today's middling standards of transplanting medium-sized trees with all the technological know-how available, the accomplishments of the nineteenth-century tree-movers were gargantuan. In particular, William Barron, one-time head gardener to the Earl of Harrington of Elvaston Castle, Derbyshire, achieved much distinction for his high percentage of success in moving very large trees during the latter half of the century. The transplanted yew in the churchyard at Buckland-in-Dover, Kent, is perhaps his most famous living monument.

The Buckland Yew was stationed very close to the west end of St. Andrew's Parish Church, and according to Loudon and an account given of it by the Rev. W. T. Bree in the 1850s it was shattered by lightning in the eighteenth century at the same time as the church steeple rising above it. Descriptions of the tree some time after the event are little short of horrific: "Dead portions of the tree seem to evince a disposition to slough out, like fragments of carious bone separating from the flesh, but they are kept in position by the living wood lapping over it and clasping them firmly. The encasing of the old dead wood of the rotting tree by that of more modern formation is well displayed, and in one part of the southern limb the mortified is completely enclosed by the living. The trunk twists and interlaces, suggesting the idea that it has been ripped open, exposing to view its very entrails. A fanciful resemblance to some anatomical preparation of an animal trunk, of which the viscera are displayed and preserved entire."

Although there is no reliable means of proving it, the yew is reputed to be over a thousand years old, ante-dating the Norman conquest. Whatever the age, condition and value of the tree at the time of the decision to extend the west end of the church in 1878, there were many who objected to its removal, and alternative suggestions were thrashed out: the chancel could have been pulled down and rebuilt 20 ft. further eastwards and a new crossing inserted, or another aisle could have been built on the south side. The wrangling went on for several years, but at the end of 1879 William Barron, then self-employed as Barron & Son of Barrowash, Derby, was asked to travel to Buckland to give his opinion of the likelihood of a successful transferring of the tree to another site in the churchyard, in order that the western extension of the church (the most popular decision) could be built. He came, and unhesitatingly gave it as his opinion that the tree could be moved and that it would continue to flourish.

Barron fixed the best time for such a delicate operation as being the month of February. An agreement was reached, the treeman insisting that it would be necessary to limit the number of spectators who might flock to the churchyard to see such a wonderful sight. Accordingly a decision was made to close the churchyard during the end of February 1880, but with the corollary that when all was ready for the actual removal of the tree the public would be admitted by ticket at a charge of two shillings and sixpence each! The undertaking excited universal interest and attracted the press and many writers to record the success or failure of such a controversial venture. Barron described other large trees he had moved as "chickens compared to the Buckland Yew", but he remained undaunted.

The operations started on February 24th, by digging a trench on all sides of the root 4 ft. wide and leaving a large central block of earth 18 ft. long by 16 ft. broad. The trench was finally 5 ft. deep and a long cutting was made from the old site to the proposed new one, 62 ft. to the west, forming a gradual ramp to within a foot of the surface. The large block of earth around the root system was then tightly bound on all four sides with planks of timber held together with chains, straw being inserted between the timber and earth for the purpose of binding the whole. As soon as all was ready, the gang of men began tunnelling under the tree, making four "drifts" from back to front, and into these were placed four huge blocks of timber between which were inserted strong battens. Between the battens and the blocks rollers were set. The earth was then cut away between the baulks of timbers, leaving the whole mass of roots and tree, estimated to weigh fifty-five tons, resting on the rollers. The horizontal bough was propped by heavy timbers and then anchored on to a timber-dray. Above the place where the tree was to be rehoused three wind-lasses or crabs, such as were used for hauling the bathing-machines of the time, were erected, and from them chains and blocks were fastened to a plank bolted on to the front of the baulks under the tree.

Unfortunately, as soon as the vital part of the operation began, the chains snapped under the strain one after another. Stronger tackle was procured, and at last, on Wednesday, March 3rd, at about 5 pm, after eight days of Herculean labour, the tree began to move. Darkness set in and the work was suspended. Next day, with almost imperceptible motion, the huge mass travelled forward with many a stoppage and hitch, but before dusk it arrived within a yard of its destination. The last yard was quickly covered on the morning of March 5th and the indomitable Mr. Barron was vindicated.

Before the work of unpacking the roots began, photographs were taken of the scene and the conglomeration of bits and pieces enveloping the base of the tree. Then turves were packed between the baulks: powerful jacks raised the latter from their positions and the rollers were extracted. The spaces left were again stocked with good topsoil and turves, and the whole root then covered up with soil to a proper level, with a little extra to allow for settlement.

The undertaking had had its crises and surprises. At the first movement of the tree, a rumbling sound was heard and a brick vault close against the trunk caved in, taking with it a large chunk of the block of earth attached to the tree. Such a mishap would have depressed most people, but Barron rose to the occasion. Within an hour he had constructed a support for the side of the root which might have split and so ruined the operation. Afterwards, Barron admitted he had feared the tree might split asunder about his ears, but to his great credit and to the disappointment of the cynics and sceptics the ancient tree held together. The cost of the project has never been published in detail, but thanks to the acumen of the promoters in insisting upon a ticket admission for the general public, supplemented by other proceeds of the publicity and reporting, the "great cost" was easily defrayed, with possibly a bonus for the church extensions. The latter were duly carried out in 1880 at an estimated cost of £1,862. And, despite the buffetings of the 1970 blizzard, the yew still surveys the scene as of old—inscrutably.

Chapter Ten

————————∞∞∞∞OQOOOO∞∞∞————————

Past, Present and Future

The green garment of these islands having been ripped, patched and re-tailored endlessly throughout the centuries, first by invaders and settlers, then by the quirky moods and necessities or indulgences of peasant, priest, feudal king or dilettante landowner was, from the early nineteenth century onward, succeeded by a reaction that re-wove it into a great variety of newly discovered trees from the rest of the world. A new and enterprising hobby of plant and seed collection became the vogue, sponsored by various societies and the already established botanic gardens. The West North American outback became a veritable wild arboretum from which tenacious explorers extracted the seeds and saplings of impressive "new" trees, mostly conifers. Adventurous nurserymen wandered dangerously the length of the Pacific coast from Alaska down to the southern border of Mexico, often risking attack from hostile natives and suffering extremes of climate.

The names of these men, some of whom never returned, after being responsible for despatching the material they discovered to the home-land, still grace the titled of the specimens they sent. Douglas Fir, Jeffrey's Pine, Veitch's Fir and Lobb's Thuya are a few which have been allocated an appropriate Linnaean classification. The discovery of every such tree must have had a history and romance of its own, which in some cases has been documented. By the middle of the nineteenth century, when communications were revolutionized by the advent of the steamship and railways, China, and eventually Japan, were also to contribute to our increasing collections of plants and trees.

To describe the comings and goings of men and trees from all quarters of the globe, both in the last two centuries and in the beginning of the present one, cannot fully be dealt with here. Of the hundreds of species which found their way into our gardens, nurseries and arboreta, only a brief list is given in Appendix I, together with the native trees of the British Isles and their further distribution in other parts of Europe and Asia.

The quest for exotic trees resulted firstly in trial plantings in this country for experimental as well as ornamental purposes, but, as it became clear that many of the introductions would grow as well here as in their native climates, the commercial advantages of growing them were not ignored. During Victorian times three important organizations were inaugurated to lay the foundation for the further study of both seed collection and new forestry practices. These were: the Oregon Association, a small group of Scotsmen with interests in the potential commercial harvest of North American forests; the Royal Scottish Forestry Society, and the Royal Forestry Society of England, Wales and Northern Ireland.

The last named was established at a meeting in Hexham Town Hall, Northumberland, in 1882, under the title of the English Arboricultural Society; its members consisted of a handful of enthusiastic foresters who foresaw changes to come in timber-growing policies and the need for far-sighted plans if our woodlands were to remain an economic asset. The Society initiated examinations for woodmen and foresters as early as 1895, and the correspondence between professionals, together with the publishing of papers, became part of the "Transactions". The landowners and administrators of the timber plantations of those days had for some time chiefly been using larch, spruce and Scots Pine in their plantations, these conifers often being mixed with suitable hardwoods as pioneer species to assist the latter to establish. Sometimes the conifers would be the sole crop, either of one species or mixed. The conservative emphasis was, however, still on growing broadleaved trees, the conifers perhaps being removed as soon as the main crop had made headway, to be used as small timber or for general use on the estates.

The time-honoured methods for building up the resources of home timber ostensibly for commercial and private use were not completely adequate or did not produce sufficient stocks of trees, as was demonstrated by the overwhelming demands of the First World War, a catastrophe which depleted the woods considerably and meant importing large quantities of vital material at great cost and hazard. After the Armistice, the Government passed an act recommending a national policy for forests. The Forestry Commission was formed, its terms of reference being to ensure that a constant supply of timber would be available for the nation in the future. The process of planting available marginal land, and the re-furbishing of badly-gapped old forests began, only to be thwarted in midstream by the Second World War. The dauntless Commission continued as best it could, often under financial stress and bedevilled by the dictates of successive governments. New forests were created, hillsides and braes practically devoid of topsoil became peppered with the ubiquitous green dots of conifers forming new and often aesthetically disliked chequerboard designs in the old landscapes of the highlands and the downs.

Some existing private woodlands were purchased by the Commission in the hope of restoring them or replanting them with fast-growing commercially productive trees—thuya, Sitka and Norway spruce, hemlock and fir, pine and larch, and, it must be said, a good deal of oak and beech where better soils were available. Birch was commonly established between the blocks of conifers as a precaution against the spread of fire. The thinnings of these plantations are sold from time to time, the finest trees being left to mature as the final crop, which would not, in the main, be realized for about eighty years after planting. Small returns are coming in all the time now, and the national estate is beginning to enjoy a little dividend from its investment.

In England and Scotland today a lament can be heard from the conservationists who campaign vigorously against the supplanting of old oak and beech woods by "dark satanic poles"—which, the computer decides, are more "viable" investments on the land available. The ecologists among these dissenters also point out that the indigenous broadleaved trees support the greatest number of insect species most beneficial to the natural balance of woodland life. One hypothesis is that the relative number of insect species associated with trees reflects the varying abundance of those trees in particular countries throughout geological eras. This means that the native species of tree would have the most insects relying on them, and the more recently introduced or naturalized the fewest. Appendix V, which comprised part of a paper given by T. R. E. Southwood of the Department of Zoology, Imperial College, London, shows the comparative series of the numbers of insect species on various deciduous and coniferous trees in Britain and European Russia. It is uniquely interesting since it mirrors not only the periods of comparative indigenousness of the various tree species but also the passage of time since the introduction of alien species.

In turn the ornithologists and mycologists fear for the extinction of their subjects from the losses of the great oak and beech woods. All the marvellous balance of Nature evolved so painstakingly yet prodigally throughout the Quaternary period would be destroyed, they say; even the armies of bacteria in the rich forest floor would be dispersed and so eventually adversely and irrevocably affect the texture of life, both for man and beast. There are those who argue that the wholesale felling of established forests of hardwoods must inevitably increase the risk of flooding, since rainfall would not be intercepted and retarded by the foliage or branches of trees, and would run off the ground too quickly, causing sudden flooding to streams and rivers and, incidentally, carrying off a good deal of irrecoverable topsoil with it. On level forest ground denuded by the axe, rainwater would cause a stagnant swamp, for there would be no natural humus of the forest floor to absorb and retain it. At worst, all these enlightened arguments point to soil erosion—the nightmare of "progressive" agriculture, the disappearance of many species of flora and fauna, disease affecting all life, and eventual shortage of food.

Before it is asserted that such calamities could not occur in these islands because of our still considerable heritage of trees, it would be well to reflect on the experiences of other lands once well forested. As late as 1938, at Kopuawhara, in New Zealand, a great wall of water swept down the river, overwhelming the occupants of a camp, wiping out cattle, sheep, destroying bridges, farms and homes. The indiscriminate removal of a hillside forest nearby was the cause. When the Missouri flooded in 1937, it carried away nearly 9,000,000 tons of topsoil in a single day, as a direct result of intensive cultivation and widespread tree-felling over many years. The land became barren and useless.

So let us remember that our own tree cover is little more than six per cent, and however much the plans of the Forestry Commission and the private woodland owners may clash with the views of the aesthetes and bird-watchers, we must temper our interests with the sober fact that trees ensure our well-being and prosperity as well as being a pleasurable amenity.

No less a threat to a balanced environment is that created by our expanding population and its affluent activities of work and leisure forever insisting on bigger and better motorways, car-parks, housing estates, sports facilities, etc. Let us bear in mind also the pollution caused by the Moloch of industry, remorselessly poisoning the air we breathe, our water supplies and the good earth we live by. It is calculated that during the next twenty years one new town for every 70,000 persons will have to be built every few months if we are all to be housed adequately. The computers have calculated that to offset the past and present loss of trees and topsoil, an additional 20,000,000 trees will have to be planted to ensure a tolerable existence for us all. The machine does not recommend what species of trees these should be. The choice will have to be a rational one, for it is too evident already that there is an obsession for planting cherries, sorbus varieties, and others of merely ornamental and shortlived characteristics which only serve to emphasize a suburban ethos. Space will be all-important if the larger varieties are to be planted, as they will require spreading-room and a water catchment area to suit their sizes. One big tree is worth a dozen small ones, and the hybrid fancies of the nurserymen, "tailored trees" as they are often called, only conjure up an Orwellian irony in face of our urgent needs. Fortunately, our mentors are awakening from the nightmares of past errors to recognize the rôle of trees in our destinies and to take steps to further conservation of what remains by more enlightened planning and renewal.

There are other schemes afoot, however, by which it is hoped to create wind barriers of hardy trees, not entirely suited to our natural scene, in strategic positions on open land. Praiseworthy as this may be, such types of planting would lack the virtues of the homely hedgerow we know, for the reasons already given.

The hedgerows of the British Isles, the broadleaved woodlands of the estates, the remaining natural wholeness of the old forests, and the remnants of the old Scottish pine forests are therefore all under pressure from our expanding population in one form or another, so alarmingly accelerated since the earliest inhabitants made their first clearings. Another aspect of their disappearance is the question of their importance to our future well-being and health. There was once a theory that the process of leaf photosynthesis purified the atmosphere, but it has now been discounted. Yet it is an obvious truism that the air in forests and parks is cleaner than in dust-laden streets. Blocks of trees act as filters, trapping dirt and impurities, and for this reason a screen of trees to windward is beneficial. The same benefits of hedgerows to cattle and other stock might be paralleled by those given to us humans by nearby trees, the most obvious being the braking of cold winds, and as a guard against severe frosts. By their need for water, trees depress the water table which would otherwise cause health troubles. It might seem paradoxical, perhaps, to add that trees also raise and contain the water table and thus prevent soil erosion. Many deserts bear witness to this. The soil of forest floors contains little albuminoid matter or salts suitable for harmful bacterial growth, the humus thus produced by tree litter being antagonistic to pathogenic bacteria, destroying them by micorrhyzal processes.

Most sanatoria are built either among trees or planted up with trees at the building stage. The effects of such an environment can only have beneficial effects on patients.

The importance of the amenity tree is little more than psychological, especially in towns, although it is surprising how many birds are attracted to them. But the overall effects of future vast new developments on virgin or agricultural land, where many trees may have to be removed, may threaten the natural order of rainfall or climate. Water tables may fall over wide areas, due to the dam of building foundations and roadways which divert gravitational drainage and contribute to the loss of absorbent catchment areas. Further results can be trees dying from thirst, especially older specimens whose roots are unable to seek water sources.

Another distinctive threat comes from the plough. Modern farm machinery exists to produce more and more short-term crops for its progressively-minded masters. What is more the latter can see no productivity in hedgerows. Thanks to modern plant hire, it takes little time to demolish these troublesome obstructions and the accompanying large trees growing from them. The elms, oaks and ashes of the old farmlands form the principal panorama of the countryside of Britain. They are slowly becoming fewer in number. One quarter of the total standing volume of timber in Britain now is in the hedgerows, and it is probably the tree group which makes the highest impact aesthetically.

To the tourist industry the hedgerow tree of Britain is a priceless asset. It is typical of England, at least Shakespeare's England, and not least the nostalgia of the exile or the descendants of many a pioneering immigrant. To drive through England's countryside is like driving towards a distant forest which one never reaches. The bounds of the forest recede as they are seen, while its attainment dissolves into a pattern of hedgerow trees. Admirers of our landscape claim it is the ideal they ought to emulate, and look at it as a kind of spontaneous genius, unwitting, perhaps, yet valid. Some agriculturists will argue that the removal of hedgerows merely takes us back to the landscape of the days before the enclosures. That argument is misleading. Before the enclosures, the open fields were bounded by a densely wooded countryside, and untouched wilderness teeming with microflora and microfauna.

The sober fact is that our farming soils are the direct result of the debris of old forests, hundreds of years of leaf-mould and decayed material. Those forests have so dwindled that their beneficial ecology is now minimal. There are other biological arguments to support the great importance of the hedgerow trees and hedges. Still air is necessary for the retention of warmth and moisture in the soil. Hedgerows protect crops and soil, not only from the cold but from the drying winds, which also encourage excessive transpiration in crops, resulting in the stunting of growth. Further, an unsheltered area discourages pollination by insects, whose flights are disturbed by winds. In East Anglia a complete revision of irrigation schemes may yet have to be carried out due to the removal of hedgerows.

Yet there is little sign that any lesson has been learnt—the hedges are not being replaced. It is an extraordinary state of affairs, when many countries in Europe are replanting hedges after experiencing loss of crops and fertility, to realize that this country is not yet following suit in the light of this latter-day wisdom. Hedgerows also supply shelter for both stock and those "policemen" of the fields, hedgehogs, weasels, polecats and birds, not to mention the vegetation, litter and weeds which grazing animals need to enhance their diet. The value of shade from hot sun needs no elaboration, nor does the advantage of restrictive "folding" of stock in progressive and controlled grazing.

The acceptance of hedgerow trees as important units in a well-conceived and all-embracing forestry management plan would ensure that the heritage will not be lost. Were farmers to be given the same management grants as the forestry fraternity, and advised freely on schemes to promote the growth of the "free" hardwoods of the field boundaries, then an encouraging start could be made. Selected saplings of ash, oak and elm are not hard to find within the miles of hedges still standing. They have only to be reprieved from the bill-hook and hedge-cutter and allowed to grow above the trimmed tops to be easily recognized by the most unintelligent hedger. The farm forest is one method which presents itself.

The particular claims that pine woods have a therapeutic value, and that exudations and emanations from the pine needles and resin have an antiseptic and germicidal quality were once taken seriously, but such theories have not been proved tenable. Yet who shall say that in some mysterious way inhaling of pine scented air does not have an invigorating effect? The context of a healthy soil and clean air should surely be beneficial to the human metabolism.

In these many related matters there are signs that public conscience is at last stirring. Perhaps new-found leisure is at last giving people time to think. Perhaps, too, a quarter of a century of comparative peace allied to the shedding of Empire and other outward distractions have helped in this most sensible introspection involving our happiness and environment. The urgency and the new enlightenment are here, and we need a second John Evelyn to teach and lead us.

But time is the chief remaining adversary. Unless we catch up with the balding face of Britain, our land will become a development desert. How soon after that will come the storm that will sweep away thousands of tons of topsoil from the tilled and parched farmland? Even as these words are written, the news of an area of desolation a mile wide by fourteen miles long is reported from the Wisbech area of Cambridgeshire following a freak storm.

The weakened branch needs to fall before the alert is sounded, lest the last tree should fall and the dying earth turn sour. For we can no longer, like our pastoral ancestors, fold up our tents and steal away when today's pastures are exhausted—there will be none in our tomorrows. A note of hope is that the United States, the world's most civilized nation despite or because of its social traumas, is now beginning to appreciate its great parks and forests to such a degree that exploitation and vandalism are replaced by caring, and the dust bowl that pricked the nation's conscience will never happen again.

It is a cliché that what America does today we copy a decade later. Let us hope that it is demonstrated in this context—and that we reduce the time interval.

Domesday Oak, Ashton Court, Bristol.

Appendix I

ORIGINS, HABITATS AND RECORDS OF INTRODUCTIONS OF FOREST AND GARDEN
TREES IN THE U.K. AND IRELAND

	Country of Origin	*Notes*
Alder (Common)	Indigenous, Europe and Western Asia, N. Africa	
Alder (Grey)	Europe	Rare in British Isles until 1782.
Ash (Common)	Indigenous	Common in Europe except far north. Parts of India.
Ash (Manna)	S. Europe and Asia Minor	Introduced by Dr. Uvedale in 1710.
Beech (Common)	Indigenous in England but not Scotland	Beech not common in Ireland until 1794. Place names taken from Beech: Buckingham, Bickleigh, Boking, Buxton.
Beech (Upright)	Original trees struck from cuttings of tree at Dawyck House, Peebleshire	Known as the Dawyck Beech.
Beech (Purple)	Hanleiter Forest, Sonderhausen, Thuringia, Germany. Forest of Darney in the Vosges	
Birch (Common)	Indigenous, Europe and Central and Northern Asia	
Birch (Silver)	Indigenous, Europe, N. and E. Asia	
Birch (Paper)	United States, parts of Canada	Introduced in 1750.
Box	Indigenous, Western Europe, Mediterranean regions, Caucasus and Persia	
Caucasian Wingnut	Persia and Armenia	Introduced about 1805.
Elm (Common)	Of doubtful origin. May be indigenous from trees in S.W. England	
False Acacia	United States E. of Rockies, Nova Scotia and Ontario	Introduced by Jean Robin in 1601 to France, and in 1624 to Britain.
Wild Cherry (Gean)	Indigenous. Most of Europe except parts of Spain, Italy and Russia	
Hornbeam	Indigenous in South of England, and most of Europe	

Horse Chestnut	South-eastern Europe	Introduced in 1615.
Horse Chestnut (Indian)	North-west Himalayas, India	Introduced in 1851.
Indian Bean Tree	Parts of Eastern United States, Florida and Georgia	Introduced in 1726 by Mark Catesby.
Hawthorn	Indigenous to parts of England, Europe, Asia Minor, Caucasus, Algeria, Morocco, Persia, Afghanistan, Himalayas	
Holly	Indigenous. Also Western and Southern Europe, Persia, China in various similar forms	
Honey Locust	Pennsylvania, Ontario, Michigan, Alabama, Mississippi	Introduced in 1700 by Bishop Compton.
Judas Tree	Mediterranean regions, Judea	Cultivated by Gerard about 1596.
Judas Tree (Canadian)	Parts of Canada down to Virginia, United States	Introduced in 1730.
Juniper (Common)	Indigenous, Northern Europe, Northern Asia, North America	
Juniper (Chinese)	China, Japan, Mongolia	Introduced in 1804 by William Kerr.
Laburnum	Central Europe	Introduced in 1596 by John Tradescant.
Lime (Common)	Probably a hybrid between the Large- and Small-Leaved Lime	Cultivated during 17th century.
Lime (Large-leaved)	Central and Southern Europe	Not indigenous to Britain. Introductory date uncertain.
Lime (Silver)	Bosnia, South-eastern Europe	Introduced in 1767.
Lime (Small-leaved)	Indigenous, also in Europe	
Maple (Ash-leaved, or Box-elder)	North America	Introduced in 1688.
Maple (Field)	Indigenous to England only. Becoming naturalized in Scotland	Very rare in Europe.
Maple (Norway)	Northern Europe, scattered throughout S.E. Europe	Introduced in 1683.
Maple (Sugar)	Eastern North America, Canada, Kansas, Texas	Introduced about 1740.
Monkey Puzzle	Chile, S. America	Introduced in 1795 by Archibald Menzies. The seeds were sown on board homebound ship

Monkey Puzzle		and the plants cultivated by Sir Joseph Banks. First five plants planted at Kew.
Mulberry (Black)	Eastern Asia	Introductory date about 1548, but evidence of earlier plantings in England. *Morat* was an Anglo-Saxon word, and a favourite drink of those times. Morus=Mulberry.
Mulberry (White)	China	Introduced in 1596.
Oak (Common)	Indigenous. Europe and parts of Asia	Two species: Pedunculate and Sessile.
Oak (Cork)	Mediterranean regions, Morocco, Algeria, Tunis	Introduced about 1700.
Oak (Holm)	Mediterranean regions, Morocco, Algeria, Tunis and Southern India, Asia	Introduced in 16th century. Thomas Cromwell reputed to have destroyed certain holm oaks at Dissolution.
Oak (Pin)	Eastern United States	Introduced about 1800 by Messrs. Fraser.
Oak (Red)	Eastern Canada and United States	Introduced about 1739 by Phillip Miller.
Oak (Scarlet)	Quebec, Maine, Nova Scotia, and Pennsylvania	Introduced in 1690.
Oak (Turkey)	Southern Europe, Asia Minor, Syria, Italy and the Doubs Department of France, Hungary	Introduced between 1738 and 1748.
Palm (Chusan)	Eastern Asia	Chinese variety sent by Robert Fortune.
Paulownia	China, Korea and Japan	Introduced in 1838.
Plane (Oriental)	S.E. Europe, parts of India	Introduced about 1550.
Plane (Western)	Eastern United States	Introduced about 1634.
Poplar (Aspen)	Indigenous. Widely distributed over Europe, N. Africa, Siberia, China, Japan and Himalayas	
Poplar (Black)	Indigenous. Europe	
Poplar (Black Italian)	Hybrid cross between American and European tree	Uncertain source—probably France.
Poplar (Lombardy)	Banks of River Po, Italy	Originated as sport from a single tree. Introduced into France 1749, and into England at St. Osyth's Priory, Essex, in 1758 by the Earl of

Poplar (Lombardy)		Rochford, Ambassador in Turin.
Poplar (White)	Europe, scattered parts of North Africa.	Introduced about 1750.
Sophora	China and Chusan	Introduced in 1753 by James Gordon.
Strawberry Tree	Mediterranean regions, parts of N. Africa and S.W. Ireland	Introduced from Ireland in the middle of the 16th century.
Sweet Gum	Wide distribution in United States especially in South	Introduced in 1681 by John Banister.
Spanish Chestnut	Southern Europe, parts of North Africa and Persia	Probably introduced by Romans.
Sycamore	Parts of Europe, especially South-east	Found in Scotland in about 1480, also in N. Wales and Cheshire. Not indigenous but becoming naturalized.
Tree of Heaven	China	Introduced from China in 1751. Sent by Père d'Incarville from Nanking. (French Jesuit Missionary.)
Tulip Tree (American)	Ohio, Florida, United States, parts of Canada	John Tradescant obtained plants about middle of 17th century.
Tulip Tree (Chinese)	ʼChina	Introduced by E. Henry Wilson in 1901.
Walnut (Black)	Middle United States	Introduced in 1650.
Walnut (Common)	Greece, Albania, Persia and across to China	Probably introduced by Romans.
Willow (Crack)	Indigenous from Central Scotland southwards. Europe and Western Asia	Not indigenous in Ireland.
Willow (Goat)	Indigenous. Also Europe, Siberia, China, Korea	
Willow (Weeping)	China	Introduced by a Mr. Vernon in 1748.
Willow (White)	Indigenous except in far North of Scotland. Indigenous to Ireland	

CONIFERS (others)

Cedar (Algerian)	Algeria and Morocco	Introduced by Lord Somers about 1845.
Cedar (Deodar)	Himalayas, India	Introduced in 1831, by the Hon. W. Leslie Melville.

P

Cedar (Lebanon)	Lebanon, Syria, Asia Minor Tauric Mountains	Introduced between 1630 and 1645.
Cypress (Arizona)	Arizona	Introduced by Charles Sprague Sargent via the Arnold Arboretum, Boston, Mass. in 1882.
Cypress (Dawn)	Szechuan, China	Discovered in 1941. A deciduous conifer, not propagated in Britain until 1948.
Cypress (Lawson)	S.W. Oregon and N.W. California	Seed sent by William Murray from Sacramento River in 1854. Main supply of seed distributed by Lawson's Nursery, Edinburgh, 1855.
Cypress (Leyland)	Hybrid between Nootka Cypress and Monterey Cypress	Hybrids occurred in 1888, at Leighton Hall, Welshpool.
Cypress (Mediterranean)	Persia, Syria, Greece, Rhodes, Crete, Cyprus	Introduced about 1546, via Italy.
Cypress (Monterey)	Monterey, California, U.S.	Introduced in 1838 by A. B. Lambert.
Cypress (Sawara)	Central and S. Japan	Introduced in 1861 by J. G. Veitch.
Cypress (Sitka)	West Coast of United States, North of Oregon to Alaska	Discovered in 1793 by A. Menzies, seed not sent until 1850 via Botanic Garden at St. Petersburg.
Cypress (Swamp)	Florida, United States	Introduced from Florida by John Tradescant in 1640.
Fir (Caucasian)	Caucasus and Black Sea areas	Introduced in 1848.
Fir (Common Silver)	Central and Southern Europe	Introduced in 1600 by S. Newdigate.
Fir (Douglas)	Western North America	Discovered by Archibald Menzies in 1795; not introduced until 1827 by David Douglas.
Fir (Giant)	North-west coast of America	Introduced in 1831 by David Douglas.
Fir (Greek)	Cephalonia and scattered parts of Greece	Introduced in 1824 by Sir Charles Napier.
Fir (Japanese)	Shikoku and Kiusiu, Japan	Introduced in 1861 by J. G. Veitch.
Fir (Noble)	West Coast of North America	Introduced in 1831 by David Douglas.
Fir (Red)	Mt. Shasta and Trinity	Introduced in 1851 by

Fir (Red)	Mountains, Oregon, U.S.	John Jeffrey.
Fir (Spanish)	Southern Spain	Introduced in 1839 by Capt. Widdrington.
Gingko (Maidenhair)	China	Introduced in 1754 to Kew Gardens.
Hemlock (Eastern)	New Brunswick, Wisconsin, and south to Alabama	Introduced in 1736 by P. Collinson.
Hemlock (Western)	S.W. Alaska southwards down coast to California	Introduced in 1851 by J. Jeffrey.
Incense Cedar	Oregon, Sierra Nevada to Lower California	Introduced in 1853 by J. Jeffrey.
Japanese Cedar	China and Japan	Introduced in 1842 by Captain Sir Everard Home.
Larch (European)	Alps and Central Europe	Introduced about 1620.
Larch (Japanese)	Japan	Introduced in 1861 by J. G. Veitch from Nippon.
Pencil Cedar	Nova Scotia, New Brunswick, Georgia, Alabama, Dakota, Nebraska, Kansas, Tennessee	Cultivated in 1664 by John Evelyn.
Pine (Aleppo)	Mediterranean regions. North Africa	Introduced in 1683 by Bishop Compton.
Pine (Arolla)	Siberia and Central Europe	Introduced in 1746 by the Duke of Argyll.
Pine (Austrian)	Austria, Serbia, Hungary	Introduced in 1835 by Messrs. Lawson of Edinburgh.
Pine (Bhutan)	Himalayas and west to Afghanistan. East to Nepal	Introduced in 1823 by A. B. Lambert.
Pine (Corsican)	Southern Europe and parts of Western Asia	Introduced in 1759.
Pine (Lodgepole)	Columbia River, Washington State, U.S.	Discovered by David Douglas at Cape Disappointment in 1825, but not introduced until about 1852.
Pine (Macedonian)	Bulgaria, Macedonia	Introduced in 1864.
Pine (Maritime)	Mediterranean regions	Introduced at the turn of 17th century.
Pine (Mountain)	Central and S. Europe	Introduced in 1779 by John Blackburn of Warrington.
Pine (Monterey)	Monterey Peninsula. Parts of California, offshore isles	Introduced by David Douglas in 1833.
Pine (Stone)	Mediterranean regions, Spain and Portugal across to Asia Minor. Rare in N. Africa	Introduced in about 1540.

Pine (Scots)	Indigenous, especially in Scotland. N. Europe. Parts of Siberia to the Armour River	Place names: Cragguish, Altnaguish, Dalguise. Gaelic for pine = *gius*. Much more widely distributed in England and Ireland in the past.
Pine (Sugar)	Oregon and California, U.S.	Introduced by David Douglas in 1827.
Pine (Umbrella)	Japan	Introduced by J. G. Veitch in 1861.
Pine (Weymouth)	Eastern North America, East of Rocky Mountains, Canada, N. United States	Introduced about 1705 and planted at Longleat, Wilts.
Pine (Yellow)	British Columbia, Nevada, Utah, Colorado, Arizona, Texas	Introduced by David Douglas in 1827. Another variety of the tree introduced by John Jeffrey in 1853.
Redwood	Oregon, United States Monterey, California	Introduced in 1853 by Knight and Perry, through the courtesy of Dr. Fischer of the St. Petersburg Botanic Gardens. The claim that K. T. Hartweg sent seed home in 1846 is disputed.
Spruce (Brewer's)	Northern California and S.W. Oregon	Introduced in 1897 by courtesy of Arnold Arboretum, Boston, Mass.
Spruce (Common)	Pyrenees, Alps, Balkans, S. Germany, Scandinavia, Poland and Western Russia	Introduced in middle of 16th century.
Spruce (Hondo)	Fuji, Mitake, Ugo Chokarsan, Japan	Introduced by Mr. Maries, collector for J. G. Veitch in 1861.
Spruce (Serbian)	Drina Valley, Serbia, Bosnia, S.E. Europe	Introduced to Kew in 1889.
Spruce (Sitka)	West Coast of N. America, especially S.E. Alaska	Originally discovered by Archibald Menzies, but introduced by David Douglas in 1831.
Thuya (Giant)	Western N. America from Alaska down to California and Montana	Discovered by Née, who was aboard with Malaspina on voyage round the world between 1789 and 1794. Not introduced until 1853 by William Lobb.

Wellingtonia (Big Tree)	Western slopes of Sierra Nevada, California	Official introduction 1853 by J. D. Matthew and W. Lobb.
Yew (Common)	Indigenous. Europe, Asia and North Africa	Place names: Youghal= yew wood. Dromanure= yew hill. Glenure=yew-glen. Mayo=yew-field.
Yew (Irish)	Fermanagh, N. Ireland	Original Tree from which cuttings taken at Florence Court, 1780.

Biographical Notes to Appendix I

BANKS, SIR JOSEPH, F.R.S. (1743–1820). President of the Royal Society. Accompanied Captain Cook to the South Seas in 1768. Introduced many tropical plants.

BANISTER, JOHN. A missionary in Virginia, compiled a catalogue of American plants. Killed by falling from a rock while collecting material in 1692.

CATESBY, MARK (1679–1749). An enthusiastic naturalist who travelled in North America from 1712 to 1726. Master of the art of etching. Produced *Hortus Americanus Europaeus*, unpublished until 1767, and *Natural History of Carolina*.

COLLINSON, PETER (1693–1768). An amateur arboriculturist who introduced new plants to his garden at Mill Hill, near Hendon, London, and which is now a school. He was a successful draper and a Quaker.

COMPTON, HENRY (1632–1713). Bishop of London from 1675 to 1713. Collected plants from all over the world and his garden at Fulham contained the greatest number of specimens in England.

DOUGLAS, DAVID (1798–1834). Sent by Horticultural Society in 1824 to Western North America to collect plants. Born near Perth, he studied at the Botanic Garden in Glasgow and was recommended as a plant collector. Worked in Columbia River and California areas for several years, sending home new seeds. Killed in the Sandwich Islands by falling into a trap intended for wild bulls.

FORTUNE, ROBERT (1812–1880). A Scotsman, sent by Horticultural Association to China in 1843 to collect plants. Returned to England 1846. Appointed Curator of Chelsea Physic Garden; resigned 1848 to establish tea plants in India. Laid foundation of tea industry there.

GERARD, JOHN (1545–1607). Trained as surgeon and apothecary. In London he established a botanic garden at Holborn. Published his *Herbal* in 1597.

GORDON, JAMES. Nurseryman established at Mile End, London, 1750.

HARTWEG, K. T. (1812–1871). A German, sent by Horticultural Society to Mexico in 1836. Sent many half-hardy plants and several new conifers to Europe.

JEFFREY, JOHN (b. 1830). The Oregon Association, formed of Scots gentle-men, despatched Jeffrey to Western North America in 1850 to collect seed. Reached collecting grounds in 1851 and worked his way down to California. After two years of zealous exploration he quit his assignment and joined an expedition to explore Arizona, and completely disappeared.

KERR, WILLIAM. Sent from Kew to China in 1803.

MENZIES, ARCHIBALD (1754–1842). As a young man studied in Botanic Garden, Edinburgh, but obtained a diploma as a surgeon. Became assist-ant-surgeon in the Navy and accompanied George Vancouver, a British navigator under Captain Cook, on his celebrated voyage round the world. Discovered and collected many new plants.

MILLER, PHILLIP (1691–1771). Curator of Physic Garden at Chelsea.

NAPIER, GENERAL SIR CHARLES. Governor of Cephalonia.

ROBIN, JEAN and VESPASIAN. Gardener to Henry IV of France in 1601; his son was arborist to Louis XIII in the Jardin des Plantes in 1635.

SARGENT, CHARLES SPRAGUE. Collector for the Arnold Arboretum, Boston. Writer on the flora of North America and Japan.

TRADESCANT, JOHN. A Dutchman who came to England about the end of the sixteenth century. Gardener to Charles I (1629). Travelled in Eastern Europe and North Africa collecting plants. His son travelled in Virginia, North America, introducing many new specimens.

UVEDALE, DR. (1642–1722). A master of Enfield Grammar School about 1670. Devoted so much time to his garden that he was threatened with dismissal. He commissioned one of his ex-pupils to bring plants of Cedar of Lebanon from the Mountains of Lebanon. The Enfield Cedar was re-puted to have been such a specimen brought back in a carpet-bag. This tree was felled in 1927.

VEITCH, J. GOULD (1839–1870). Of the nursery business of the same name, he discovered and sent home new conifers. The Veitch nursery also sent William Lobb to North America in 1849, resulting in important dis-coveries. Lobb (1809–1863) had previously explored the flora of South America and collected many rare and new trees and plants. He died of paralysis in San Francisco.

WILSON, HENRY. Travelled in China for Messrs. Veitch and for Harvard University between 1899 and 1911. Introduced about 400 new species of plants.

Appendix II

SOME NOTABLE AND RECORD TREES OF THE BRITISH ISLES

Linnaean Classification	English Name	Height (as at 1970)	Girth	Location
Abies Alba	Common Silver Fir	151 ft.	12 ft. 2 in.	Powis Castle, Montgomerys.
Abies Grandis	Grand Fir	175 ft.	16 ft. 3 in.	Cairndow, Argyll.
		110 ft.	19 ft. 9 in.	Lochanhead, Dumfries.
Abies Nordmanniana	Caucasian Fir	134 ft.	14 ft. 3 in.	Powerscourt, Co. Wicklow
		90 ft.	15 ft. 1 in.	Powerscourt, Co. Wicklow
Abies Procera	Noble Fir	150 ft.	11 ft.	Duncraig Castle, Ross
		110 ft.	15 ft. 11 in.	Cortachy Castle, Angus
		105 ft.	16 ft. 5 in.	Blair Castle, Perths.
Araucaria Aracauna	Monkey Puzzle	87 ft.	11 ft. 11 in.	Endsleigh, Devon
		78 ft.	12 ft. 2 in.	Bicton, Devon
Cedrus Atlantica	Algerian Cedar	132 ft.	8 ft. 10 in.	Bowood, Wilts.
		87 ft.	21 ft.	Corsham Court, Wilts.
Cedrus Deodara	Deodar Cedar	103 ft.	18 ft. 2 in.	Bicton, Devon
		120 ft.	9 ft.	New Forest, Hants.
Cedrus Libani	Cedar of Lebanon	132 ft.	17 ft. 7 in.	Petworth House, Sussex
		85 ft.	26 ft. 11 in.	Blenheim Park, Oxford
Chamaecyparis Lawsoniana	Lawson Cypress	126 ft.	9 ft. 10 in.	Endsleigh, Devon
		102 ft.	12 ft. 8 in.	New Forest, Hants.
Chamaecyparis Nootkatensis	Nootka Cypress	97 ft.	9 ft. 5 in.	Eridge Park, Sussex
		93 ft.	10 ft.	Westonbirt, Glos.
Chamaecyparis Obtusa	Hinoki Cypress	83 ft.	8 ft. 5 in.	Bedgebury, Kent
Chamaecyparis Pisifera	Sawara Cypress	75 ft.	8 ft. 4 in.	Killerton, Devon
Cryptomeria Japonica		121 ft.	8 ft. 11 in.	Woodhouse, Devon
		92 ft.	17 ft. 5 in.	Boconnoc, Cornwall
Cupressocyparis Leylandii	Leyland Cypress	103 ft.	8 ft. 3 in.	Bicton, Devon
Cupressus Macrocarpa	Monterey Cypress	120 ft.	19 ft.	Tregothnan, Cornwall
		105 ft.	22 ft. 7 in.	Montacute House, Somerset
Cupressus Sempervirens	Italian Cypress	71 ft.	8 ft. 5 in.	Fota, Co. Cork
		63 ft.	12 ft. 2 in.	Nettlecombe, Somerset
Gingko Biloba	Maidenhair Tree	93 ft.	8 ft. 7 in.	Linton Park, Kent
		73 ft.	13 ft. 7 in.	Maesllwch, Radnors.

Linnaean Classification	English Name	Height as at 1970	Girth	Location
Juniperus Chinensis	Chinese Juniper	61 ft.	7 ft. 9 in.	Highnam Court, Glos.
Juniperus Virginiana	Pencil Cedar	53 ft.	8 ft.	Mamhead, Devon
		56 ft.	9 ft. 4 in.	Killerton, Devon
Larix Decidua	European Larch	43 ft.	10 ft. 4 in.	Ham Manor, Sussex
		142 ft.	9 ft. 7 in.	Parkhatch, Surrey
		111 ft.	18 ft. 6 in.	Monzie Castle, Perths.
Larix Eurolepsis	Hybrid Larch	101 ft.	6 ft.	Murthly Castle, Perths.
Larix Leptolepsis	Japanese Larch	65 ft.	7 ft. 6 in.	Dawyck, Peebles
		120 ft.	4 ft. 7 in.	Fonthill, Wilts.
		88 ft.	9 ft. 3 in.	Munches, Kirkcudbright.
Librocedrus Decurrens	Incense Cedar	117 ft.	9 ft. 6 in.	Oakley Park, Salop.
		110 ft.	12 ft. 5 in.	Lythe Park, Surrey
Metasequoia Glyptostroboides	Dawn Cypress	52 ft.	2 ft. 6 in.	Savill Gardens, Surrey
Picea Abies	Norway Spruce	140 ft.		Dunkeld, Perths.
		138 ft.	10 ft. 4 in.	Strathallan, Perths.
Picea Breweriana	Brewer's Spruce	48 ft.	4 ft. 8 in.	Vernon Holme, Kent
		38 ft.	6 ft.	Kilmacurragh, Co. Wicklow
Picea Omorika	Serbian Spruce	48 ft.	4 ft. 7 in.	Murthly Castle, Perths.
		54 ft.	6 ft. 1 in.	Headfort, Co. Meath
Picea Sitchensis	Sitka Spruce	164 ft.	15 ft. 7 in.	Murthly Castle, Perths.
Pinus Contorta	Lodgepole Pine	92 ft.	9 ft. 5 in.	Bodnant, Denbighs.
		88 ft.	9 ft. 10 in.	Bodnant, Denbighs.
Pinus Coulteri	Coulter's Pine	98 ft.	12 ft. 8 in.	Titley Court, Herefs.
Pinus Jeffreyi	Jeffrey's Pine	116 ft.	10 ft. 8 in.	Powerscourt, Co. Wicklow
Pinus Nigra Austriaca	Austrian Pine	112 ft.	11 ft. 7 in.	Petworth House, Sussex
		88 ft.	13 ft.	Bicton, Devon
Pinus Nigra Maritima	Corsican Pine	147 ft.	10 ft. 8 in.	Stanage Park, Radnors.
		125 ft.	14 ft. 3 in.	Arley Castle, Worcs.
Pinus Peuce	Macedonian Pine	91 ft.	11 ft. 5 in.	Stourhead, Wilts.
Pinus Pinaster	Maritime Pine	114 ft.	10 ft. 4 in.	Garnons, Herefs.
Pinus Pinea	Stone Pine	85 ft.	15 ft.	Sheffield Park, Sussex
		68 ft.	10 ft. 10 in.	Embley Park, Hants.

Linnaean Classification	English Name	Height	Girth (as at 1970)	Location
Pinus Radiata	Monterey Pine	144 ft.	12 ft. 2 in.	Cuffnells, Lyndhurst, Hants.
Pinus Sylvestris	Scots Pine	60 ft.	18 ft. 1 in.	Spye Park, Wilts.
Pinus Wallichiana	Bhutan Pine	105 ft.	5 ft. 10 in.	Redleaf, Kent
		85 ft.	11 ft. 8 in.	Pitt House, Devon
Pseudotsuga Menziesii	Douglas Fir	180 ft.	13 ft. 6 in.	Powis Castle, Montgomerys.
		105 ft.	23 ft. 3 in.	Eggesford, Devon
Scadiopitys Verticillata	Umbrella Pine	70 ft.	4 ft. 5 in.	Benenden, Kent
		45 ft.	5 ft. 4 in.	Pennyhill, Surrey
Sequoia Sempervirens	Coast Redwood	138 ft.	11 ft. 11 in.	Castlehill Estate, Instioge, Co. Kilkenny
		120 ft.	22 ft. 2 in.	Endsleigh, Devon
Sequoiadendron Giganteum	Wellingtonia	165 ft.	20 ft. 5 in.	Crichel Down, Dorset
		108 ft.	29 ft.	Broadlands, Kent
Taxodium Distichum	Swamp Cypress	117 ft.	14 ft. 9 in.	Close Walks, Cowdray, Sussex
Taxus Baccata	Yew	85 ft.	8 ft. 3 in.	Stonefield, Argylls.
Thuya Plicata	Western Red Cedar	135 ft.	12 ft. 8 in.	Belladrum, Inverness.
		107 ft.	15 ft. 9 in.	Leaton Knolls, Salop.
Tsuga Canadensis	Eastern Hemlock	109 ft.	9 ft. 5 in.	Benmore, Argylls.
Tsuga Heterophylla	Western Hemlock	157 ft.	11 ft.	Golden Grove, Carms.
		120 ft.	16 ft. 8 in.	
BROADLEAVED TREES				
Acer Campestre	Field Maple	78 ft.	8 ft. 8 in.	Mote Park, Maidstone, Kent
		60 ft.	12 ft. 11 in.	Fairlawne, Kent
Acer Dasycarpum	Silver-leafed Maple	100 ft.	8 ft. 5 in.	Westonbirt, Glos.
		90 ft.	12 ft. 2 in.	Tortworth, Glos.
Acer Griseum	Paper-bark Maple	45 ft.	2 ft. 9 in.	E. Bergholt Place, Suffolk
		40 ft.	5 ft. 3 in.	Hergest Croft, Herefords.
Acer Platanoides	Norway Maple	90 ft.	7 ft. 11 in.	Westonbirt, Glos.
		60 ft.	13 ft. 6 in.	Glendurgan, Cornwall
Acer Pseudoplatanus	Sycamore	112 ft.	21 ft. 5 in.	Drumlanrig, Castle, Dumfriess.
		85 ft.	22 ft. 4 in.	Birnam, Perths.

Linnaean Classification	English Name	Height	Girth as at 1970	Location
Aesculus Hippocastanum	Horse Chestnut	125 ft.	13 ft. 4 in.	Busbridge, Surrey
		125 ft.	19 ft. 2 in.	Petworth, Sussex
Ailanthus Altissima	Tree of Heaven	95 ft.	8 ft. 11 in.	Endsleigh, Devon
		82 ft.	12 ft. 2 in.	Selborne, Hants.
Alnus Glutinosa	Alder	85 ft.	12 ft. 4 in.	Sandling Park, Kent
Betula Verrucosa	Common Birch	102 ft.	7 ft. 9 in.	Woburn, Beds.
Castanea Sativa	Sweet Chestnut	58 ft.	11 ft. 7 in.	Worlingham, Suffolk
		118 ft.	11 ft. 9 in.	Godington Park, Kent
		64 ft.	27 ft. 4 in.	Carshalton, Surrey
Catalpa Bignonioides	Indian Bean	60 ft.	4 ft. 8 in.	Batsford Park, Glos.
Eucalyptus Globulus	Blue Gum	138 ft.	19 ft. 11 in.	Glengariff, Cork
		98 ft.	14 ft. 6 in.	Derreen, Co. Kerry
Fagus Sylvatica	Beech	142 ft. (Pollard)	8 ft. 9 in.	Yester House, E. Lothian
		100 ft.	12 ft. 11 in.	Burnham, Bucks.
var. atropunicea	Purple Beech	100 ft.	11 ft.	Brockhall Park, Northants.
		88 ft.	6 ft.	Linton Park, Kent
var. fastigiata	Dawyck Beech	82 ft.	12 ft. 7 in.	Wakehurst Place, Gask House, Perths.
var. laciniata	Fern-leaf Beech	95 ft.	10 ft. 8 in.	Drumlanrig Castle, Dumfriess.
var. pendula	Weeping Beech	148 ft.	10 ft. 6 in.	Duncombe Park, Yorks.
Fraxinus Excelsior	Ash	105 ft.	22 ft. 2 in.	Godinton Park, Kent
Juglans Nigra	Black Walnut	95 ft.	14 ft. 7 in.	Pusey House, Oxon.
		80 ft.	19 ft. 10 in.	Much Hadham, Herts.
Juglans Regia	Common Walnut	87 ft.	17 ft. 8 in.	Laverstoke Park, Pilton, Northants.
		60 ft.	21 ft. 6 in.	
Liquidambar Styraciflua	Sweet Gum	93 ft.		Kew, London
		74 ft.	9 ft. 9 in.	Escot, Devon
Liriodendron Tulipifera	Tulip Tree	115 ft.	19 ft. 1 in.	Taplow Court, Bucks.
Nothofagus Obliqua		98 ft.	6 ft. 9 in.	Bodnant, Denbighs.
		79 ft.	8 ft. 7 in.	Caerhayes Castle, Cornwall
Platanus Acerifolia	London Plane	125 ft.	21 ft.	Carshalton, Surrey
		114 ft.	26 ft. 4 in.	Ely Cathedral, Cambs.

Linnaean Classification	English Name	Height as at 1970	Girth	Location
Populus Canescens	Grey Poplar	120 ft.	16 ft. 6 in.	Marlfield, Tipperary
Populus Nigra	Black Poplar	126 ft.	9 ft. 5 in.	Peper Harrow, Surrey
var. italica	Lombardy Poplar	115 ft.		Holyport, Bucks.
		118 ft.		Marble Hill, Twickenham, Middx.
Populus Serotina	Black Italian Poplar	100 ft.	16 ft. 8 in.	Leighton, Montgomerys.
Populus Trichocarpa	Balsam Poplar	140 ft.	21 ft.	Fairlawne, Kent
Prunus Avium	Gean	120 ft.		Arley Castle, Worcs.
		102 ft.	8 ft. 4 in.	Woburn, Beds.
		55 ft.	14 ft. 9 in.	Studley Royal, Yorks.
Quercus Borealis	Red Oak	115 ft.		West Dean, Sussex
		100 ft.	19 ft. 8 in.	Cassiobury Park, Herts.
Quercus Cerris	Turkey Oak	128 ft.	23 ft. 5 in.	Knighthayes, Devon
		65 ft.	26 ft. 5 in.	Chertsey, Surrey
Quercus Coccinea	Scarlet Oak	85 ft.	7 ft. 7 in.	Tortworth, Glos.
		65 ft.	9 ft. 1 in.	Chiltley Place, Hants.
Quercus Ilex	Holm Oak	92 ft.	13 ft. 11 in.	Killerton, Devon
		80 ft.	17 ft.	Killerton, Devon
Quercus Robur	Common Oak	120 ft.	11 ft. 5 in.	Studley Royal, Yorks.
		(Pollard)	37 ft. 6 in.	"Majesty" Oak, Fredville Pk, Kent
		(Pollard)	39 ft. 8 in.	Bowthorp, Lincs.
Quercus Petraea	Sessile Oak	135 ft.	14 ft. 3 in.	Whitfield, Herefs.
		90 ft.	29 ft. 1 in.	Shobdon, Herefs.
Quercus Suber	Cork Oak	60 ft.	10 ft. 4 in.	Tregrehan, Cornwall
		56 ft.	14 ft. 7 in.	Sharpham House, Devon
Robinia Pseudoacacia	Locust Tree	89 ft.	9 ft. 8 in.	Kew, London
		75 ft.	16 ft. 8 in.	Frogmore, Berks.
Tilia Cordata	Small-leaf Lime	113 ft.	13 ft.	Oakley Park, Salop.
		(Pollard)	21 ft. 10 in.	Algakirk, Lincs.
Tilia Petiolaris	Silver Pendant Lime	107 ft.	10 ft. 3 in.	Strathfieldsaye, Hants.
Tilia Platyphyllos	Big-leaf Lime	104 ft.	12 ft. 6 in.	Embley Park, Hants.
		100 ft.	16 ft. 3 in.	Titley Court, Herefs.
Tilia Tomentosa	Silver Lime	90 ft.	12 ft. 9 in.	Tortworth Church, Glos.

Linnaean Classification	English Name	Height *as at 1970*	Girth	Location
Tilia Vulgaris	Common Lime	145 ft.	12 ft. 4 in.	Duncombe Park, Yorks.
		80 ft.	21 ft. 3 in.	Bramshill, Hants.
Ulmus Carpinifolia	Smooth-leaf Elm	118 ft.	10 ft. 10 in.	Kensington Gardens, London
var. cornubiensis	Cornish Elm	118 ft. (Pollard)	12 ft. 8 in.	Knightshayes, Devon
		20 ft.	2 in.	Enys, Cornwall
var. sarniensis	Wheatley Elm	121 ft.	11 ft. 9 in.	Wilton, Wilts. On A30
Ulmus Glabra	Wych Elm	125 ft.	12 ft. 6 in.	West Dean, Sussex
Ulmus Hollandica	Dutch Elm	80 ft.	20 ft. 4 in.	Tendring Hall, Essex
		111 ft.	16 ft. 2 in.	Saltram House, Devon
var. vegeta	Huntingdon Elm	88 ft.	14 ft. 10 in.	Kew, London
		110 ft.	11 ft. 8 in.	Oxford, Oxon.
Ulmus Procera	English Elm	90 ft.	17 ft. 4 in.	Westonbirt Village, Glos.
		122 ft.	19 ft. 4 in.	Youngsbury, Ware, Herts.
Zelkova Carpinifolia		30 ft.	27 ft. 10 in.	Carshalton, Surrey
		114 ft.	17 ft. 11 in.	Pitt House, Devon
		83 ft.	23 ft.	Croome Court, Worcs.
Pterocarya Fraxinus	Caucasian Wingnut	105 ft.	17 ft. 7 in.	Melbury Park, Dorset
ADDITIONAL CONIFERS				
Pinus Strobus	Weymouth Pine	128 ft.	8 ft. 5 in.	Puck Pits, New Forest, Hants.
		102 ft.	16 ft. 5 in.	Strathfieldsaye, Hants.
Pinus Radiata	Monterey Pine	140 ft.	12 ft. 2 in.	Cuffnells, Hants.
		80 ft.	21 ft. 9 in.	Bicton, Devon
Pinus Ponderosa	Western Yellow Pine	128 ft.	14 ft.	Powis Castle, Montgomys.

Appendix III

Many of these are on private property and written permission may have to be obtained beforehand before visiting. Some properties are occasionally open to the public, others are accessible only during summer months and notice is given of "open" times. A few are National Trust properties, but not always open to the public. The following codes apply:

† Occasional access at advertised times.

†† Usually open especially in summer months.

* No access without permission or prior arrangement.

(N.T.) National Trust.

ENGLAND

Woburn	Bedfordshire†
Frogmore	Berkshire†
Savill and Valley Gardens	Berkshire††
Windsor Great Park	Berkshire††
Bristol Zoo	City of Bristol††
Ashton Park	City of Bristol††
Dropmore, Burnham	Buckinghamshire†
Cambridge Botanic Gardens	Cambridge, Cambs.††
Boconnoc	Cornwall*
Caerhayes Castle	Cornwall†
Carclew	Cornwall*
Cotehele, Calstock	Cornwall (N.T.)
Penjerrick	Cornwall†
Tregothnan	Cornwall†
Muncaster Castle	Cumberland†
Chatsworth	Derbyshire††
Arlington Court, Lynton	Devon†
Bicton	Devon††
Dartington Hall	Devon†
Endsleigh	Devon*
Exeter University Campus and Halls of Residence	Devon†
Killerton	Devon††
Knightshayes	Devon†
Mamhead Park	Devon*
Poltimore Hospital	Devon*
Powderham Castle, Exeter	Devon†
Saltram House, Plympton	Devon†
Watcombe, Torquay	Devon†
Abbotsbury	Dorset††
Forde Abbey	Dorset†
Melbury Park	Dorset*

Minterne House	Dorset†
Audley End, nr. Saffron Walden	Essex††
Batsford Park, Batsford	Gloucestershire†
Highnam Court, Highnam	Gloucestershire†
Tortworth (Prison)	Gloucestershire*
Speech Ho. Arboretum, Forest of Dean, Coleford	Gloucestershire†† Forestry Commission
Stanway Park, Stanway	Gloucestershire†
Westonbirt Arboretum	Gloucestershire†† Forestry Commission
Bolderwood, Lymington	Hampshire††
Elvetham (I.C.I.)	Hampshire*
Exbury	Hampshire††
Herriard House, Herriard	Hampshire†
Highclere House	Hampshire*
Jermyn's Ho. Arboretum, Romsey (Hillier's)	Hampshire††
Laverstoke Park	Hampshire*
Osborne House, I.O.W.	Hampshire††
Pylewell House, Lymington	Hampshire†
Stratfieldsaye	Hampshire*
Croft Castle, Croft	Herefordshire†† (N.T.)
Eastnor Castle	Herefordshire††
Garnons, Mansel Gamage	Herefordshire†
Hergest Croft	Herefordshire††
Titley Court, Titley	Herefordshire*
Cassiobury Park, Watford	Hertfordshire††
West Lodge Park, Hadley Wood	Hertfordshire†† Hotel patrons
Bedgebury Pinetum	Kent†† Forestry Commission
Benenden Grange	Kent*
Benenden House (School)	Kent*
Cobham Hall, Cobham	Kent*
Linton Park, Linton	Kent†
Mote Park, Maidstone	Kent††
Scotney Castle, Lamberhurst	Kent††
Revesby Abbey, Revesby	Lincolnshire†
Brockesley Park	Lincolnshire†
Chiswick House	London†
Greenwich Park	London††
Holland Park	London††
Hyde Park and Kensington Gardens	London††
Kenwood, Highgate	London††
Kew Royal Botanic Gardens	London††
Marble Hill, Twickenham	London††
Osterley Park, Hounslow	London†† Trees grown from seeds or cuttings of historic trees
Ravensbury Park, Morden	London††
Syon House	London††

Waterlow Park, Highgate	London††
Holkham Hall	Norfolk†† Access half-days
Althorp, Brington	Northants.†
Alnick Castle	Northumberland*
Cragside, Rothbury	Northumberland†
Kyloe Woods	Northumberland*
Wallington Hall, Cambo	Northumberland†
Trent College, Nottingham	Nottinghamshire*
Blenheim Park, Woodstock	Oxon.††
University Parks, Oxford	Oxon.††
Bath Botanic Gardens	Somerset††
Dunster Woods, Dunster	Somerset†
Hinton House, Dinnington	Somerset*
Mells Park, Mells	Somerset*
Nettlecombe Court, Nettlecombe	Somerset*
Victoria Park, Bath	Somerset††
Sandon Park, Sandon	Staffordshire†
Trentham Park, Trentham	Staffordshire†
Bury St. Edmunds Abbey	Suffolk††
East Bergholt Place	Suffolk†
Claremont, Esher	Surrey* (N.T.)
Kitlands, Leith Hill	Surrey*
Knaphill Nursery, Woking	Surrey††
Moss's Wood, Leith Hill	Surrey††
Peper Harrow	Surrey*
Riverside, Richmond	Surrey†
Sunningdale Nursery	Surrey††
Winkworth	Surrey††
Wisley Arboretum, Wisley	Surrey†† Royal Horticultural Society
Borde Hill, Haywards Heath	Sussex†
Chiddingly	Sussex*
Highdown, Goring-by-Sea	Sussex††
Petworth House	Sussex†† (N.T.)
Sheffield Park, Fletching	Sussex†† (N.T.)
Wakehurst Place, Ardingly	Sussex†
Warnham Court, Warnham (G.L.C. School)	Sussex*
West Dean, Sussex	Sussex†
Corsham Court, Corsham	Wiltshire††
Bowood, Calne	Wiltshire*
Longleat, nr. Warminster	Wiltshire††
Stourhead	Wiltshire†† (N.T.)
Wilton House, Salisbury	Wiltshire††
Bramham Park, Bramham	Yorkshire†
Duncombe Park, Helmsley	Yorkshire††
Grantley Hall, Winksley	Yorkshire†
Fountains Abbey and Studley Royal, Ripon	Yorkshire††

WALES
Bodorgan, Anglesey	Wales†
Bodnant	Denbighshire†† afternoons
Hafodunos (School)	Denbighshire*
Roath Park, Cardiff	Glamorgan††
Powis Castle	Montgomeryshire††
Stanage Park	Radnorshire*

SCOTLAND
Benmore Younger Botanic Gardens	Argyllshire†
Stonefield	Argyllshire†
Strone, Cairndow	Argyllshire†
Culzean Castle	Ayrshire†
Brodick Castle	Bute† (N.T.)
Rossadhu	Dunbartonshire*
Edinburgh Royal Botanic Gardens	Edinburgh†
Smeaton House, E. Lothian	East Lothian*
Whittinghame	East Lothian* Forestry Commission and School
Yester House	East Lothian*
Hermitage, Inverness	Inverness††
Balladrum	Inverness*
Durris House	Kincardine†
Cairnsmore, Kirkcudbright	Kirkcudbrights.*
Glenlee Park	Kirkcudbrights.*
Kirkennan	Kirkcudbrights.*
Munches	Kirkcudbrights.*
Lee Park	Lanarkshire*
Oxenford Castle	Midlothianshire*
Gordon Castle	Morayshire†
Candor Castle	Nairn†
Kilrevoch Castle	Nairn*
Dawyck	Peebleshire†
Blair Castle	Perthshire†
Blair Drummond	Perthshire†
Dunkeld House	Perthshire†
Gask House	Perthshire*
Keir House	Perthshire*
Murthly Castle	Perthshire*
Taymouth Castle	Perthshire*
Strathallan	Perthshire*
Duncraig Castle	Ross and Cromarty*
Fairburn	Ross and Cromarty*
Skibo Castle	Sutherland*
Hopetoun House	West Lothian†
Castle Kennedy, Lochinch Castle	Wigtownshire††
Logan	Wigtownshire††

IRELAND

Adnagashel	Co. Cork†
Glengarriff (Ilnacullen)	Co. Cork†
Castlewellan	Co. Down†
Tullymore Park	Co. Down†
Botanic Gardens, Glasnevin	Dublin†
Ashburne House	Co. Kerry†
Muckross Abbey, Killarney	Co. Kerry††
Ashford Castle, Cong	Co. Mayo†
Birr Castle	Offaly†
Dunganstown	Co. Wexford†† Kennedy Memorial Park
Mt. Usher	Co. Wicklow†
Powerscourt	Co. Wicklow†

Appendix IV

A CATEGORIZED LIST OF FURTHER TREES, NOT DEALT WITH IN TEXT,
OF HISTORICAL AND BOTANICAL INTEREST

† Tree Lost

LANDMARKS

Stowe, Buckinghamshire	Two-mile-long avenue of elms from Buckingham–Brackley Road to Corinthian Arch, entrance to school.
Bostock Green, Davenham, Cheshire†	Bostock Oak. Centre of county.
Tresillian, Cornwall	Long avenue of holm oaks.
Badminton, Gloucestershire	Beeches and limes bounding estate. Fitzgerald and Duchess Oaks, both girthing approximately 27 ft.
Birdlip, Gloucestershire†	Foston's Ash. Landmark at fork of roads from Birdlip to Bisley. Inn of same name close by.
Cheltenham, Gloucestershire†	Maud's Elm. Famous elm of great girth now lost.
Lassington, Gloucestershire†	Lassington Oak was 600 years old, girthed 30 ft.
Painswick, Gloucestershire	Pollarded tree of 24 ft. girth.
Woodthorpe, Lincolnshire†	Oak reported to have borne leaves in 1938; girth 37 ft. Was a landmark to navigators on North Sea. Calculated to have been over 1,000 years old.

Bridgham, Norfolk†	Bridgham High Tree. A poplar planted to guide travellers on the heath.
Mile Oak, Tamworth, Staffordshire†	Mile Oak. Gave name to district.
Betchworth, Surrey	Beeches known as "Betchworth Clump".
Cobham, Surrey	Cedar of Lebanon at Pain's Hill once claimed to be tallest cedar in England.
Pear Tree Farm, Whitesmith, Lewes, Sussex	Pear tree of great girth; 300 years old.

LITERARY ASSOCIATIONS

Oaker Hill, Derbyshire	One of twin sycamores. Subject of Wordsworth's poem, "A Tradition of Oaker Hill".
Stinsford, Dorset	Yew tree adjacent to grave of Thomas Hardy.

WAR

Sloden Enclosure (New Forest), Hampshire	Clumps of yews, descendants of trees used for bow-making.
Walford, Herefordshire	Avenue of 23 lime trees. At the foot of each was the name of a soldier killed during Parliamentary Wars.
Hinckley, Leicestershire†	Tablet marks the site occupied by Captain Shenton's Oak. John Shenton, an officer of Charles I's army, hid in this tree to escape capture by Parliamentary forces in 1646.
Eaton Constantine, Shropshire†	Watch Oak; commemorated by an inscribed tablet fixed to the wall of a house nearby: "The Watch Oak, blown down in 1850". Tree used as a look-out for Cromwell's troops coming from Shrewsbury, and later to watch for coaches on this old highway from Shrewsbury.
Shelton Oak Priory, Shropshire†	Shelton Oak. Traditionally the tree which Owen Glendower climbed on July 21st, 1403, to watch the Battle of Shrewsbury. The claim has always been in dispute, as Glendower was supposed to have been at Carmarthen at the time. The priory was previously named Glendower's Cottage. Offspring acorn planted in 1884 in Shrewsbury Quarry.
Kempsey, Worcestershire†	Revolution Elms in churchyard. Several elms planted to mark accession of William and Mary. Planted in 1688 to commemorate the "Bloodless Revolution".

Meiklour, Perth, Scotland	Largest beech hedge in British Isles: 95 ft. high and 580 yds. long. Average girth of trees only 4 ft. Planted in 1745 by workmen who left to fight at the Battle of Culloden. They never returned.

CRIME AND PUNISHMENT

Lower Star Post, Buckinghamshire	Meeting place of two avenues in pine forest, once a haunt of highwaymen.
Came Down, Dorset†	Culliford Tree. Ancient Court Tree.
Alderton, Gloucestershire†	Dabb's Elm. Sheep stealer named Dabb hanged from tree.
Totteridge, Hertfordshire	Ancient Yew. Old Hundred Court meeting place.
Calderstones Park, Liverpool, Lancashire	Allerton Oak. Court Tree. Plaque: "A thousand years ago Allerton did not possess a courthouse, and it is believed that the sitting of the Hundred Court was held under the spreading branches of the tree."
Brigstock, Northamptonshire†	Bocase Tree. Stone commemorates the tree which was Forest Court meeting place.

RELIGION

Appleton, Cheshire	Descendant of Glastonbury Thorn, q.v., planted by Adam de Dutton in 12th century. Practice of "Barning the Thorn" used to be on June 29th. Tree was "dressed".
Eastham (St. Mary's), Cheshire	Ancient yew reputed to be 1,300 years old. Saxon font nearby. Original early Christian preaching site.
Lorton, Cumberland	Wesley's Yew. John Wesley preached under this tree on May 28th, 1725.
Avington, Hampshire†	Gospel Oak; fell about 1893. Last bounds beaten here in 1880. Stood near Hempage Wood. Reported to have been used by St. Augustine in 6th century as a preaching tree.
South Hayling (St. Mary's), Hampshire	Ancient Yew, reputed to be over 1,000 years old. Early Christian shrine.
Blackburn, Gib Lane, Livesay, Lancashire†	Ash in poor condition known as Crucifixion Tree. Triple-trunked, suggesting an anchor; supposed to symbolize the Trinity, Christ and the Two Robbers. Between 100–150 years old.
Preen, Shropshire	In churchyard. Hollow, will hold 21 men

Preen, Shropshire	standing upright. Estimated 1,000 years old. Reported to be grown on ancient Druidical site.
Shawbury, Shropshire	Oak standing at High Ercall. Age unknown. Used by Methodists about 150 years ago as preaching site. The practice was discontinued in 1854. Known as a Gospel Oak locally. Methodists were forbidden to hold services in their homes by the local landowner, and, land not being available for a chapel, services were conducted on the land beneath the tree.
Combe, Suffolk	Gospel Oak; dead trunk still stands in Holy Oak farmyard, near church.
Lavenham, Suffolk†	Gospel Oak. Burned down or struck by lightning during 1944.
Norbury Park (Mickleham), Surrey	Group of ancient yews called Druids' Grove, two of which are over 20 ft. in circumference.
Abberley, Worcestershire†	Oak marked spot on St. Augustine's route and where he had meetings with the Celts.
Alfrick, Worcestershire†	Another oak reputed to be a preaching site of St. Augustine.
Guarlford, Worcestershire†	Friar's Elm, on Guarlford Road, A440, on side of common. Dead stump 40 ft. in girth with 30 ft. tree growing from base. Here a priest distributed bread to the poor. About fifty years ago Vicar would head a procession on Good Friday from church to tree. (Spiked fence erected around continuity tree.)
Lapworth, Worcestershire†	Originally a Gospel Oak until 1958, this was the gathering place for the sale of pigs on the third Thursday in March.
Sedburgh, Yorkshire	George Fox (1624–91), founder of Quakers, preached under this yew.
Ystradgynlais, Brecknock, Wales	Yew kept pruned well below the belfry as there is a prophecy that "when the smallest yew in the churchyard grows as high as the belfry the end of the world will come".
Penpont, Brecon, Wales	Circle of yews on site of an older circle of yews (now gone). Many churches in England and Wales have similar circular designs so that the "devil cannot enter at any corner". Churchyards often circular in construction echoing the stone circle, tumulus or barrow.

HEALING AND THE OCCULT

St. Mellion, Cornwall† — Amy Tree. Oak which stood on an island at cross-roads. Said to have been originally a stake thrust through the heart of a suicide named Amy, buried on same site of his death.

ROYAL ASSOCIATIONS

Lullingstone, Kent — Mulberries used for silkworms to provide Elizabeth II's coronation robes.

FAMOUS PEOPLE

Beaconsfield, Buckinghamshire† — Large walnut tree near tomb of Edmund Waller, 17th-century poet.

Doveridge, Derbyshire — Yew reputed to be 1,400 years old. Tradition that Robin Hood was betrothed to Maid Marian under tree.

Mamhead, Devon — Large yew in churchyard. James Boswell took an oath under tree never to get drunk again. Promise not kept, as "a little wine hurried him on too much".

Meopham, Kent — Two mulberries planted by John Tradescant, gardener to Charles I.

Castle Donnington, Leicestershire† — Chaucer's Oak. Was 44 ft. girth. Chaucer stayed near here with his patron, the Duke of Lancaster, and wrote under tree.

15, Gray's Inn Rd., London — Reputed to have been planted by Sir Francis Bacon. A Catalpa tree.

Keats's Grove, London, N.W.3 — Mulberry in Keats's garden, 250 years old.

Dryden's Oak, Blakesley, Northamptonshire† — Dryden's Oak at home of poet for a time.

Stowmarket, Suffolk — Mulberry planted by Milton at his home. Threatened recently by demolition.

Tillington, Sussex — "Bishop's Clump". Planted at East Lavington by Samuel Wilberforce.

West Grinstead Park, Sussex† — Pope's Oak. Vestige only remains. The poet wrote "The Rape of the Lock" under it while staying with Caryll family. Remains standing in National Stud land.

Lowther Park, Westmorland — Trees planted by Kaiser Wilhelm.

Kirkleatham, Yorkshire† — Kirkleatham Oak. Planted to commemorate bravery of Tom Brown at Battle of Dettingen.

MISCELLANEA

Childrey Rectory, Berkshire — Cedar of Lebanon planted in 1646 by Dr. Edward Pococke, Rector, and Professor of Hebrew and Arabic at Oxford.

Mapledurham House, Berkshire	Horse chestnut with other tree species growing inside area of layered branches.
Wokingham, Berkshire	Mulberries planted in 17th century to assist local silk industry.
Dropmore, Buckinghamshire	Magnificent arboretum including long avenue of cedars and a descendant of the Royal Oak from Boscobel.
Ely (Palace School), Cambridgeshire	Large London plane claimed to be 290 years old.
Hildersham, Cambridgeshire	Large walnut on village green near church.
Marton, Cheshire†	Ancient oak split into three parts. Reputed to have been 1,000 years old and the largest oak in Cheshire.
Falmouth, Cornwall	Banana trees seen growing in the open.
Pencarrow, Cornwall†	First Monkey Puzzle tree, so named by a visitor to the Molesworth property here.
St. Dominic, Cornwall†	Hunter's Oak. Branches pointed four ways. Coins planted under replacement oak. Tree so named because hounds met here.
Trematon, Cornwall†	Granny's Tree. Was familiar landmark on Burraton–Saltash Road, at junction of three roads. Known as Jousting Place. Tree supposed to have been planted over a general killed in an unknown war. Smugglers made their way to Granny's Tree to deposit contraband in nearby tunnel.
Canford, Dorset	Mungay Oak. Sweet Chestnut of 40 ft. girth.
Colchester Castle, Essex	Sycamore on top of castle to commemorate Battle of Waterloo.
Epping Forest, Essex	The Grimston Oak, largest oak remaining in the forest. Commemorates G. S. Grimston, Sussex cricketer and one-time forest verderer.
Hempstead, Essex†	A gigantic oak measuring 53 ft. in circumference at its slimmest point on the trunk. Tree lost about 1870. The acorns from it were sold for £2 per year.
St. Osyth Priory, Essex	Remains of first Lombardy poplar introduced in 1758.
Woodford Green, Essex	Another Cedar of Lebanon in the grounds of Hart's Hospital; planted 1641 and claimed as first planting of species. Trunk mutilated but tree otherwise in excellent condition.
Cirencester and Kingscote, Gloucestershire	Best example of beech trees in British Isles.

Coleford, Gloucestershire	Speech House. Two-mile avenue of spruce trees. Very large old hollies. Oak planted to commemorate Prince Consort (from the seed of Panshanger Oak, Panshanger, Herts., *q.v.*).
Newland, Gloucestershire†	Newland Oak. Vestige only. Was largest oak in British Isles until 1956. 46 ft. girth.
Standish, Gloucestershire	In hospital grounds. Two ancient oaks of great girth, vestiges of Kingswood Forest.
Burley, Hampshire†	Twelve Apostles. Vestiges only of large oaks. Also Ridley Wood, beeches unlawfully pollarded in 1571 by tenant of enclosure.
Chilton Condover, Hampshire	Yew avenue 40 ft. wide and half a mile long; 350 years old.
Eversley, Hampshire	Scots Pines originating about 1680.
Lyndhurst, Hampshire	Bolderwood. King and Queen Oaks. Indian Cedar planted in 1861, now over 120 ft. in height. Natural regeneration of Douglas Fir. Plantation of Indian Cedars. Fine 156 ft. Wellingtonia Gigantea and a superb Noble fir.
Eyeworth Wood (New Forest), Hampshire	Queen Beech. Reached by foot-track from Cadnam–Fordingbridge Road.
Mark Ash Wood, Hampshire	Queen Beech, 18 ft. 1 in. girth at 4 ft.
Mark Ash Wood (New Forest), Hampshire	Knightwood Oak, 22 ft. girth.
Southampton Common, Hampshire†	Three great common elms felled as a safety precaution: Faith, Hope and Charity. The largest was Charity.
Twyford, Hampshire	Yew clipped in umbrella shape.
Eardiston, Herefordshire	Remains of elm trunk 25 ft. circumference.
Eastnor Castle, Herefordshire	Several specimens of Algerian Cedar of differing habit which may have been planted about the time of introduction of tree (*q.v.*).
West Lodge Park, Hadley Wood, Barnet, Hertfordshire	Very old Strawberry tree, fine Swamp cypress and avenue of 170 limes. This hotel has many other fine trees.
Cobham Hall, Cobham, Kent†	Once possessed four ash trees of great height. The cricket Ashes supposed to have been kept at the Hall. Also avenue of limes 1,000 yards long.
Sissinghurst Place, Kent	One of the finest Durmast oaks in England. Reputed to be 500 years old; 79 ft. high, girth 19 ft. 4 in.
Speke Hall, Liverpool, Lancashire	Two sentinel yews in courtyard. Possibly old Hundred Court trees.

Thorpe Hall, Louth, Lincolnshire	Large sycamore named Seven Sisters. Now has only six limbs, one blown off in gale.
Witham-on-the-Hill, Lincolnshire	Old hollow oak, known as Bowthorpe Oak; qualifies as the largest-girthed British oak standing—39 ft. 6 in.
Bushey Park, Middlesex	Triple avenue of chestnuts and limes.
Marble Hill, Middlesex	Large Black Walnut 16 ft. 3 in. girth, 91 ft. in height.
Lowick, Northamptonshire†	Lowick Oak, which fell in 1968, had a girth of 25 ft. and height of 90 ft.
Tichmarsh, Northamptonshire†	Cedar of Lebanon. Reported to have been planted in Rectory garden in 1627, a contradiction of introductory date.
Dulverton, Somerset	One of finest sycamores in British Isles, in very good condition. In churchyard.
Bagot's Park, Staffordshire	Bagot's Walking Stick. Very tall oak, straight and clean of branches to a great height. *q.v.* Duke's Walking Stick, Sherwood.
	†Beggar's Oak was said to be one of finest in England, but was felled. Tradition: a former Lord Bagot met a beggar under tree and refused him alms, the beggar cursed his family, saying that firstborn would not survive. Another explanation: tree so named because it was meeting place of beggars and deerstealers of Needwood Forest.
	†Cliff Oak, felled in 1933. Supplied the panelling of *Queen Mary* liner.
Hawstead Place, Suffolk	Reputed to have been the earliest Oriental plane trees planted in England.
Eastwick, Gt. Bookham, Surrey	Eastwick Sycamore, 15 ft. girth, 40 ft. high. In grounds of County Primary School. Estimated to be 200 years old. Chosen to depict school crest.
Esher Place, Surrey	Tulip tree planted by Bishop Compton, 1685.
Weybridge, Oatlands Park Hotel, Surrey	Another claim for first planting of Cedar of Lebanon. Planted early 17th century, supposedly by Prince Henry, son of Charles I.
Buxted, Sussex	Avenue of limes planted *c.* 1630.
Witley Rectory, Surrey	Fine specimen of London Plane 21 ft. girth and 115 ft. in height.
Goodwood Park, Sussex	Fine Cedar of Lebanon of very large girth.
Levens Hall, Westmorland	Avenue of oaks recently reprieved from motorway development. Famous examples of topiary. Landscaped by Le Notre.

Bradford-on-Avon, Wiltshire	Fine specimen of false acacia in church-yard. Fine specimen of tulip tree at the Priory.
Corsham Court, Wiltshire	Very wide-spreading yew overshadowing graves. A notable Oriental plane.
Savernake Forest, Wiltshire	Grand Avenue. Although badly gapped now, still contains some exceptionally fine old beeches planted *c.* 1720.
Tisbury, Wiltshire	Yew of great girth claimed as largest in British Isles. In churchyard.
Bewdley, Worcestershire†	Whitty Pear Tree. Original now lost, but small successor grows at side. Was known as Sorb Tree or Quicken Pear, a large and hitherto unknown species of sorbus noted as far back as 1678 by certain authorities. This specimen is also known as the Wyre Forest Service Tree. One raised from the original stands at Arley Castle and now measures 66 ft. with a girth of 10 ft. 2 in.
Nidd Valley, Cowthorpe, Yorkshire†	Cowthorpe Oak. Once largest oak in British Isles, 45 ft. circumference at 3 ft. from ground.
Inverewe, Wester Ross, Scotland	A magnolia at one time recorded as the largest in the British Isles. (On National Trust property.)
Isle of Mull, Scotland	McCulloch's Tree. Fossil of tree stump protected as a monument. Fifty million years old.
Houth, Dublin, Eire	An English elm. According to Department of Lands, believed to be the oldest introduced tree in Ireland.
Tollymore, Co. Down, Eire	Specimen of Dwarf Spruce. Stock tree from which all other plants of this "accident" have been perpetuated. Now 200 years old. Discovered by the Earl of Clanbrassil on his estate (now Forest Park). Now only 17 ft. high.

Appendix V

† Deciduous
* Coniferous

Tree	Britain	Russia
Oak†	284	150
Willow†	266	147
Birch†	229	101
Hawthorn†	149	59
Poplars†	97	122
Apple†	93	77
Pine*	91	190
Alder†	90	63
Elm†	82	81
Hazel†	73	26
Beech†	64	79
Ash†	41	41
Spruce*	37	117
Lime†	31	37
Hornbeam†	28	53
Larch*	17	44
Fir*	16	42
Holly	7	8

Index

Acknowledgements

I am most grateful to the following correspondents for assisting in research.

Adams, R. H.: Addis, Lt. Cdr. C. P.: Alldrick, Stella M.: Allen, Mrs. K.: Allen, Mrs. L. E.: Allison, Mrs. C.: Anderson, Miss L. F.: Archer, G.: Arden, J.: Armstrong, J. C.: Austin, Mrs. M. M.

Bagnall, The Rev. C. H.: Baker, Mrs. P.: Banks, Miss V.: Barnett-Saunders, C. F.: Beale, T. Edward: Beattey, A. R.: Beazer, Cyril H.: Beer, W. H.: Bennett, Mrs. A. E.: Bennett, Mrs. N.: Blaber, R.: Blair, Sir James Hunter, Bt.: Blaxland, The Rev. L. B.: Bogie, B.: Boston, Miss S. Bourne, S. H.: Boyd, Mrs. A. M.: Bradley, Alexander: Bradley, Mrs. E. F. Losco: Bradley, Mrs. F. E.: Braithwaite, Mrs. M. W.: Bray, Mrs. I. M.: Bray, Mrs. R.: Brearley, Mrs. J.: Bristol Evening Post: British Broadcasting Corporation: British Red Cross Society, Ely: Brooks, Christine M.: Brown, Mrs. A. O.: Brown, M. C.: Bunce, Mrs. B. H.: Butterfield, Mrs. R. P.

Carey, M.: Lady Carlile, J. P.: Carter, Mrs. C.: Catt, George: Cawston, Mrs. S. M.: Chadwick, Mrs. D.: Champion, The Rev. F. C.: Chapman, Friar D. A.: Cheales, The Rev. H. S.: Churcher, D. M.: Clark, F. L.: Clark, J. F.: Clark, Nelson Ltd.: Clarke, Miss L. A.: Clarke, Sir Ralph K.B.E.: Clay, Dr. R. C. C.: Coen, T.: Cole, V.: Coleman, S. W.: Coleclough, Miss M.: Collacott, Cecil T.: Collier, Mrs. B.: Collis, Miss A. M.: Comer, M.: Commemorative Tree Company: Cook, S. J.: Corser, Miss G. J.: Cowie, Mrs. M. R. R.: Cox, Mrs. E. W.: Crawford, Mrs. M. E.: Croot, Arnold: Cross, Capt. R. G.: Crow, R. C.: Crowe, A. J.: Cusse, J. M.

Davidson, W. A.: Davies, Mrs. C.: Davies, Mrs. G.: Davies, Paul: Davis, Miss W. L.: Deakin, R. H.: Lord Ducie: Dunk, F.: Dunmore, Mrs. E. E.

Eckford, P. D. S.: Edmonton Hundred Historical Society: Ellen, Mrs. D. M. R.

Farris, H. O.: Field, J. J.: Finlay, J.: Fitton, Wing Cdr. A. K.: Flanders, L.: Ford, I. N.: Forestry Commission: Fox, The Rev. F. T.: Foxell, H. D. G.: Fraser, Mrs. E.: Fryer, K. J.: Furneaux, F. S., M.B.E.

Gardner, B. L.: German, Miss M.: Girling, H.: Glover, Miss H. E.: Godfrey, Mrs. H.: Godfrey, M.: Goodier, The Rev. S. A. R.: Goodinge, A. W.: Goslin, V.: Gould, Maurice: Graham, Miss S.: Gregory, Lt. Cdr. C. G.: Gush, A. J.

Hance, P. J.: Harlick, R. S. B.: Harmsworth, Sir Geoffrey, Bt.: Harris, Mrs. E.: Harris, E. G.: Hart, J. W.: Hart, K. D.: Harvey, G.: Hatchett, Anita: Hawes, Major-General L. A.: Hawthornthwaite, E. J.: Hayman, Capt. P. M. C.: Hayward, Mrs. S.: Hazeldine, J. M.: Henderson, The Rev. W. Paton: Herstmonceaux Parish Council: Hill, L. C.: Hill, Mr. & Mrs. S.: Hinchcliffe, John C.: Hiscott, G. L.: Horne, Nicholas, A.I.I.P.: Horswell, K. M.: Houlston, Mrs. E. H.: Hyne, Sarah.

Ibbetson, Ruth: Ireland, J. Alec: Irvine, R. T. M.

Jones, B. G.: Jones, E. Emrys: Jones, Miss J. I.: Jones, Mrs. M. B.: Joy, G.

Kay, Miss D.: Keller, Mrs. E. M.: Kendall, F.: Kennerley, Miss M.: Kenney, Ruth: Kitchener, D. H.: Knap Hill Nurseries, Ltd.: Knowles, Mrs. J. B.

Lainchbury, G.: Lavender, J. H.: Lawrence, L.: Leathart, P. S., M.B.E.: Lee, W. G.: Looseley, A.: Lovegrove, R.: Lovell, R.: Lubran, A.: Lyons, P. A.

McCloy, Mrs. E. M.: Macdonald, Donald J.: Mackay Brown, Mrs. C.: Macrae, K.: Macrae, M.: Major, M.: Madge, H. E.: Mann, C. E.: Marks, Violet: Mauger, D.: Maulden, Cdr. J. W., O.B.E.: Maxwell, L. E. L.: Meade-Waldo, Mrs. M.: Merry, S. C.: Meynell, G.: Midson, S.: Milligan, Spike: Mills, Mrs. E. M.: Milne, Mrs. P.: Ministry of the Environment: Mitchell, Alan: Mobsby, Mrs. M.: Moore, M.: Morgan, Joan (Henley Society): Morland, T. E.: Muir, N.: Murray, M. A.

Nathan, T. J.: Neale, W. E.: Neill, Miss E.: Neilson-Taylor, G. J.: Newman, Miss F. E.: Nixon, Jean M. V.: Noel, J.: Northover, P. R.: Nuttall, Mrs. M.

Ormsby, A. G.

Palmer, C. C.: Pape, Miss H.: Parlett, The Rev. Gordon A.: Patterson, Mrs. A. A.: Patterson, Mrs. L.: Pearce, Miss L.: Pearson, Dorothy L.: Pendrell Smith, Colin: Philipson, Miss D.: Plumley, Mrs. G.: Pollard, M. W.: Pratt, G.: Pringle, Mrs. C.: Purser, H. R.

Quayle, J. C.

Ramuz, Mrs. R.: Redfern, R. A.: Redman, Miss A. I.: Reilly, Mrs. M.: Richards, T. A.: Rider, A. J.: Riddlestone, Mrs. A.: Riley, Miss Jean: Roberts, Mrs. G.: Robertson, G. M.: Robinson, C. J.: Ross, Mrs. R. G.: Rowe, A. E.: Royal Horticultural Society: Rusden, P. T.: Russell, Mrs. T. H. D.

Searle, A. F.: Seel, Mrs. E. G.: Shaw, Mrs. A. N.: Sheridan, Freda: Shillingford, A. G.: Shirlaw, Mrs. F.: Shute, G.: Simons, Mrs. C. M.: Slade, L. H.: Smith, Mrs. E.: Smith, Miss N. A.: Smyth, Miss V. V.: Spence, G.: Stevenson, Miss K. T.: Sturgeon, E. A.: Sutton, Mrs. G.: Sutton, Mrs. Graham: Symns, A. M.

Thompson, F. S.: Thurstan, Major W. F. F.: Thwaites, Edward: Titlay, Mrs. A.: Tomkins, M.: Tonge, Miss B.: Topham, B.: Trollope-Beller, T. F.: Tuck, Col. A. A. N.: Turner, W.: Twelvetrees, Mrs. E.: Tyrell, S. J.

University College London: Usher, R. N.

Vyner, J. E. T.

Ware, S. C.: Watson, Mrs. D.: Watson, Miss M.: Wells, D. V.: Westbrook, E. M.: Whale, R. C.: Wheatley, F.: Wigley, L. E.: Williams, E. (Wilmslow Rostrum Club): Williams, Mrs. G.: Wills, F. B.: Wilmshurst, Hilda M.: Wilson, D. Mcleod: Wilson, E.: Wilson, P. J., B.Sc.: Wilyman, W. E.: Wood, Mrs. M. E.: Woodgate, Florence: Wray, Mrs. Ann: Wright, E. C. S.: Wright, Dr. S.

Yeomans, S. E.: Yorkshire Post: Youle, Mrs. J. E.: Young, Mrs. J. S.

£5.00